GLOBAL HISTORY
STAREVIEW

STRATEGIC
TEST–ACHIEVEMENT
REVIEW

Authors:

Sue Ann Kime   **Paul Stich**

Editor:

Wayne Garnsey

Illustrations and Artwork:
Eugene B. Fairbanks

Cover Design:
Wayne Garnsey & Paul Stich

N & N Publishing Company, Inc.
18 Montgomery Street   Middletown, New York 10940
(800) NN4 TEXT
www.nandnpublishing.com   email: nn4text@warwick.net

Credits

Thanks to our many colleagues who have contributed their knowledge, skills, and years of experience to the making of our endeavor. To these educators, our sincere thanks for their assistance in the preparation of this manuscript:

Kenneth Garnsey   Fran Harrison
Howard Van Ackooy   Maureen Van Ackooy

Reference

Top-rate references are most important to consistency in word and fact. We are grateful to the authors, editors, contributors, and publishers of two of the finest resources:

The American Heritage Dictionary© – fundamental definitions and appropriate word usage [available on CD-ROM, SoftKey Multimedia Inc, Cambridge, MA]
2000 Grolier Multimedia Encyclopedia© – date and information varifications [available on CD-ROM, Grolier Interactive Inc, Danbury, CT]

© Copyright 2001
N & N Publishing Company, Inc.
18 Montgomery Street   Middletown, New York 10940
(800) NN4 TEXT
www.nandnpublishing.com   email: nn4text@warwick.net

ISBN # 0-935487 70 0
3 4 5 6 7 8 9 10 11 12 13 14 15 BMP 2005 2004 2003 2001

Printed in the United States of America, Book-mart Press, NJ

SAN # 216 - 4221

TABLE OF CONTENTS

LESSONS . . . . .PAGE
1   APPROACHES FOR THE GLOBAL HISTORY EXAM 5-28
2   GEOGRAPHIC INFLUENCES ON GLOBAL HISTORY 29-58
3   ANCIENT WORLD: CIVILIZATIONS & RELIGIONS – (4000 BC – 500 AD) 59-80
4   EXPANDING ZONES OF EXCHANGE & ENCOUNTER – (500 - 1200 AD) . . .81-102
5   GLOBAL INTERACTIONS – (1200 – 1650 AD) 103-126
6   THE FIRST GLOBAL AGE – (1450 – 1770 AD) 127-146
7   AN AGE OF REVOLUTIONS – (1750-1914 AD) 147-166
8   A HALF CENTURY OF CRISIS & ACHIEVEMENT – (1900 – 1950 AD) 167-186
9   THE WORLD SINCE 1945 187-212
10 GLOBAL CONNECTIONS & INTERACTIONS – (PRESENT TO THE FUTURE) 213-230

11 GLOBAL HISTORY PRACTICE EXAM ONE 231-250
12 GLOSSARY & INDEX 251-288

THEMES & CONCEPTS

HISTORY
Change
Choice
Culture
Diversity
Empathy
Identity
Interdependence

GEOGRAPHY
Environment & Society
Human Systems
Physical Systems
Places & Regions
Uses of Geography
World in Spatial Terms

POLITICAL SCIENCE
Citizenship
Civic Values
Decision-Making
Government
Human Rights
Values

ECONOMICS
Economic Systems
Factors of Production
Needs & Wants
Scarcity
Technology

4 MILLION PLUS YEARS

Hominids in Africa
(4 million)

Neolitic Revolution
(60,000)

4000–

2000–

Ancient Civilizations & Religion
(4000 BC – 500 AD)

1000–

BC
0–
AD

Expanding Zones of
Exchange and Encounter
(500–1200)

1000–

2000–

APPROACHES
FOR THE
GLOBAL HISTORY
EXAM

Global Interactions (1200–1650)

First Global Age (1450–1770)

Age of Revolutions (1750–1914)

Half Century of Crisis & Achievement (1900–1950)

The World Since 1945

Global Connections & Interactions (Present to Future)

PREFACE

Stonehenge – PhotoDisc©

You are reading this because there is a serious challenge before you – a difficult final examination in global history and geography. You need help in sorting through the concepts, the ideas, the relationships, and the facts presented as you study the history of human existence. Lessons 2 through 10 of this book concentrate on major themes and historical details that relate to them.

Before plunging into all that history, this lesson requires you to take some time to analyze the task itself. It looks at the blueprint or layout of the examination. If you know the task, you can effectively organize your review time and focus your energy.

EXAM BLUEPRINT

Part I – Objective Response (55 points): 50 multiple choice questions

Part II – Subjective Response (45 points) composed of:

1 Thematic Essay (15 points)

1 Document-Based Question (DBQ, 30 points) composed of:

Part *A* – scaffolded short answer questions on 4 to 8 documents (15 points)	Part *B* – essay based on Part *A* documents and outside knowledge (15 points)

EXAM HINTS

On multiple choice questions, often you can eliminate answers:
• that are *too extreme* – watch out for answers that contain "all," "none," or "only"
• have no logical connection to the question

Never leave any questions blank. There is no penalty for guessing.

When you take practice exams, time yourself.

PART I: MULTIPLE CHOICE QUESTIONS

On global history and geography tests, there are many kinds of multiple choice questions. There are very few straight, factual recall questions (e.g., "The current U.N. Secretary General is ..."). Most questions are "compound questions." This means they require (a) some basic knowledge, and (b) an application of that knowledge. Here are some approaches to correctly answering various types of multiple choice questions.

Example 1 – Compound Question Structure:
  In both the former Yugoslavia and the former Soviet Union, the
  desire for self-determination is resulting in increased
  1   collectivization
  2   ethnic conflict
  3   economic equality
  4   educational opportunities

In Example 1, the *basic knowledge* (a) is knowing that **self-determination** means a desire for local independence and sovereignty. However, there is a second level of thinking involved. You must *apply* (b) that basic knowledge to current events in the former Yugoslavia and the former Soviet Union. Those former nations have split into many smaller ones created by the desire of **ethnic groups** (people sharing a common and distinct racial, national, religious, linguistic, or cultural heritage) for their own countries. So ethnic conflict (answer #2) has increased due to the desire for self-determination.

There are a number of other types of multiple choice questions used on global history examinations. Commonly, multiple choice questions ask you to complete a statement. Often these questions will ask you to identify a cause (see Example 2), or identify an effect (see Example 3).

Example 2 – Complete a statement:
  A major reason for the decline of the Roman Empire was
  1   a series of military defeats in Africa
  2   political corruption and instability of the government
  3   the abolition of slavery throughout the Empire
  4   continued acceptance of traditional religions

Example 3 – Analyze a situation:
  After World War II, the Soviet Union established satellites in
  Eastern Europe to
  1   support the remaining fascist governments in Eastern Europe
  2   preserve capitalism in Eastern Europe
  3   preserve democratic governments in Eastern European nations
  4   expand its power and control over Eastern Europe

Up to 20% of the multiple choice questions will measure your ability to comprehend visual data (maps, graphs, charts, cartoons). Example 4 shows one type, but because these questions have become more popular, the next section of this introduction goes into greater detail on them.

Example 4 – Analyze data:
What is a valid conclusion based on the information provided in the graph?
1   The Philippines had a higher fertility rate than Afghanistan did.
2   In most instances, nations with higher literacy rates tend to have lower fertility rates.
3   The literacy rates for South Asian nations are higher than the literacy rates for Southeast Asian nations.
4   Southeast Asian nations have a higher rate of population growth than any other region in the world.

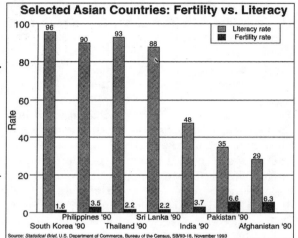

Some multiple choice questions test your knowledge of concepts. In this type, you are presented with a series of situations and asked to identify the one that clearly illustrates one of the "big ideas" of global history such as absolute monarchy, feudalism, laissez-faire, or nationalism. You will have to know some definitions and be able to recognize them at work. You will find a general list later in this lesson. You will also find them identified in the content of Lessons 2 through 10 as well as in the appendix at the back of the book.

Example 5 – Identify a concept at work:
Which statement best reflects the effect of mercantilism on the colonies in Latin America?
1   Markets in the colonies were closed to manufactured goods from the mother country.
2   Land was distributed evenly among the social classes.
3   Industries in the colonies manufactured the majority of finished goods for the mother country.
4   The wealth of the colonial power increased at the expense of the colony.

Another popular type of multiple choice question gives multiple clues in the stem and asks you to find similarities or make comparisons. In this type you are presented with a series of situations or leaders and you must look for a common thread. The simplest approach is to look for something you know is true or false about one of the situations or persons. If it is false, you can eliminate that answer. If it is true, see if it can be universal enough to be applied to the others. It could be the common thread you need. Try this with Example 6. Besides identifying the correct answer, be aware of *why* you rejected the other answers.

Example 6 – Compare similar situations that occurred at different times:

Which statement best explains the periods of the Gupta Empire of India, the Golden Age of Greece, and the Renaissance in Italy?
1   Winning wars always inspires scientific and artistic achievement.
2   A combination of wealth and time of relative peace often leads to cultural achievement.
3   A dictatorship usually encourages cultural growth and development.
4   Periods of censorship are needed for a nation to achieve cultural and scientific greatness.

THE GROWING POPULARITY OF DATA-BASED QUESTIONS

Questions based on some "visual stimulus" (a chart, a graph, a map, a cartoon) are very popular on tests, because they help to assess a broad range of skills beyond historical knowledge. On Part I, often more than one multiple choice question will be asked on a visual's data. The first is often a very basic, straightforward question to test your skill at extracting information from the data. The second question usually asks you for an explanation, analysis, comparison, or relation of the data to a set of historic circumstances.

Cover the question(s) – A simple technique is to cover the question(s) related to the visual with your hand or scrap paper and just look and think about the visual. Ask yourself some questions, such as:

- What does the data represent?
- What point is being made?
- What do you know about the time period involved?

When you uncover the questions, you may be surprised at how this simple "brainstorming technique" has helped. Try it as you look at the different examples of data-based questions that follow.

Put trouble on hold – Also, as you look at the following examples, take note of the particular type of data that gives you trouble. You will want to practice this type of question more than others.

When you actually take the test, remember to do Part I in pencil so you can make changes easily. Also, when you actually take the test and you are not sure of the answer, it is best to put down a *tentative* answer, circle the question number, and check back on it later. Let time work for you. Wait until you have "warmed up" and had some time to look over the examination to finalize your answers. When you have "settled in," you will be less tense than when you first started. By then, you will be thinking differently, and you will be able to address questions more logically. Try to see data-based questions as "gifts." Remember, the answer is in the visual and it is something *obvious* – rarely is it tricky or obscure.

Example 7 – Maps:

One reason Italian city-states were able to dominate the trade pattern shown on the map was that they were

1. centrally located on the Mediterranean Sea
2. situated north of the Alps
3. unified by the Hanseatic League
4. located on the trade routes of the North Sea

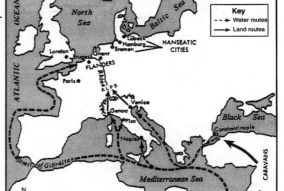

Trade Routes (13th – 15th centuries)

Example 8 – Graphs (pie):

Which is an accurate statement based on the information in the graphs?

1. The population of the world will double between 1990 and 2025.
2. The distribution of the world's population by regions will remain the same between 1990 and 2025.

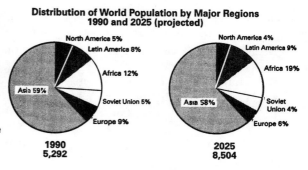

Distribution of World Population by Major Regions
1990 and 2025 (projected)

1990
5,292

2025
8,504

3   By 2025, there will be a major shift in population from the for-
     mer Soviet Union to Europe.
4   By 2025, Africa's percentage of the world's population will
     increase more than any other region's percentage.

Example 9 – Graphs (bar):
Which statement is best supported by the data in the graph?

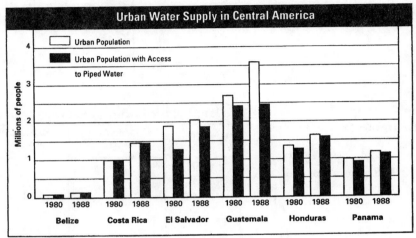

Source: Frederick S. Mattson, CDM and Associates, Arlington, VA

1   The urban areas of Honduras and Panama require the largest
     supply of water in Central America.
2   Belize and Costa Rica are meeting the water needs of their
     urban population.
3   Urban water supplies are declining in many Central American
     countries.
4   Most Central American countries experienced a decrease in
     urban population between 1980 and 1988.

Example 10 – Graphs (line):
Which action will help slow
the trend indicated in the
graph?
1   expanding food produc-
     tion
2   increasing industrial-
     ization of Less
     Developed Countries
3   using alternative ener-
     gy sources
4   lowering the price of
     gasoline world wide

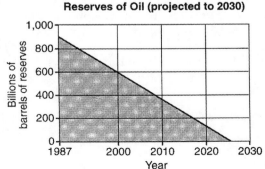

CHARTS & TABLES

Example 11 – Charts:
From which point of origin was the broadest dispersion?
1   Pakistan
2   Turkey
3   Syria
4   Palestine

World Refugees (1988)		
Original Home	**Current Home**	**Total**
Afghanistan, Iran	Pakistan	3,595,000
Palestine	Jordan, Gaza Strip, Syria, West Bank	1,980,000
Iran, Iraq	Turkey	301,000

Example 12 .1 – Tables:
According to the table at the right, the lowest birthrates are mostly found in
1   Western Europe
2   North America
3   Southeast Asia
4   Africa

National Birthrate Table (1994 approx.)		
Nations	Birthrate (per 1,000 females)	Infant Mortality Rate (per 1,000 births)
Uganda	51	104
Somalia	50	122
Angola	47	137
Cambodia	46	112
Ethiopia	46	110
Pakistan	40	109
Canada	14	6.8
France	13	6.7
Denmark	13	6.6
Italy	10	8.3
Germany	10	5.9
Japan	10	4.4

Example 12.2 – Tables:
Which is a valid generalization based on the information in the table above right?
1   In developing nations, the infant mortality rate decreases as the birthrate increases.
2   Industrialized nations have lower birthrates and infant mortality rates than developing nations do.
3   Decreasing the infant mortality rate will limit population growth in developing nations.
4   Industrialized nations have higher population densities than developing nations do.

CARTOONS

Example 13 – Cartoon:
Why were the leaders of Western
Europe surprised by the event
addressed in this cartoon?

WONDER HOW LONG THE HONEYMOON WILL LAST?

FDR Library

1   The Soviet Union and Nazi
Germany were both democratic
regimes.
2   The ideologies of these two
nations were at opposite ends
of the political spectrum.
3   The Soviet Union had a long
history of close relations with
Great Britain.
4   Since 1935, the official government policy of the Soviet Union
had supported isolationism.

TIMELINES

Example 14 – Timeline:
Which period of
European history is
represented by this
timeline?
1   Enlightenment
2   Middle Ages
3   Reformation
4   Commercial
Revolution

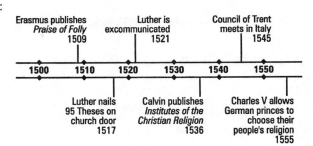

READING PASSAGES

"Yesterday, your Ambassador petitioned my Ministers
regarding your trade with China ... Our Celestial Empire pos-
sesses all things in great abundance and lacks no product within its own borders. There is, therefore, no need to import any
product manufactured outside by barbarians in exchange for
our own goods."
– Emperor Ch'ien Lung of China to King George III of Britain, 1793

Example 15.1 – Reading Passage:
In the view of the Emperor, which foreign policy action was in the
best interest of China in 1793?
1   maintaining economic isolation
2   expanding foreign trade
3   increasing international interdependence
4   developing into a colonial power

Example 15.2 – Reading Passage:

Based on the previous passage, which type of attitude does the Emperor display?

1 empathetic
2 ethnocentric
3 imperialistic
4 militaristic

EXAM HINTS

Speaker Questions:
Cover the questions then read the four statements, ask yourself:

- What is the general topic under discussion? (different kinds of government systems)

- Who are these people? (A = nationalist / socialist / Nazi; B = communist, isolationist / ethnocentric / Maoist; C = Confucian rules of proper behavior according to role played in society; D = natural law concept from Enlightenment /Rousseau).]

SPEAKER A-B-C QUESTIONS

Speaker A: Nationalism, democracy, and socialism are the goals of my party.
Speaker B: We must rid our country of all foreign influences and return to the true principles of communism.
Speaker C: A good ruler will rule by example, not by decree.
Speaker D: The laws of nature, not government, should rule society.

Example 16.1 – Speaker Question:

Which speaker's statement best reflects the ideas of China's Cultural Revolution?

1 *A*
2 *B*
3 *C*
4 *D*

Example 16.2 – Speaker Question:

The speaker's statement that best reflects an ideal of Confucianism is

1 *A*
2 *B*
3 *C*
4 *D*

EVENTS LIST (or group of newspaper headlines)

> *"Germany Recognizes the Independence of Slovenia"*
> *"United States Establishes Diplomatic Relations with Croatia"*
> *"Latvia Joins the United Nations"*

Example 17 – Headlines:
These headlines illustrate the
1   collapse of governments of these nations
2   strength of the Russian Empire
3   beginning of a united Europe
4   increase in international support for self-determination

USE YOUR "SENSE OF HISTORY"

A final thought on multiple choice questions:

Use the general awareness of history you have built up over the years. There are certain things that have happened in the world over the five centuries of recorded history. There is a logical flow to the patterns of human civilization. Whether you are aware of it or not, down deep most global history students have a sense of how governments, religions, and quality of life improvements such as technology have evolved. Put your awareness of these patterns and your broad chronological consciousness to work. No matter what the form of the question or type of visual presented, there are going to be answers suggested that are just plain wrong. Your "sense of history" will tell you that these answers do not square with your grasp of what has happened. If you keep the "big picture" of human experience in mind, it will help you see whether a multiple choice answer is appropriate.

PART II: WRITING QUESTIONS (ESSAYS)

Both the thematic essay and the document-based question require thought and preparation before writing. This "prewriting" is a vital part of the writing process and helps you focus on the task. You need to summon the writing skills you have acquired not just in social studies but in your English classes too. You should arrange your answers in a simple outline:

- **Introduction Paragraph** – The introduction is critical. It must state your purpose, your controlling thought – your **thesis** (proposed answer that you will argue in the essay).

- **Body Paragraphs** – The body is a series of paragraphs in which you must present evidence in support of your thesis.

- **Conclusion Paragraph** – Lastly, there should be an an effective conclusion in which you must restate your thesis, summarize your ideas, and re-emphasize evidence that proves them.

In the model essays below, there are suggestions for prewriting as well as ideas about effective writing.

EXAM HINTS

Watch spelling, grammar, and punctuation. The easier and clearer your work is to read, the easier it is to grade; therefore, the higher the points received.

Keep things in perspective. Remember that the point values matter, too. On all examinations, the designation of points on a question indicates how much time and effort to spend on a particular section. On the Global History & Geography Examination, the 50 multiple choice questions on Part I are worth 55 points, but you are only half way through the exam when you complete them. There are still 45 points of writing to do on Part II. The DBQ's (Document-based Questions) Part *A* is a series of short answers about each of the individual documents. It is really a 15-point prewriting exercise designed to give you ideas to incorporate into the Part *B* essay. You should also remember that Part *B* of the DBQ and thematic essay are worth exactly the same number of points (15).

At any rate, the point values should tell you that the overall effort and length of the two essays should be about equal. Students lose a "good chunk of credit" when (1) they put most of their effort into the thematic essay, and/or (2) spend too much time "figuring out" the DBQ's Part *A* short responses. In either case or a combination of both, the students do not have enough time left to write an effective response on the DBQ essay.

EXAM HINTS

On Part II, often visuals are used for one or two of the documents on the Document Based Questions. Use the same "cover and brainstorm" technique mentioned earlier. Cover the question, then just look and think about the visual for a moment. Ask yourself some mental questions about what you have before you uncover the question. The "prethinking" gives you a "mind set" to approach the actual question.

Look at Part II for a few minutes. See if there is any information or vocabulary from Part I that you might use on Part II and make a note of it in the margin.

SAMPLE THEMATIC ESSAY DIRECTIONS AND ANSWER

Directions:
Write a well-organized essay that includes an introduction, several paragraphs explaining your position, and a conclusion.

Theme: Religion and human affairs

> Throughout global history, religions have played a role in the development of regions.

Task:

> - Decide how strong the influence of religions has been on people's lives and the course of history.
> - Support your opinion by discussing the influence of *three* religions.
> - Use specific examples to explain how *each* religion shaped the culture and historic development of a region.

Suggestions: You may use any religion from your study of global history. Some suggestions you might wish to consider include the impact of Hinduism on India, the effect of Christianity on Medieval Europe, the influence of Islam on the Middle East, the effect of Judaism on Israel, the impact of Protestantism on Western Europe, the influence of Shintoism on Japan. **You are *not* limited to these suggestions.**

ANSWER:
   Writing Strategy for this essay: After you have written your introduction and stated your thesis, divide the body into logical paragraphs and a final, concluding paragraph. For each religion, be sure to

- identify region or nation which practiced the religion
- use specific examples to explain how a belief affected the region
- use transitional phrases to link each paragraph to the thesis

★ REVIEW – SAMPLE THEMATIC ANSWER

INTRO & THESIS PARAGRAPH

(THESIS =) Historical evidence shows that religions have had a major influence on people's lives and the course of history. For centuries, Hinduism, Buddhism, Judaism, Christianity, Protestantism, Shinto, and Islam have all made great impacts on many regions of the world. (TRANSITION =) Evidence of the influence of the Hindu, Christian, and Islamic religions shows they have been very powerful forces in shaping world events.

EVIDENCE PARAGRAPH A

In ancient India between 1500 BC and 500 AD, the Hindu beliefs in dharma – the sacred duty that one owes to family and social class – led to a rigid caste systems and acceptance of one's lot in this life. As it evolved, dharma led to untouchables being prohibited from contact with others, wasting talent and intellect in the development of Indian society. The strength of these beliefs brought stability to the society and avoidance of civil strife. But, the rigid social structure led traditionalists to resist innovations such as the Green Revolution's use of animal fertilizers.

EVIDENCE PARAGRAPH B

(TRANSITION =) Another example of religion's power to create a strong social foundation is the cultural bond for stability that Christianity brought as the troubled Roman Empire weakened in the 4th century AD. Christianity's beliefs in the divinity of Jesus, the Trinity, and universal brotherhood attracted many converts. At first, Roman emperors persecuted Christians because their beliefs undermined belief in the emperors' divinity. Yet, early Christians chose to become martyrs rather than renounce their beliefs or accept the paganism of the Roman Empire. When it was impossible to stamp out the Christian movement, the Emperor Constantine issued the Edict of Milan (313 AD), allowing toleration. The Roman Christian Church became the main unifying institution of Western Europe from the fall of the Roman Empire until the Protestant Reformation (5th-16th centuries AD). European Christians even launched exhausting Crusades in the 11th and 12th centuries to reconquer the Middle East in the name of the Church.

EVIDENCE PARAGRAPH C

(TRANSITION =) The desire for stability and consistency in a changing world was also a factor in the acceptance of Islam in the Middle East. Islam calls for a community of believers with common laws to govern a way of life. Islam grew into a culture with guidelines and rules for life in all its aspects and dimensions. During the 7th and 8th centuries, Islamic leaders unleashed formidable armies to spread the faith in a series of sweeping jihads. During the Umayyad Dynasty in the 7th and 8th centuries, scholars developed the doctrine that faith alone did not make a person a believer, and that anyone committing grave sins was an unbeliever destined to hell. They applied this argument to the leaders of the community, holding that caliphs who were grave sinners could not claim the allegiance of the faithful. In the 1970s, this concept influenced Shi'ite fundamentalists to purify Iranian society by overthrowing the Shah and establishing an Islamic Republic (1979).

CONCLUSION PARAGRAPH

Hinduism, Islam, and Christianity created codes of ethics and rules of behavior that became accepted in large areas by large numbers of people for long periods of time. The rules created by these religions brought long-lasting order and stability to their respective societies that can still be seen today. Therefore, religions play a major role in the development of human societies. Even today, conflicts among adherents of certain religious beliefs still lead to wars, migrations, and human suffering.

SAMPLE DOCUMENT BASED QUESTIONS (DBQs)

DIRECTIONS AND ANSWERS

These questions test your ability to analyze information, organize it, and use it to present a point of view. Follow the same structural rules as for writing thematic essays. The exception is that you have to incorporate references to and analyses of the Part *A* documents.

- **Introduction paragraph** – must contain your **thesis** (the position you are trying to prove), some details which set the scene, and transition to the first paragraph.

- **Body paragraphs** – must organize, compare, and show how the document(s) prove your thesis and include additional historical information.

- **Final paragraph** (**conclusion**) – must summarize your ideas and use quotations to re-emphasize how you think the evidence has proven your thesis.

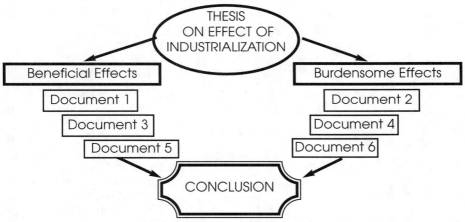

Directions: The following question is based on the accompanying documents (1-6). Some of the documents have been edited for the purposes of this exercise. The question is designed to test your ability to work with historical documents. As you analyze the documents, take into account both the source of the document and the author's point of view.

- Write a well-organized essay that includes an introduction with a thesis statement, several paragraphs explaining the thesis, and a conclusion.
- Analyze the documents.
- Use all the documents and refer to them by title, author, or number.
- Use evidence from the documents to support your thesis position.
- Do not simply repeat the contents of the documents.
- Include specific related outside information.

Historical Context: Industrialization significantly altered modern civilization. The documents below present views of the influence of industrialization on modern times.

Task: Decide whether industrialization was a beneficial or a burdensome change and support your opinion with the documents below and your knowledge of global history and geography.

Part *A* – Short Answer

The documents that follow relate to early 19th century industrialization. Examine each document carefully, then answer the question that follows it.

Document 1

TECHNOLOGICAL MILESTONES OF THE INDUSTRIAL REVOLUTION			
	Inventor	**Invention**	**Effect**
TEXTILES	John Kay (1704-1764)	Flying Shuttle	Doubled speed of weavers
	Richard Arkwright (1732-1792)	Water Frame	Used water power; factories developed; could spin 48-300 threads at once
	Samuel Crompton (1753-1827)	Spinning Mule	Combined jenny and water frame; could spin fine thread
TRANSPORTATION	James Watt (1736-1819)	Steam Engine	New source of power allowed many applications and the location of factories in different places
	George Stephenson (1781-1848)	Steam Locomotive	Faster land transportation
	Thomas Telford (1757-1783) and John McAdam (1756-1836)	Hard Surfaced Roads	Faster land transportation in all kinds of weather

1   What effects did the items shown by this chart have on life in the late 18th and early 19th centuries?

   (sample answer) The inventions moved textile production out of the home (domestic system) into factories and increased productivity.
   Transportation improvements allowed textiles to be distributed to markets more rapidly.

Document 2

2   What problems exist in the flax mills?

(sample answer) Dust creates sickness among workers. High temperature of processing water scalds and burns child laborers.

> "I would seriously ask any gentleman who has himself gone through a modern flax mill, whether he can entertain the slightest doubt that the occupation, as now pursued, must, in many cases, be injurious to health and destructive of life? In many departments of the mills, the dust is great, and known to be injurious. In those in which fine spinning has been introduced, the air has to be heated, as in certain cotton mills; the flax has also to be passed through water heated to a high temperature, into which the children have constantly to plunge their arms…"
>
> – British Parliament, *Sadler Committee Report*, 1832

Document 3

3   Which group(s) is Marx blaming for the problems of workers?

(sample answer) Marx blames the machines, the supervisors, most of all the bourgeois owners, and the bourgeois state.

> "Owing to the extensive use of machinery and to division of labour, the work of the proletarians has lost all individual character… He (the worker) becomes an appendage (part) of the machine, and it is only the most simple, most monotonous, and most easily acquired knack, that is required of him. … Not only are they (the workers) slaves of the bourgeois class, and the bourgeois state; they are daily and hourly enslaved by the machine, by the overlooker, and above all, by the individual bourgeois manufacturer…"
>
> – Karl Marx, *Communist Manifesto*, 1848

Document 4

4   What side effect of rapid industrialization is shown by this drawing?

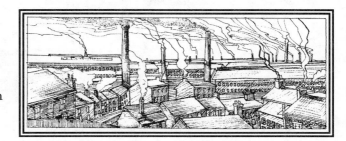

(sample answer) Factory towns grew too fast and became unhealthy places to live because of the pollution.

Document 5

5   According to Ashton, how has industrialization improved the life of the workers?

(sample answer) Ashton says the rate of pay gradually raised incomes; the status of women improved, debt declined, and unions were formed to fight for better conditions.

"Most of the factory operatives were engaged at rates of pay which raised family incomes above those of an earlier generation. As women and girls became less dependent on their menfolk they gained in self-respect and public esteem. As the factories moved to the towns, or towns grew up about the factories, the practice of the long pay gave way to weekly or fortnightly disbursements, …and the indebtedness of workers to employers declined. Since the operatives were no longer isolated cottagers it was easier for them to form unions and to defend their standards of hours and wages; and it became possible to enlist in the fight against abuses …"
- T.S. Ashton, *The Industrial Revolution, 1760-1830*

Document 6

6   According to Bronson, why were workers in an industrial society better off than in an agricultural society?

(sample answer) Bronson says governments took responsibility for protecting workers' safety, wages increased, and the general quality of life improved.

"The conditions in the cities were not as bad as some social historians have led us to believe. National and local governments introduced laws to make factories safer and more sanitary. As demand for mass produced goods grew and new factories opened, demand for workers pushed wages upward. After paying the rent, many workers had money for entertainment in music halls. Cities became places of opportunity and personal development in ways that had never been possible in the old closed agrarian society."
- Michael R. Bronson, *An Industrial Century*, 1927

Part *B* – Essay Response

Your essay should be well organized with an introductory paragraph that states your thesis as to the effects of industrialization. Develop and support the reasons for your thesis in the next paragraphs and then write a conclusion. In your essay, include specific historical details and refer to the specific documents you analyzed in Part *A*. You may include additional information from your knowledge of global history and geography.

DBQ ORGANIZATIONAL NOTES

[1] Be sure to restate the task as you begin.
[2] Take a clear position on what you want to prove.
[3] Clearly show where your argument will go next.
[4] Use specific information from the documents.
[5] Add information from your own knowledge of global history.
[6] Refer to documents by number, author, or title.
[7] Try to group the documents to reinforce each other.
[8] Restate your thesis as part of the conclusion.
[9] Use brief quotes from the documents to strengthen your conclusion.

☆ REVIEW – SAMPLE DBQ ANSWER

The Industrial Revolution was far more than an economic change [1]. It had many social and political effects. It wrenched the slow, quiet, seasonally ordered life of farmers into a fast-paced machine-dominated society that had clanking, high speed production as its key characteristic. ([2] THESIS =) While the transformation from an agricultural life to an industrial one was not without suffering, industrialization generally had a beneficial influence on society in the long run. ([3] TRANSITION =) When change is rapid, radical, and widespread enough to affect all elements of society, it will be disruptive to peoples' lives.

INTRO & THESIS PARAGRAPH

By the 1830s, entrepreneurs were applying the technology of the inventions and processes of the late 18th century shown in Document 1 [6]. The new business class (bourgeois) was combining inventions such as Kay's Flying Shuttle, Hargreaves' Spinning Jenny, Arkwright's Water Frame, and Cartwright's Power Looms to accelerate growth in the textile industry [4]. Rapid transportation improved by Stephenson's locomotives and McAdam's roads allowed raw materials to be moved to the factories and finished goods to be moved to market at a very fast pace [4].

DOCUMENT 1 EVIDENCE

([3] TRANSITION =) Yet the faster pace of production made life in the factories difficult and often unsafe. Document 2 [6] shows that the British Parliament's 1832 Sadler investigation of the linen making factories discovered dangerous air and water conditions wearing out workers [4]. Parliamentary actions led to government safety regulations and restrictions on child labor [5]. The rapid growth of industry also led to changes in the general air quality [5]. Sketches from the era like that shown in Document 4 [6] indicate that pollution became a problem. High concentrations of coal burning furnaces produced pollution and made the air quality of cities like London and Manchester deteriorate [5].

DOCUMENTS 2 & 4 EVIDENCE

([3] TRANSITION =) Protests against what was happening to life arose. Reformers wanted rapid changes to stop the suffering of the workers. Government was dominated by the wealthy and the factory owners who held back the pace of reform fearing it would diminish production [5]. Workers became more and more militant and angry. Document 3 [6] is an example of the kind of protests that spurred cries for reform. Karl Marx [6] blamed the bourgeois entrepreneurs for the suffering of the workers [4] and gave rise to angry

DOCUMENT 3 EVIDENCE

★ REVIEW – SAMPLE DBQ ANSWER (CONTINUED)

protests, and desire for socialist governments that would look to the needs of the proletariat or working class [5]. The fear of the militant socialist and communist revolution led governments to enact reforms even though the bourgeoisie opposed them [5].

DOCUMENTS 5 & 6 EVIDENCE

([3] TRANSITION =) As industrialization continued in the 19th century, the pace of reform also increased. Document 5 [6], an evaluation by historian T.S. Ashton [6], says that workers began to form unions to fight for better conditions [4]. Strikes often became violent, but the bourgeois and government slowly yielded to the movement for better conditions. In Document 6 [6], Michael Bronson [6] notes that economic forces such as the demand for workers also raised wages and made life better for the working classes by the beginning of the 20th century [4].

CONCLUSION PARAGRAPH

Documentary evidence shows the change was disruptive and there was great suffering during the 19th century; but evidence also shows the long term positive effects outweigh the short term negative ones [8]. Through improved technology, production increased and life gradually got better throughout the society. As Ashton [9] shows, workers were in contact with each other and they had more time and wealth "to enlist in the fight against abuses." Industrialization made the world a better place. As historian Michael Bronson [9] says, "Cities became places of opportunity and personal development in ways that had never been possible in the old closed agrarian society."

Notice

The DBQ essay uses the same basic outline as the thematic essay. What is different is that the Part A documents, short answer ideas, and additional relevant information have to be incorporated.

USING THIS BOOK FOR REVIEW

Now you have an idea of the parts of the examination and the types of questions on it, and you see the task before you in a clearer light. The next step is to understand how this book will help you to prepare for the examination.

Geographic Influences Lesson – You need to concentrate on the essential concepts, ideas, and patterns of events. While the bulk of the examination is devoted to historical concepts and patterns, geography plays a powerful, universal role in the shaping of human affairs. It is important that you see how geography touches every era of global history, including the present. So that you can carry this geographic knowledge through the chronological eras, this is where the review begins – Lesson 2 is on geographic influences. Lessons 3 through 10 deal with content studied in the major chronological eras of global history. Finally, there is a full practice examination.

Standard Lesson Structure – Lessons 2 through 10 are structured in similar fashion, although they are of different lengths. For consistency, each lesson begins with an overview of the main political, economic, and social occurrences of the era. From there, the lessons go into detail on the interplay of the forces that shaped the era. Along the way, there are illustrated charts and profiles to help visualize and deepen the broad patterns shown in the lesson. **Graphics are extremely important**, and they are often used to provide "mental triggers" to help you visualize key ideas and events.

Lesson Assessment – At the end of each lesson is an assessment that will train you for the examination as well as deepen ideas about what you have read. The assessment features multiple choice questions similar to the actual test questions. You should do the questions and look back in the lesson and the glossary (last pages in the book) for those of which you are unsure.

Emphasis on Writing Questions – It is a fact that students lose a higher percent of credit on the Part II written responses than on the Part I multiple choice questions. Each lesson's assessment has a thematic essay. To succeed on the examination, you must practice prewriting, planning, and outlining the written responses. At the end of each lesson, the "Practice Skills for DBQs" will strengthen your ability to deal with the longer version of the DBQ on the examination. For guidance, it is worth referring back to the model thematic essay and model DBQ you have just seen in this introductory lesson. Be sure to work the answers out on scrap paper first. Getting your ideas on paper – no matter what the order of ideas – is one of the most vital parts of the writing process.

ESSENTIAL CONCEPTS

Concepts are "core ideas" that are essential to mastering global history. They are guaranteed to appear on every examination. The list that follows merely presents the terms to perhaps jog your memory. It is artificial to define them here. They are only valuable if they are presented in context – associated with historic people, places, and things. However, you should be on the lookout for them throughout this book. As you progress through the review lessons, you will find them introduced and defined as their associated content is presented. Concepts include:

Political

Absolutism, Anarchy, Appeasement, Civil Disobedience, Colonialism, Communism, Constitution, Democracy, Dictatorship, Divine Right, Fascism, Feudalism, Genocide, Imperialism, Isolationism, Manorialism, Monarchy, Nationalism, Oligarchy, Parliamentary, Republic, Revolution, Self-determination, Socialism, Sovereignty, Theocracy, Totalitarian

Geographic (Physical)

Altitude, Climate, Continent, Cordillera, Current, Hemisphere, Island, Isthmus, Latitude, Longitude, Maps, Monsoon, Mountain Range, Peninsula, Plain, Plateau, Region, River Valley, Spatial Relationships, Steppe, Strait, Topography, Savanna,Tundra

Economic

Barter, Capitalism, Command Economy, Commercial Revolution, Diversification, Gross Domestic Product, Income, Industrialization, Interdependence, Investment Capital, Laissez-faire, Less Developed Country, Market Economy, Marxism, Mercantilism, Per Capita, Scarcity, Socialism, Subsistence Farming, Supply and Demand, Surplus, Traditional Economy, Unionism

Environmental

Desertification, Deforestation, Green Revolution, Greenhouse Effect, Strip Mining

Social

Birth Rate, Culture, Cultural Diffusion, Diversity, Ethnocentrism, Golden Age, Humanism, Infant Mortality Rate, Literacy Rate, Modernization, Racism, Social Darwinism, Social Mobility, Traditionalism, Urbanization, Westernization

Religious

Animism, Buddhism, Christianity, Dogma, Ethics, Fundamentalism, Heresy, Hinduism, Islam, Judaism, Monotheism, Moral, Piety, Polytheism, Ritual, Scripture, Sect, Shinto, Taoism

"THE MAIN THING IS ... DON'T GET EXCITED"

Some students get very frantic as examinations loom. They put pressure on themselves that drives them into an emotional state that is counter-productive. Here are some important ideas to keep you calm and help you make the most of a big task:

Allow sufficient time – Any review of a course as broad as global history and geography is going to take time. It cannot be done quickly, and it cannot be done alone. So, give yourself time. On your own, work in a quiet environment, get rid of distractions, and always have pen and paper handy. The act of writing helps cement ideas in your consciousness.

Get Verbal Feedback – During *some* of your review, you might try working one-on-one with a friend or parent. Verbal feedback and dialog about the content helps build your confidence. Above all, take it slowly – in small doses, a few pages at a time.

Work With Your Teacher – This book was designed to be used under a teacher's supervision and advice in the classroom and at home. Each of the lessons is intended to be read in one or two nights and followed up in class the next day. Perhaps your teacher will have you attempt to prewrite a thematic essay or DBQ at home and then work on writing the actual essay the next day in class. Perhaps you will start the prewriting process by brainstorming in a cooperative group in class and finish an essay for homework. There are many ways to approach the review, but use your teacher's system – and don't look for short cuts. At this point, there aren't any.

Lean on a Textbook – When you are working on your own, remember to have your textbook handy. It has much more material and background than this brief review book. When you feel you need more depth to understand something, use your textbook as a reference book. Go to the index and look up key words, then skim the text material connected with them. Look carefully at the textbook page. Just the appearance of the page or some illustration should remind you of when you originally studied the material. Take some time to jot down a few notes about the event, person, or movement from the text. Write them in the margin of this book so they are there when you are going over the material later.

There is no single, right method for review. There are many possible ways to review. Your teacher is the best guide for designing the review procedure. The key is working at the material calmly, systematically, and gradually over several weeks.

STRATEGIC
TEST-ACHIEVEMENT
REVIEW

Now,
Shoot For The Stars!

4 MILLION PLUS YEARS

Hominids in Africa
(4 million)

Neolitic
Revolution
(60,000)

GEOGRAPHIC INFLUENCES ON GLOBAL HISTORY

4000–

2000–

Ancient Civilizations & Religion
(4000 BC – 500 AD)

1000–

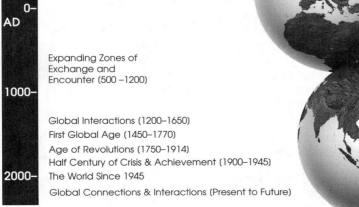

BC
0–
AD

Expanding Zones of
Exchange and
Encounter (500 –1200)

1000–

Global Interactions (1200–1650)
First Global Age (1450–1770)
Age of Revolutions (1750–1914)
Half Century of Crisis & Achievement (1900–1945)

2000–

The World Since 1945

Global Connections & Interactions (Present to Future)

INTRODUCTION

Geography is the study of the Earth and its features. It also studies the distribution of life on the Earth, including human life and the effects of human activity. Therefore, it is a critical element in any course in global history.

Geographic features have a significant impact on where and how people live. When studying history, geography helps explain the relation of the natural environment to the human environment. Relationships to climate, water, landforms, and mineral deposits shape how people live and act toward others.

A modern instance of geographic factors altering relationships is environmental conditions. For example, nations have industries whose pollution becomes airborne (e.g., acid rain) and affects conditions in other countries. Less developed countries balk when pressed by others to cut down their industrial pollution, claiming they need income to raise their standard of living.

Studying the natural environment reveals much about how civilizations develop (e.g., river valleys as cradles of civilization). Location can indicate what motivates a nation (e.g., Russia's traditional desire for navigable Baltic and Black Sea ports).

Climate has often played a key role in human development. It shapes culture (e.g., desert dwellers are usually nomadic; monsoons govern the agriculture of the Indian Subcontinent). In each world region, the general climatic conditions govern human progress.

To understand geography's importance in the scope of global history, it is important to study the elements of geography: human geography, physical geography, political geography, migration, and trade. Understanding the impact of geography on people and places will make it possible to answer questions about the role it has played throughout human history.

- Human geography involves the examination of the distribution of life on the Earth, including human life and the effects of human activity.

- Physical geography includes the study of landforms (mountains, islands, etc.), climate, water, location, and mineral resources. They may determine an area's livelihood and may also affect culture as people adapt to their environment.

- Political geography studies regions and other groupings of people that might include tribes, ethnic groups, religious groups, and nation states.

- Migration examines the movement of humans from one area to another and the factors which influence that movement.

- Trade involves the movement of goods and services from place to place to meet the economic needs and wants of human society.

Since a **region** is a large portion of the Earth's surface, encompassing many inhabitants, being precise about what defines it is often difficult. Regions are usually unified by physical or human characteristics such as language and culture (e.g., Latin America) or a political system (e.g., the Roman Empire).

In history, perceptions of regions change often. Historians redefine them as circumstances change. For example, since a number of early civilizations developed in the Tigris-Euphrates-Nile area, historians referred to the region as the "Fertile Crescent." Historians refer to the area influenced by classical Greco-Roman Era as the "Mediterranean World." Although the followers of Islam can be found in every country on the globe, a huge, sweeping region from North Africa to Pakistan and into Indonesia is religiously identified as the "Islamic World." Thus, regions shift and overlap. Their definition depends on the times and the contexts in which they are being studied. In this study of global history, seven key regions are primarily in focus:

- Western Europe
- Eastern Europe, Russia, and Central Asia
- Latin America
- The Middle East
- Africa
- South and Southeast Asia
- East Asia

Knowing the locations and the general geographic features and climates of these regions is helpful to a student of global history. A brief survey of the geography of these regions is useful before starting a review of the chronological eras of humankind.

SELECTED GEOGRAPHIC TERMS

Term	Explanation
Meridian	An imaginary great circle passing through the North and South geographic poles; lines of longitude measured East or West to 180 degrees of the Prime Meridian (0° – running through Greenwich, England)
Parallel	Any of the imaginary lines representing degrees of latitude that encircle the earth parallel to the plane of the Equator (0°) measured North and South to 90 degrees (geographic poles)
Hemisphere	Either the northern or southern half of the Earth as divided by the Equator, or the eastern or western half as divided by a meridian
Continent	One of the principal land masses of the Earth, including Africa, Antarctica, Asia, Australia, Europe, No. America, and So. America
Region	A large portion of the Earth's surface unified by physical or human characteristics such as language, culture, economic activity, or a political system
Ocean	Any of the principal divisions of the Earth's salt water surface (71%), including the Atlantic, Pacific, and Indian Oceans, their southern extensions in Antarctica, and the Arctic Ocean
Sea	A relatively large body of salt water completely or partially enclosed by land
Strait	A narrow channel joining two larger bodies of water
Bay	A body of water partially enclosed by land with a mouth accessible to the sea
Gulf	A large area of a sea or ocean partially enclosed by land
Lake	A large inland body of fresh water or salt water
River	A large natural stream of water emptying into an ocean, a lake, or another body of water
Mountain	A significant natural elevation of the Earth's surface having considerable mass, generally steep sides
Cordillera	Extensive chain of mountains or mountain ranges, especially the principal mountain system of a continent
Valley	Elongated lowland between ranges of mountains, hills, or other uplands, often having a river or stream running along the bottom
Hill	A small, but well-defined natural elevation
Plateau	An elevated, level expanse of land; a tableland
Plain	An extensive, level, usually treeless area of land
Savanna	Flat grassland of tropical or subtropical regions
Peninsula	A piece of land that projects into a body of water

WESTERN EUROPE

WESTERN EUROPE DATA BOX

MAJOR PHYSICAL FEATURES

Bodies of Water – North Sea, Baltic Sea, Mediterranean Sea, Adriatic Sea, Aegean Sea, English Channel, Strait of Gibraltar

Rivers – Rhine River, Seine River, Thames River

Mountains – Alps, Pyrenees, Apennines

Plains – Northern European

Climate – Varies among mild Mid-Latitude Rainy (Koppen* C-types moderated by North Atlantic Drift), temperate Mid-Latitude Wet and Dry (D-types); and Polar (E-types).

ECONOMIC RESOURCES

Mineral Resources – coal, iron, bauxite, North Sea petroleum

Agricultural Products – wheat, livestock, vegetables, fruit

Industrial Products – service industries (banking and financial), machine and metal products, textiles, chemicals, automobiles, steel

---

*The climate types referred to in the "Data Box" (at the right) are based on the broad climate classifications developed by Wladimir Peter Koppen (German, 1846-1940) in the *Handbook of Climatology*.

SELECTED GEOGRAPHY & HISTORY LINKS

Location – Western Europe is surrounded by water on three sides with several peninsulas, and no one is more than 450 miles from salt water. Access to waterways led to commerce, trade, exploration, and colonization (ancient Athens, Portugal, Spain, England, France, Netherlands).

Rhine River – This river system is a major carrier of goods for the European Union. Louis XIV of France sought the Rhine River as a natural

KOPPEN CLIMATE TYPES*
(ADAPTED)

Tropical Rainy (A-types)
Af – highland, wet all year
Aw – even amount wet and dry
Am – tropical and humid

Dry (B-types)
Bs – steppe, low but even rainfall
Bw – hot, low rainfall

Mid-Latitude Rainy (C-types)
Cs – highland, wet all year
Cw – even amount wet and dry
Cf – rainy, mild winter

Mid-Latitude Wet & Dry (D-types)
Dw – wet and dry, cold winter
Df – rainy, cold winter

Polar (E-types)
ET – tundra
EF – ice cap

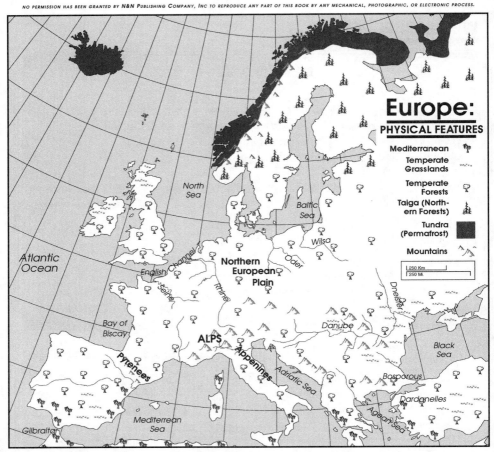

boundary for France in 4 major wars (17th-18th centuries). It was viewed as an obstacle to troop movements during World War II (1939-1945).

Alps – These mountains were an obstacle overcome by Hannibal's army in its attack on the Roman Empire (3rd century BC). They were a factor in Switzerland's ability to declare neutrality. Also, water deposited soils from mountains creating fertile river valleys for crops and livestock.

Mediterranean Sea – It is a major artery for transportation, communication, and cultural diffusion. In ancient history, Athens used it to trade and establish colonies from Spain to Egypt, and in the Middle Ages the Crusaders used it to cross to the Holy Land (11th to 13th centuries). During the Renaissance, it helped to provide Europe with products and ideas from Asia and the Eastern Mediterranean. It was a vital link – a "lifeline" of the British Empire to the East. The narrow straits of Gibraltar and the Dardanelles and Bosporus guard entrances and desire for control of them was a factor in wars such as the War of Spanish Succession, the Crimean War, and World Wars I and II.

FOCUS: GREAT BRITAIN

Location – The English Channel historically provided protection from invasion (last successful invasion by water was that of William the Conqueror in 1066) and enabled Britain to avoid involvement in some European wars. Britain's water surroundings led to the development of a large navy begun under the Tudors. Sailors' familiarity with waters and seamanship helped to defeat the Spanish Armada (1588).

Good ports – Ports such as London and Portsmouth led to early development of commerce and trade which in turn spurred the domestic system and industrialization. Good ports also encouraged colonization of places from the Americas to India.

Mining Coal in Northern England
PhotoDisc©

Coal and iron resources – These were critical factors in the early development of factories (18th century). Coal heated steam powered machinery, trains, and ships. Early harsh working conditions in mines (Ashley Report) led to reforms and government assumption of some responsibility for working conditions.

Rivers and streams – They were early sources of power for machinery and part of canal systems used for inexpensive transportation for heavy products such as coal.

EASTERN EUROPE, RUSSIA, CENTRAL ASIA

SELECTED GEOGRAPHY/HISTORY LINKS

North European Plain – It was a major invasion route used by Napoleon (18th-19th centuries) and Hitler (1939-1945). Its significance is demonstrated by the struggles for control among Russia, Prussia, and

---

EASTERN EUROPE, RUSSIA, AND CENTRAL ASIA DATA BOX

MAJOR PHYSICAL FEATURES

Bodies of Water – Black Sea, Aral Sea, Caspian Sea, Lake Baikal, Pacific Ocean, Arctic Ocean

Rivers – Danube, Don, Volga, Amur, Lena, Ob, Yenisei

Mountains – Carpathians, Caucasus, Urals

Plains – Northern European, Siberian

Climate – Varies among dry steppe and desert (Koppen B-types) in Central Asia, mild Mid-Latitude Rainy (C-types) in interior Europe and Asia, temperate Mid-Latitude Wet and Dry cold winters (D-types) in E. Europe, and Polar (E-types) along the Arctic coast.

ECONOMIC RESOURCES

Mineral Resources – coal, iron, bauxite, natural gas, petroleum

Agricultural Products – wheat, corn, rye, potatoes, sugar beets, livestock

Industrial Products – food processing, textiles, chemicals, armaments, heavy machinery

---

Russia, E. Europe, & C. Asia:
PHYSICAL FEATURES

Temperate Forests	Desert
Taiga (Northern Forests)	Temperate Grasslands
	Tundra (Permafrost)
	Mountains

0 Miles 800

Austria and the resulting partitions of Poland (18th century). It is also a fertile farm area.

Danube River – This river is a major artery for trade and commerce in Eastern Europe. Cereals, ores, and petroleum of southeastern Europe enter world trade to be exchanged for manufactured goods. It is also used for irrigation, as a source for hydroelectric power, and for fishing. It was a highway to the west for Huns, Slavs, and Magyars, and a route for cultural diffusion from Germany.

Population – Historically, the area has contained diverse ethnic and religious populations. This has been a cause of wars, genocide (Armenians during World War I, Jews during World War II), and ethnic cleansing (post Cold War in Yugoslavia). For example, in the former Yugoslavia there were large numbers of Serbs, Croats, Bosnians, Slovenes, and Kosovar Albanians and major religious groups including Orthodox Christians, Roman Catholics, and Muslims.

FOCUS: RUSSIA

Climate – The cold climate has made it difficult for invading armies (Napoleonic Wars and World War II). The lack of ice-free ports has led to expansion. The settlement of Siberia, the wars of Peter the Great (18th century) and Catherine the Great (18th century) were in part designed to gain access to warm water ports. Russian expansion toward Turkey, Iran, China, and India also had this as a goal.

Rivers – The vast distances in Russia make rivers an important avenue for transportation, commerce, and cultural diffusion. The Volga/Don system with its interlocking canals is very important in eastern Russia where it provides transportation from the Baltic Sea to the Black Sea. However, in the vast region of Siberia, the major rivers flow north toward the Arctic and have limited value. (The exception is the Amur River in the Russian Far East.)

Semi-frozen evergreen forests of the Subarctic Taiga, just south of the Tundra in Siberia, Russia   *PhotoDisc©*

Mineral resources – Russia may have the best mineral resource base of any country on Earth. It has large supplies of platinum, nickel, iron, petroleum, and 40% of the world's natural gas reserves. Climate conditions limit access to many of these resources, and recent economic disruptions have further limited exploitation of the resources.

Population – In the former Soviet Union, there were about 100 ethnic groups speaking 80 different languages. As the Cold War ended, many of these groups sought and obtained independent republics (Uzbeks, Estonians). In other instances, civil wars resulted as people tried to free themselves from Russian control (Chechnya) and ethnic groups warred among themselves over disputed territories (Azerbaijanis and Armenians).

Isolation – The cold climate combined with the Mongol invasion (13th century) combined to isolate Russia from Europe during the Renaissance. This limited Russian access to the changes occurring in Europe during this time. Also, the autocracy (single person government with limited control) of the Mongol rulers may have contributed to tsarist policies.

LATIN AMERICA

LATIN AMERICA DATA BOX

MAJOR PHYSICAL FEATURES
Bodies of Water – Caribbean Sea, Atlantic Ocean, Pacific Ocean, Panama Canal
Rivers – Amazon River, Orinoco River, Rio de la Plata
Mountains – Andes, Sierra Madres
Plains – Pampas of Argentina, Llanos of Venezuela, Gran Chaco of Brazil
Climate – Varies greatly among Tropical Rainy (Koppen A-types) in the Caribbean, Central America, and northern South America), Dry (B-types) along the west coast of South America and through the Andes, mild Mid-Latitude Rainy (C-types) in the southern half of South America. In the Andes, there are also vertical climates determined by elevations: tropical wet and dry in low areas (tierra caliente), temperate warm-and-cool seasons above 3,000 ft. (tierra templada), and cool nights and winters above 6,000 ft (tierra fria).

ECONOMIC RESOURCES
Mineral Resources – petroleum, natural gas, copper, iron, manganese, tin, silver, gold
Agricultural Products – coffee, bananas, sugar cane, livestock, cacao, cotton, tobacco, maize, wheat
Industrial Products – food processing, textiles, leather products, transportation equipment, appliances, steel, aluminum

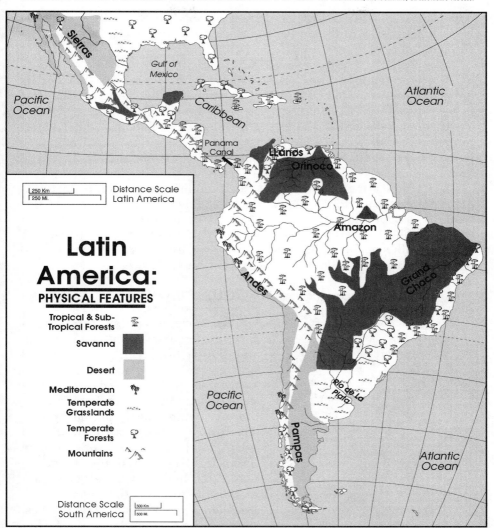

SELECTED GEOGRAPHY/HISTORY LINKS

Andes Mountains – Second only to the Himalayas in height, the Andes *Cordillera* limits east-west travel and only a few narrow passes pierce them. The mountain area from Peru south is rich in natural resources. Native Americans adopted terracing of mountain areas in order to grow crops. The Andes blocked long-term unification of Spanish South America as Gran Colombia under Simón Bolívar in the 19th century.

Pampas of Argentina – This large grassland area became known as the "breadbasket" of South America because of its grain production. It was also famous for beef production which became a major export for

Argentina. The agricultural products available led the British to invest large amounts in railroads to transport the foodstuffs to the ports for shipment abroad.

Panama Canal – The Canal was built in 1903 after Panama won its independence from Colombia with U.S. support. The Canal cut the time needed to go from the Atlantic to Pacific Oceans and also helped ships to avoid the dangerous waters in the Strait of Magellan. However, super-tankers, aircraft carriers, and other large ships cannot go through the narrow locks. The U.S. transfers ownership to Panama in 2000.

Urbanization – Mexico City with 19 million people is the most populous city in the world; one in five Brazilians live in Rio de Janeiro or Sao Paulo. The continuing movement of people from rural areas to cities in search of jobs and better educational opportunities for their children is a serious challenge. Major cities are surrounded by **barrios** (shanty towns) which have makeshift housing and lack the basic services.

FOCUS: BRAZIL

Dense rainforest, interior of Brazil
PhotoDisc©

Amazon River system – This river system is over 3,000 miles long, has 200 tributaries, and is second only to the Nile in size. The tropical rain forests provide products such as rubber, carnuba, and hardwoods. However, rain quickly leaches minerals from cleared land ("slash and burn"), and long-term farming on the same land is impossible. Ongoing struggles between developers and environmentalists (concerns about greenhouse effect, endangered species, native peoples, etc.) leave the future of the area in doubt.

Importation of Slaves – Early Portuguese settlers forced native peoples to work in the sugar cane fields established in the 16th century. However, they rapidly died from the hard work under often brutal conditions. This led to the importation of slaves from Africa. About 40% of the slaves imported to the Americas went to Brazil. When the gold and diamond mines were opened in the Brazilian Highlands in the 17th century, the same labor process occurred. The underclass in Brazil today has large numbers of mestizos and mulattos – descendants of the early workers. Many are tenant farmers or sharecroppers.

Opening of the interior – In 1960, the Brazilian government decided to open the interior to settlement and development of iron and bauxite deposits. A new capital, Brasilia, was built in the interior. A network of highways was begun; the most famous one was the Trans-Amazon Highway. As transportation and communication improved, education and medical care were extended to remote villages.

MIDDLE EAST

MIDDLE EAST DATA BOX

MAJOR PHYSICAL FEATURES
Bodies of Water – Mediterranean Sea, Red Sea, Persian Gulf, Straits of
            Dardanelles & Bosporus
Rivers – Nile River, Jordan River, Tigris and Euphrates Rivers, Suez Canal
Deserts – Sahara, Arabian (Rub al Khali)
Climate – Generally Dry (Koppen B-type climates) in the deserts and steppes
        (plateaus), Mediterranean areas are exceptions (where cooler and
        wetter C-types prevail).

ECONOMIC RESOURCES
Mineral Resources – petroleum, coal, iron, natural gas, phosphates
Agricultural Products – cotton, tobacco, wheat, barley, millet, fruits, livestock
Industrial Products – food processing, textiles, fertilizers, petrochemicals, diamond cutting

---

SELECTED GEOGRAPHY/HISTORY LINKS

Location – The area is a crossroads for three continents. Trade routes across the area have carried goods and ideas among Europe, Africa, and Asia. Its strategic importance has led to struggles for control between Christians and Turks, European powers, and Europeans and the native population, as well as among European powers.

Petroleum – Three quarters of the world's reserves of oil are in the Middle East. The countries which have large amounts of oil such as Saudi Arabia have a much higher standard of living than those with little or no oil such as Egypt. Struggles for control of the oil began prior to World War I. Postwar League of Nations mandates allowed Europeans to control some of the area, and other parts came under the influence of European financial interests. In the post-World War II period, OPEC was established to control production and prices. It has also used its power to

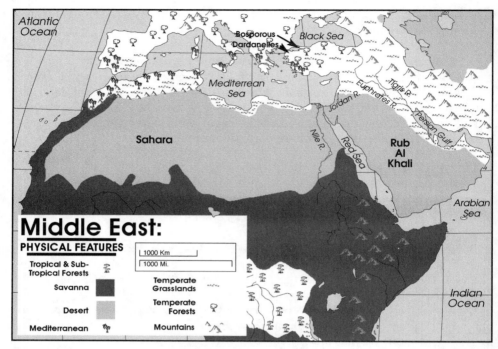

influence international affairs as in the case of the Yom Kippur War. Its policy to raise prices was a major factor in the global financial crisis of 1973. The Iran/Iraq War and the Persian Gulf War were in part caused by issues of oil control.

Water shortage – Less than 15% of the land can be farmed because of water shortages. It also limits areas of settlement and leads to dense population near water sources such as the Tigris and Euphrates Rivers. Desalination plants have been built in countries such as Saudi Arabia and Kuwait. Other countries, such as Israel, have concentrated on developing dry farming methods.

FOCUS: ISRAEL

Desert – The Israelis were able to turn desert areas into profitable farmlands. Science was applied to agriculture and irrigation, water recycling, hothouses, mechanization, and dry farming methods. It became possible to feed much of the population and export some crops.

The Israelis also recognized the need for cooperative efforts under these circumstances. This was one reason for the establishment of the kibbutz (farm or settlement) and moshav (cooperative farm settlement).

Industries – Israel must import most raw materials, but it also has a large number of skilled immigrants. Its industries take advantage of these skills to cut diamonds, produce electronic equipment and petro-chemicals, and refine petroleum.

Holy places – Places holy to Judaism, Christianity, and Islam are found in Israel. All three religions lay claim to some parts of Jerusalem which was taken over by Israel in the Six Day War (1967). This city was proclaimed the capital of Israel although this claim is not recognized by the international community. Settlement of its future is a major key to peace.

FOCUS: EGYPT

Nile River – Egypt is called the "gift of the Nile" with good reason – 95% of its population lives in the Nile Valley and Delta. The river has provided rich, alluvial soil for centuries; it is a major source of trans-portation; and has served as a route for cultural diffusion. The construction of High Aswan High Dam made it possible to control irrigation waters and flooding. In addition, it provides a source of hydroelectric power.

Suez Canal – This Canal was completed by the French in 1869 to provide a better sea route from Europe to Asia. Britain later purchased part ownership, because it was a vital link in the "lifeline of the British Empire." Gamal Abdel Nassar's (President of Egypt) decision to national-ize the Canal in 1956 led to the Suez Canal Crisis and Egyptian owner-ship. Since 1975, Egypt expanded the Canal to accommodate supertankers carrying oil and to gain additional revenue.

Population growth – Recent population growth was 2.3% per year, and population density in the Nile Valley and Delta was 3,243 per square mile. Forty-nine percent of the population is in urban areas and is increasing at twice the average national growth rate. This has led to a housing crisis, lack of basic services, and food shortages. Islamic fundamental-ists groups are actively organizing programs to meet the needs of the new city dwellers and are winning new sup-porters with which to challenge the govern-ment.

Ancient pyramids amid sands of the Sahara, Egypt
PhotoDisc©

AFRICA

AFRICA DATA BOX

MAJOR PHYSICAL FEATURES
Bodies of Water – Atlantic Ocean, Indian Ocean
Rivers – Congo (Zaire) River, Nile River, Chad River, Zambezi River, Niger River
Mountains – Atlas, Drakensberg
Deserts – Sahara, Kalahari
Landform – Great Rift Valley
Climate – In West and Equatorial Africa: Tropical Rainy (Koppen A-types) prevail,
        such as Savannas with high temperatures, but with some dry periods;
        to the north and south of the Equatorial region, Dry desert and semi-
        desert B-types prevail: very warm all year, with a small amount of rain
        in summer; on the southernmost tip there are temperate C-type Mid
        Latitude wet-and-dry areas with mild winters.

ECONOMIC RESOURCES
Mineral Resources – gold, diamonds, copper, petroleum
Agricultural Products – coffee, cacao, cotton, rubber, tea, peanuts
Industrial Products – mining, food processing, consumer products, petroleum
                refining

SELECTED GEOGRAPHY/HISTORY LINKS

Penetration of the interior – Much of Africa has a smooth coast-line and lacks natural harbors. This isolated Africans and made it difficult to trade. Many of the major rivers have rapids or falls near the coast limiting their usefulness as routes to the interior. The tropical rain forests are difficult to penetrate and often harbor serious or fatal diseases. At times, the Sahara Desert cut sub-Saharan Africa off from the north and limited access. European claims to the interior of Africa were delayed until the late 19th century.

Sahara Desert and the Sahel – The difficulty involved in obtaining water led to a nomadic lifestyle in the Sahara as people went from oasis to oasis. From the 1960s to the 1980s, desertification of the Sahel (on the fringe of the Sahara) occurred. Increased population demands and over-grazing of livestock worsened the water shortage. Government revenues were spent on relief measures and not on much needed development. Despite international efforts, starvation and disruption of life styles of the inhabitants resulted.

Slave trade – Beginning in the 16th century with the demands of the New World for labor on sugar, tobacco, and cotton plantations, the

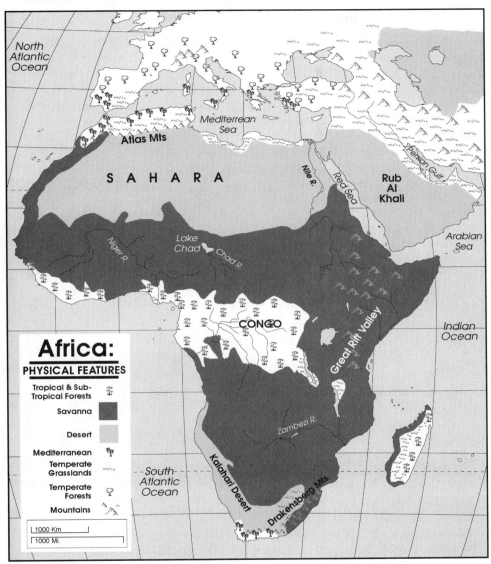

Africa:
PHYSICAL FEATURES

- Tropical & Sub-Tropical Forests
- Savanna
- Desert
- Mediterranean
- Temperate Grasslands
- Temperate Forests
- Mountains

1000 Km
1000 Mi.

slave trade cost many Africans their lives. Tribe was set against tribe in wars designed to capture prisoners to be sold to slave traders who waited at the coastal fortresses. These civil wars ended traditional social and political order and seriously diminished the population. The outcry against slavery and the often disastrous trip aboard slave trading vessels crossing the Atlantic led to the 19th century abolitionist movement, but the damage to the African life style was already done.

FOCUS: CONGO (KINSHASA)

Resources – The Democratic Republic of the Congo (formerly Zaire) is rich in resources such as copper, rubber, and cobalt. This attracted the attention of Leopold II of Belgium who used his own resources and those of private investors to gain control. Forced labor in the mines and on rubber plantations occurred to gain profits. After securing independence from Belgium, the new Congo government with Belgian aid, put down a rebellion in a breakaway province, mineral-rich Katanga. Continued reliance upon export of resources for revenue leaves Congo vulnerable to the ups and downs of the international market.

Congo (Zaire) River – This river is not navigable for the first 220 miles from the Atlantic, yet in places, it is a very important artery for transportation. Much of the Congo is tropical rain forest, and construction and maintenance of roads is very difficult.

Wildlife on the Savannas of Africa
PhotoDisc©

FOCUS: SOUTH AFRICA

Mineral resources – The Republic of South Africa mines a major portion of the 12 main mineral resources including chrome, platinum, manganese, zinc, and lead in addition to gold and diamonds. The discovery of gold and diamonds in the interior led to the Boer War. The British defeated the Boers, but established the semi-independent Union of South Africa in 1910. However, mines continued to be owned by foreigners who often exploited migrant laborers who lived far from home in mining compounds. The end of apartheid in the early 1990s saw the beginning of mining changes.

Ports – Although much of Africa has few natural harbors, the harbor at Cape Town attracted the attention of early Portuguese explorers. It was a halfway port to take on fresh water and food for the trip to Asia. Later, the Dutch seized control of the area only to lose it to Britain after the Napoleonic Wars at the Congress of Vienna (1814-1815). Modern South Africa has developed ports at Durban, Cape Town, Port Elizabeth, and East London, making it a major exporting center.

SOUTH AND SOUTHEAST ASIA

SOUTH AND SOUTHEAST ASIA DATA BOX

MAJOR PHYSICAL FEATURES

Bodies of Water – Pacific Ocean, Indian Ocean, Gulf of Tonkin, Gulf of Thailand, Luzon Strait, South China Sea, Bay of Bengal, Arabian Sea

Rivers – Ganges River, Bramaputra River, Indus River, Mekong River, Chao Phyra River, Irrawaddy River, Red River

Mountains – Himalaya Mountains, Ghats

Plateau – Deccan

Plains – Indo-Gangetic

Climate – Primarily hot, Tropical Rainy (Koppen A-types) to areas of hot, wet summers and warm, dry winters; monsoon winds from the interior of Asia bring cold-dry conditions in winter, and summer monsoons from the Indian Ocean and South Pacific bring hot, wet conditions.

ECONOMIC RESOURCES

Mineral Resources – tin, bauxite, oil, coal, iron, manganese

Agricultural Products – rubber, spices, tea, coffee, lumber, coconuts, rice, jute

Industrial Products – food processing, fishing, textiles, consumer goods, steel

SELECTED GEOGRAPHY/HISTORY LINKS

Monsoons – In general, summer monsoons bring rain to much of the area and the winter monsoons are dry. However, the winter monsoons do

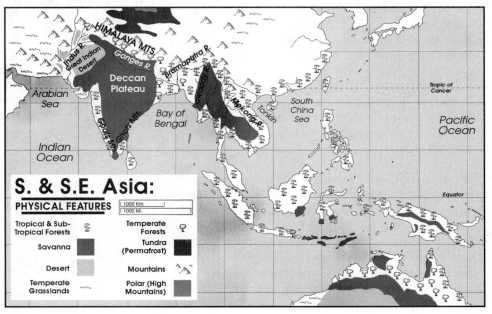

bring some rain to South Asia. The uneven rainfall has a major impact on life. Insufficient rain often means drought and famine and too much rain means flooding and destruction. Bangladesh has suffered considerable loss of life and economic damage from monsoons. Historically, 19th century merchants used the monsoon winds to carry them from China to Indonesia in the winter and back to China in the summer.

Location of Southeast Asia – Most of this area is a peninsula attached to the Asian mainland or a series of islands. As a consequence, it could be reached from land or by sea. Cultural diffusion from India led to Hinduism and Buddhism. Large numbers of Chinese migrated to the area and became a very important merchant class. The Arabs and Europeans arrived by sea attracted by the spices and other products available.

Mekong River – The source of this river is the Tibetan Highlands and it flows through China, Laos, Thailand, Cambodia, and Vietnam. It is navigable into Laos and forms boundaries for several countries. The delta in Vietnam has rich, alluvial soil, is heavily populated, and is a major rice producer.

FOCUS: INDIA

Himalaya Mountains – The eastern Himalayas block outside contact, but the western Himalayas have several mountain passes (Khyber Pass) through which invaders entered India. The Aryan invasion (c. 1000 BC) led to a mixing of cultures resulting in Hinduism, the caste system, and the Sanskrit language. Alexander the Great's invasion led to cultural diffusion from Greece and increased trade ties with the Middle East. The Muslim invasion (1200-1760) resulted in the Mughal rule which unified India and led to a golden age of culture (Taj Mahal).

Population growth – One-sixth of the Earth's population lives in India. Despite a family planning program begun in 1952, the population continues to increase. Religious reasons and the value of large farm families are partially responsible. The increasing population has led to migration to

Terraced Rice Fields, Indonesia
PhotoDisc©

urban areas, increased unemployment, and insufficient food. International efforts by the World Bank and the Food and Agriculture Organization bought the Green Revolution to India. However, parts of India still suffer from food shortages although acute famine is not a threat unless there is an unexpected natural disaster.

Deccan Plateau – This plateau comprises a major portion of the Indian peninsula. It contains much of the mineral resource base. Most of the population lives on the edges of the plateau in river valleys with heavy rain.

EAST ASIA

EAST ASIA DATA BOX

MAJOR PHYSICAL FEATURES
Bodies of Water – Pacific Ocean, Yellow Sea, East China Sea, Sea of Japan,
Rivers – Huang He (Yellow) River, Chang Jiang(Yangtze) River, Xi (West) River, Yalu River
Mountains – Himalaya Mountains, Tien Shan Range, Kunlun Mountains
Desert – Gobi Desert
Plateau – Tibet
Climate – Varies among mild Mid-Latitude Rainy (Koppen C-types) in the south, temperate Mid-Latitude West and Dry (D-types) in the north, and Wet and Dry desert (B-types) in the northern interior areas; Pacific currents also play a major tempering role in the southern and middle coastal areas.

ECONOMIC RESOURCES
Mineral Resources – coal, iron, magnesium, tungsten, petroleum
Agricultural Products – rice, wheat, barley, soybeans
Industrial Products – electronics, computers, automobiles, clothing, textiles

SELECTED GEOGRAPHY/HISTORY LINKS

River Valleys – Rivers were often the sites of early civilizations. One such civilization developed along the Huang He (Yellow) River in China over 4,000 years ago. These rivers are very important to agricultural production. Their spring floods bring much needed nutrients to the surrounding farmland, affecting the food supply. However, the Huang He River is often called "China's Sorrow" because its flooding also causes considerable damage to the dense, large population in the river valleys. Shanghai on the Chang Jiang (Yangtze) River has a population of over 12 million and continues to grow.

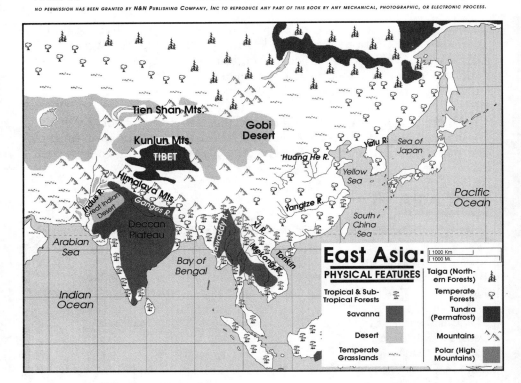

East Asia: PHYSICAL FEATURES

1000 Km
1000 Mi.

- Tropical & Sub-Tropical Forests
- Savanna
- Desert
- Temperate Grasslands
- Taiga (Northern Forests)
- Temperate Forests
- Tundra (Permafrost)
- Mountains
- Polar (High Mountains)

Isolation – Mountains and deserts to the west and north of China and the Pacific Ocean to the east made it possible for China to isolate itself from outside contact. This isolation led to ethnocentrism and the belief that all foreigners were barbarians. The Chinese referred to their country as the Middle Kingdom (remainder of the world circled around it) and made tributary states of its neighbors including Korea and the peoples to the south. The ethnocentrism later limited development and left China unprepared to meet the challenge of the Europeans in the 19th century.

Population – China's over one billion people make it the most populated country on Earth. The communists under Mao Zedong found it difficult to feed the growing number, but the establishment of communes to increase food supply resulted in a production disaster because of peasant opposition. Later, Deng Xiaoping instituted capitalist incentives to increase production. The government also enforces a program to limit the number of children. Urban dwellers are limited to one child; rural inhabitants may have two. Some exceptions are made for minority groups, but those who violate the regulations may suffer severe financial penalties.

FOCUS: JAPAN

SELECTED GEOGRAPHY/HISTORY LINKS: JAPAN

Island nation – Like Britain, Japan is an island nation. This offers the possibility of trade and cultural contacts while avoiding foreign control. Much of the cultural diffusion came from
China by way of Korea.
Buddhism, art forms,
and the tea ceremony
are examples of this dif-
fusion. In 1639, the
Tokugawa Shogunate
decided that outside
contacts, especially
European, threatened
Japan. The ports of
Japan were closed to
most foreigners until
Commodore Perry of
the U.S. Navy opened
them in 1853.

Mt. Fuji – part of Japan's rugged island terrain

PhotoDisc©

Mountains – About 85% of Japan is mountainous. This has led to intensive farming techniques and terracing in an attempt to feed the population. Japan also looks to the sea for fish to feed its people. Despite these efforts, Japan is the world's largest food importer. The fast flowing rivers which descend from the mountains are good for irrigation and hydroelectric power, but are not navigable because of rapids.

Mineral resources – Japan has some copper and small amounts of iron, but must import most of its raw materials. This lack of a good resource base was partially responsible for the aggressive expansion Japan began with the Sino-Japanese War (1894-1895) and continued through the takeover of Manchuria prior to World War II. The weak resource base also led Japan to develop industries which rely on the skill of its people. It exports finished products to pay for raw material imports.

LINKAGES

In its broadest sense, geography has had a tremendous impact on human life on the Earth. Social, cultural, and religious development, as well as population growth and movement are often related to geographic factors. They help to determine what occurs, what adaptations people make, and to what ideas they are exposed. Economically, mineral resources, agricultural products, and industries are intertwined with geographic conditions such as climate, location, and landforms. Politically, rivers, oceans, and mountains play major roles in the development of distinctive groups of human beings based on such things as tribes, ethnicity, and religious groups. Geography and history are intertwined and are major determinants of the course of human affairs.

QUESTIONS

1   A major factor in determining Russia's foreign policy throughout history was the
    1   need to secure warm water ports
    2   lack of sufficient space for the growing population
    3   search for sources of coal and iron
    4   acquisition of mountain barriers for protection

2   *Used by Crusaders to cross to the Holy Land*
     Crossed by traders to bring Far Eastern goods to Europe
     Guarded by narrow straits at each end

     These phrases best describe the
     1   South China Sea
     2   Indian Ocean
     3   Mediterranean Sea
     4   Atlantic Ocean

Base your answer to question 3 (next page) on the poem below and your knowledge of global history and geography.

3   "Towering aloft
     above the earth,
     Great Kunlun...

     In the days of summer
     Your melting torrents
     Fill streams and rivers
     Till they overflow,
     Changing men
     Into fish and turtles
     What man can pass judgement
     On all the good and evil
     You have done
     These thousand autumns?"

     – Mao Zedong - a poem written after he crossed the Kunlun mountain range on the Long March

In this poem, Mao Zedong is
1   describing the Kunlun Mountains
2   expressing his concern about the fish and turtles
3   telling of the problems encountered crossing the mountains
4   indicating his reaction to men who pass judgment

4   Britain and Japan are similar because both are
1   rich in natural resources
2   island nations
3   major oil importers
4   self-sufficient in food production

5   Less developed countries such as the Congo and Bolivia are most
likely to have industries which
1   produce high technology products
2   concentrate on the production of electronics products
3   meet basic consumer needs such as food processing
4   rely on advanced computer driven machines

Base your answer to question 6 on the map at the right and your knowledge of global history and geography.

6   What is a correct conclusion based on the information provided on the map?
1   All Western European countries were Allied Powers in 1914.
2   Russia changed sides during World War I.
3   Germany would have to fight a two-front war.
4   Britain was a neutral nation in 1914.

7   A major problem facing Eastern Europe, Russia, and Central Asia
continues to be
1   the tensions and conflicts among diverse ethnic and religious groups
2   the cold tundra or ice cap conditions throughout the area
3   the lack of good agricultural land in the entire region
4   the high mountain ranges which dominate the few valleys

8 The Incas adapted to life in the Andes Mountains by
  1 planting crops such as cotton, rice, and tobacco at high elevations
  2 using hybrid seeds and chemical fertilizers to increase production
  3 building terraces to increase available farming
  4 practicing dry farming techniques suitable for desert areas

9 Hinduism, the caste system, and the Sanskrit language are examples of cultural diffusion to
  1 Japan
  2 China
  3 Vietnam
  4 India

10 Which statement best describes the geography of Africa?
  1 Most of the continent is made up of tropical rain forests.
  2 Deserts and savannas cover almost half of the continent.
  3 Most major rivers are navigable for their entire length.
  4 The irregular coastline provides many natural harbors.

11 Japan's insular location enabled it to
  1 accept cultural ideas, but reject foreign control
  2 become self-sufficient in food and mineral resources
  3 avoid involvement in World War I and World War II
  4 develop a diverse ethnic and religious population

Base your answer to question 12 on the cartoon at the right and your knowledge of global history and geography.

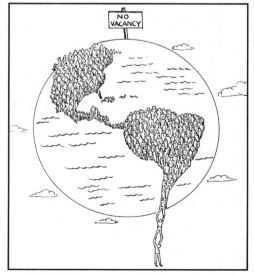

12 What would be the most appropriate caption for this cartoon?
  1 Oceans are the most source of food.
  2 The Americas are becoming overcrowded.
  3 Most people live along the coasts.
  4 Ocean pollution is a major environmental problem.

13 The Amazon River system is the subject of much controversy because
1   destruction of its rain forest threatens the world environment
2   Brazil refuses to allow settlers to remain along its banks
3   the flow of water to the Atlantic is slowed by numerous dams
4   replanting of cut trees on its banks is proceeding too quickly

14 In many less developed areas, the migration pattern is from
1   suburbs to rural regions
2   cities to suburbs
3   rural to urban areas
4   cities to farm areas

15 The Boer War, the Sino-Japanese War, and the Persian Gulf War all involved
1   issues surrounding freedom of the seas
2   struggles to achieve independence
3   disagreements over religious beliefs
4   desire to control important natural resources

THEMATIC ESSAY

Directions: Write a well-organized essay that includes an introduction, several paragraphs explaining your position, and a conclusion.

Theme: Human geography

> Throughout history, geography has had an impact on the development of nations and regions.

Task:

> Explain how geography has affected the development of three nations and/or regions.
>
> Support your opinion by citing specific examples of the impact of geography on the nations and/or regions selected.

Suggestions: You may use any examples from your study of global history and geography. Some suggestions you might wish to consider are Britain, Russia, China, Brazil, India, the Middle East, Latin America, Southeast Asia. **You are *not* limited to these suggestions**.

PRACTICE SKILLS FOR DBQ

Directions: The following task is based on the accompanying documents. The documents may have been edited for the purposes of this exercise. The task is designed to test your ability to work with historical documents. As you analyze the documents, take into account both the sources of the document and the author's point of view.

Historical Context: The Roman Empire (27 BC - 476 AD) lasted for several centuries and is generally recognized as one of the greatest civilzations of all times.

Part *A* – Short Answer

The documents that follow are related to the role that location played in the greatness of the Roman Empire. Examine each document carefully, then answer the question that follows it.

Document 1

> " How, then, could Romulus (legendary founder of Rome) with a more divine insight have made use of the advantages of a situation on the sea ...than by placing his city on the banks of a river that flows through the year with an even current and empties into the sea through a wide mouth? Thus, the city could receive by sea the products it needed and also dispose of its extra commodities. ... For practically no city situated in any other part of Italy could have been better able to command such economic advantages."
>
> – Marcus Tullius Cicero, 1st century BC orator and philosopher

1   Why does Cicero think that the location of Rome was advantageous to its development?

_____

_____

_____

_____

_____

_____

_____

_____

Document 2

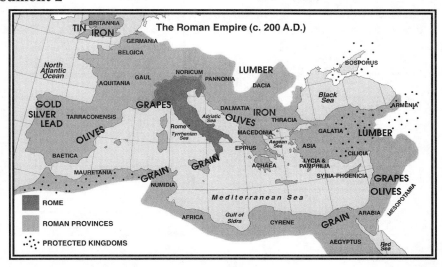

2 How did the Mediterranean Sea and the lands around it contribute to the greatness of Rome?

_____

_____

_____

_____

_____

_____

_____

Part *B* – Essay Response

Task: Using only the information in the documents, write one or two paragraphs about how location played a role in the greatness of the Roman Empire.

State your thesis:

- Use only the information in the documents to support your thesis position
- Include your analysis of the documents
- Incorporate your answers to Part *A* scaffold questions

_____

Additional Suggested Task:

From your knowledge of global history and geography, make a list of additional factors that may have contributed to the greatness of Rome.

_____

_____

_____

_____

_____

_____

_____

_____

_____

_____

_____

_____

_____

_____

_____

_____

_____

_____

_____

_____

_____

_____

_____

_____

_____

_____

_____

_____

_____

4000 BC TO 500 AD

Hominids in Africa
(4 million)

Neolitic Revolution
(60,000)

3500–

Menes unites Egypt
(3,100)

3000–

Sumerian City-states
emerge (2700)

2500–

Great Pyramids built
(2400)

2000–

Hammurabi's Code
(1792)

1500–

Aryans invade Indus
Valley (1500)

1000–

Zhou overthrows Shang
in China (1027)

Homer's *Illiad &
Odyssey* (800)

500–

Roman Republic begins (500)

Alexander spreads Hellenistic culture (325)

AD   Asoka expands Maurya rule in India (272)

0–   Octavian begins Pax Romana (31)

BC

Fall of Han Empire (220)

500–   Constantine legalizes Christianity (313)

ANCIENT WORLD: CIVILIZATIONS & RELIGIONS

INTRODUCTION

Human society emerged slowly. Over thousands of years, primitive **cultures** (total knowledge and behavior patterns of a human society) slowly evolved into civilizations. **Civilizations** are a level of society marked by complex social, economic, and political organization. The civilized organization is aided by some form of written language and scientific and technological advancement. Historians record the first civilizations arising from agricultural villages and settlements around 4000 BC.

The Great Sphinx lies near Giza, Egypt and measures 69 ft in height and 243 ft in length. It was originally built to guard the pyramid of Khafre. The Great Sphinx was later worshiped as the god Rahorakhty, "Ra of the Two Horizons."

PhotoDisc©

From 4000 BC to 500 AD, the economic, social, and political activities of humans went through many transformations. By far, the most important change came in the form of economic revolution. Moving from nomadic hunter-gathers to farmers, humans converted their entire patterns of life. Their needs and wants changed completely, and their new economic existence drove them to develop new social and political institutions.

ECONOMIC DEVELOPMENT

NEOLITHIC REVOLUTION

Prior to 10,000 BC, groups of nomadic hunter-gatherers roamed large areas in search of food. After 10,000 BC, semipermanent settlements emerged as primitive people discovered that spreading seeds and manual replanting of wild grains allowed control of some of the food supply. Historians refer to this basic economic shift – which occurred in different places at different times – as the **Neolithic Revolution**. The rise of agricultural activity led to permanent settlements. A steady food supply and permanent settlement meant better nourishment and health. Infant mortality diminished and population grew.

The Neolithic Revolution was the most profound change in the course of human existence. When agricultural **surpluses** (quantities in excess of what is needed) appeared on a regular basis, people ceased wandering and began animal husbandry (breeding and raising livestock). Early agricultural people gravitated toward river valleys for their resources.

RIVER VALLEY CIVILIZATIONS

Life in the river valleys also became more complex. Surpluses allowed some individuals to cease farming altogether and perform specialized services the communities needed (implement makers, builders, transporters, artisans, potters, weavers, masons, miners) in exchange for food and fodder. Permanent settlements were stable, but compared to mobile nomadic camps, they were vulnerable to attack and to acts of nature that ruined crops. This created a need for warriors to specialize in defenses and priests to intercede spiritually with nature to maintain prosperity. These classes then created walled cities, citadels, and temples, and the massive architectural structures of the ancient world emerged. Gradually, a merchant-trader class also arose to exchange goods over large areas.

CHARACTERISTICS OF EARLY RIVER VALLEY SETTLEMENTS:

- mild climates, generally
- availability of irrigation water and richer soils
- ease of transportation, communication, and trade
- production of agricultural surpluses
- building cities for protection and transfer of goods

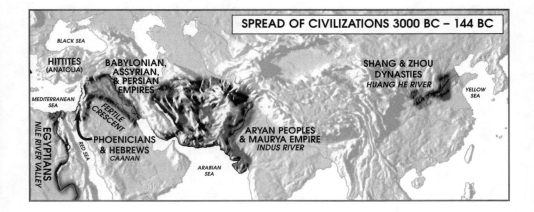

SPREAD OF CIVILIZATIONS 3000 BC – 144 BC

★ CAPSULE – RIVER VALLEY CIVILIZATIONS

- Nile River Valley Civilizations (Egypt, Kush, Northeast Africa 3000-1000 BC)
- Protected by surrounding desert
- Expanded to south (Nubia), and east (Palestine, Syria)
- Hieroglyphic writing system
- Complex religious beliefs, worshiped afterlife, polytheistic
- Pyramids, temples
- Pharaohs were divine right rulers
- 12 mo. calendar, land reclamation, irrigation, pharmacology

Indus River Valley Civilizations (India, South Asia 2700-500 BC)

- Settlements: Mohenjo-daro, Harappa, grid planned cities
- Dependence on monsoons to bring adequate rains for agriculture
- Emergence of Hindu religion and the caste system
- Sanskrit writing and language
- Hindu texts: *Vedas, Upanishad*

Huang He River Valley Civilizations (China, East Asia 2500-700 BC)

- Pictograph writing and calligraphy
- Feudal system of local lords allied to an emperor/king
- Walled cities (An'yang) to protect from outsiders
- Permanence of government (Shang, Zhou Dynasties)
- Tendency toward ethnocentrism and isolation from outside people
- Rule by "Mandate of Heaven" (a form of divine right)
- Confucian, Taoist, Legalist philosophies
- Bronze & iron implements

Tigris Euphrates River Valley Civilizations (SouthWest Asia 3000-144 BC)

- Mesopotamian city states (later united under: Sumerians, Babylonians, Hittites, Assyrians, Chaldeans, Persians)
- Cuneiform writing, wheel, copper & bronze implements, 12 month calendar, ziggurat pyramid temples, chariots, sundial, canal building
- Legal System: Code of Hammurabi
- Epic tales: *Gilgamesh*
- Aramaic as a universal language
- Zoroastrian religion: the struggle between good and evil

Other Ancient civilizations (2000-200 BC)

- After Hittites broke the power of Mesopotamia, other groups emerged in the Eastern Mediterranean:
- Hebrews (c. 1500 BC) founded Judaism; spread monotheistic religion and ethics in Canaan, created Israel c. 1000 BC
- Phoenicians (c. 1200 BC) spread streamlined 26-letter alphabet, and founded network of mighty trading cities such as Carthage

CIVILIZATIONS LINKED BY TRADE

From earliest times, agricultural settlements were linked by trade. As civilizations grew, the distances that traders traveled for profit broadened. Yet, these global adventurers brought more than goods from place to place. They brought knowledge of cultures to others. Language, customs, religions, literature, and technology all traveled with traders and diffused with their transactions. Some ancient cultures may have feared or disdained others, but knowledge about them was still widespread.

From their Eastern Mediterranean cities (Sidon, Tyre, Ugarit) the seafaring **Phoenicians** appeared in Egyptian and Mesopotamian history as early as 3000 BC. They brought cedar wood, purple dyes, glass, wine, metal weapons, and ivory. They connected Africa (Egypt and Kush) with Asia (Babylon, Syria, and Persia). Later, the Phoenicians dominated the Mediterranean from Carthage. They mixed the cultures of the ancient Middle East with those of Europe. The Phoenicians adapted a condensed alphabet from India to simplify transactions. In turn, it was adapted by the Greeks after the 9th century BC to form a base for the later languages of Europe.

In ancient times, Greek and Lydian traders from Asia Minor and Syrians and Persians from the Middle East ventured across the steppes and mountain passes of Asia. By 1000 BC, a series of trails and way stations became known as the **Silk Routes** (Silk Roads) to India and China. Caravan paths ran from the Caspian Sea through the Pamirs and the Taklamaken Desert to China's Xi'an Province. Samarkand and Tashkent became major transfer centers where caravans from east and west would exchange goods and knowledge. The Silk Routes remained a main line of commerce until the 15th century AD.

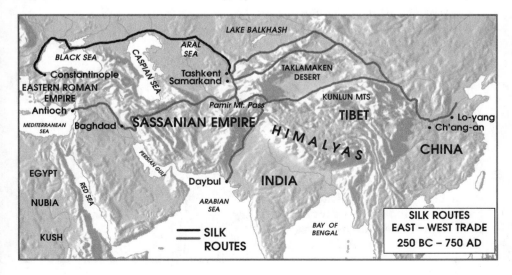

POLITICAL DEVELOPMENT

CIVILIZATIONS BECOME EMPIRES

The river valley civilizations were cradles for human advancement. As they developed, their need for additional resources – especially minerals – led to expansion beyond the valleys. **Cultural diffusion** (mixing of ideas, technologies, religions, institutions) occurred on an ever-increasing scale as societies interacted – sometimes in peace and sometimes in war.

As different civilizations clashed over land and other resources, older cities became foundations for powerful empires of the ancient world. Not only did they conquer and build cities, but they established bureaucracies and communication systems. These actions kept their conquests unified and allowed trade and cultural exchanges to flourish.

ANCIENT EMPIRES			
Period	**Empire**	**Region**	**Leaders**
539-470 BC	Persia	E. Mediterranean to Indus R.	Cyrus, Darius, Xerxes
330 BC	Macedonia	Balkans to Indus R. + Egypt	Alexander
321-297 BC	Maurya	Central India	Chandragupta Maurya
221-206 BC	Q'in	Central Eastern China	Shi Huangdi
141-87 BC	Han	Eastern China	Wudi (Liu Qi)

Agora of Ancient Athens

POLITICAL CHANGE:

CLASSICAL CIVILIZATIONS

After 1000 BC, there was active political development beyond the borders of the great empires. It set the scene for a new era of classical civilization. At the edges of the great empires, adventurous seafarers pushed beyond the protected borders. Some of these adventurers and profit-seekers became links between empires. While motivated by economic improvement, their adventurous spirit created new political units. Some founded trading colonies, pushing commercial frontiers farther and farther. Among them

CLASSICAL CIVILIZATIONS: TYPES OF GOVERNMENTS		
Type	**Who Makes Decisions?**	**Variations**
Monarchy	one person	absolute monarch, dictator, constitutional monarch
Oligarchy	a few persons	council of elders, junta; theocracy, senate
Democracy	all the people	direct democracy, representative democracy

were the **Dorians**, the **Lydians**, the **Minoans**, and the **Phoenicians**. They settled Greece, Cyprus, Crete, Sicily, and Carthage. As a group, they transmitted overlapping mixtures of language, literature, and technology through the Mediterranean Region. These new states grew in many different directions, but some of them became the bases for new political powers.

☆ CAPSULE – RIVAL GREEK CITY STATES

SPARTA

In the 10th century BC, invaders called Dorians forced independent villages on the Peloponnesian Peninsula to merge into the polis of Sparta. Spartan leaders always feared revolts by those helots (conquered servants) conquered. They developed a military-dominated, authoritarian government. All citizens were to serve and sacrifice for the state. There were two figure-head kings who commanded the army, but the real power was in a 5-person oligarchy of magistrates called the **Ephors**. The ephors dominated the council of elders and the assembly.

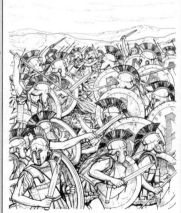

Only citizen-soldiers could hold land, with their state-assigned slaves and serfs working for them. There was no ownership – the state decided to whom the land was granted. Socially, the key virtues for citizens were obedience, courage, and modesty. The military society was strengthened by sending young boys, age 7, to live in camps for physical conditioning and military training.

Later, Sparta forced other nearby poleis into the Peloponnesian League. However, its leadership was hurt by the rigidness of a paranoid military state. It lacked the flexibility needed to meet the changing conditions in the region. In the 4th Century, Sparta maintained an uneasy peace with Philip and Alexander, but eventually it fell to the Romans.

☆ CAPSULE – RIVAL GREEK CITY STATES

ATHENS

Athens was a polis on the Attica Peninsula north of Peloponnesia. It was founded by decendents of the ancient Mycenaens called Ionians and was led by four noble tribes. Athens was surrounded by mountains with timber and minerals, but limited land for food production and the focus on cash crops (olives and grapes) forced Athens to look to the sea for its livelihood.

Athens did not grow powerful through conquest as had Sparta. Its trade allowed it to found colonies and create diplomatic alliances (the Dorian League) throughout the Aegean Sea. At first ruled by kings, periodic reforms moved Athens slowly toward a democratic government dominated by the wealthier classes. The growth of trade expanded the number of citizens in the aristocracy and broadened participation in the government. The economic variety made the society more diverse and education became more widespread, expanding creativity in the arts and sciences. Athens led the Greeks in the Persian Wars, but its regional leadership was undermined by plagues. Later it was defeated by Sparta in the Peloponnesian Wars.

None of these new civilizations were more famous than the diverse **poleis** (city states) of the Greeks, or *Hellenes* as they called themselves. Beginning as isolated communities and remaining relatively independent, it took threats of invasion from outside empires for the poleis of Hellas to join together. The Greeks developed many variations of government from monarchy to democracy but they united to face the Persians off-and-on for nearly 70 years (Persian Wars, 546-480 BC). Later, the city states even fought in alliances (Delian League, Peloponnesian League) against each other (Peloponnesian Wars, 431-404 BC) to avoid domination by a single, more powerful polis. Long periods of war exhausted their limited resources, and they eventually fell to the power of the northern king, Philip of Macedon in 338 BC.

THE POLITICAL IMPACT OF THE ROMANS

Of all the political creations of the era of classical civilizations, none have shaped western civilization more than the Romans. As a **republic** (and later as an empire), Rome's power and organization, and its language and laws created a framework and foundation for western life that lasted for centuries.

GEOGRAPHIC FACTORS MADE ROME / ITALY A FAVORABLE SITE FOR CIVILIZATION:

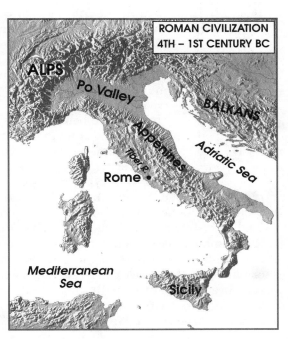

ROMAN CIVILIZATION
4TH – 1ST CENTURY BC

- Rainy, cool winters, mild, dry summers
- Good soil in the lowland valleys
- Peninsula into the center of Mediterranean Sea (2000 mile coastline)
- Protective mountain barriers in the north (Alps)
- Climate shielded by the north-south Appenine Mountain spine
- Rich natural resources (forests, copper, tin, iron, salt, building stone)

Rome's beginning in 753 BC is wrapped in myth, but the Indo-European speaking people of the Tiber Valley (Latium) were periodically overrun and plundered by the Etruscans, Samnites, and Celtic Gauls from the north. They also interacted with the Greeks in the coastal colonies to the south and absorbed their writing, architecture, and science. Italy became a melting pot of early races.

Rome began to expand. By 300 BC, it conquered southern Italy and turned on its northern neighbors. In most cases, Rome chose to form alliances with its former enemies instead of vanquishing them. Each new alliance strengthened Rome's power for the next conquest. Each city was bound directly to Rome and not allowed any other alliances. Conquered allies were allowed local self-government under Roman laws and the people were granted a limited form of Roman citizenship. Thus, Rome conquered, then diffused its culture among new people. This gave order and stability to the growing empire.

Rome itself was ruled first by Etruscan kings and then eventually by a Senate – an oligarchy composed of aristocratic nobles called **patricians**. The Roman Senate appointed military leaders, administrators (*consuls, praetors*), and magistrates. In the 5th century, **plebeians** (laborers and artisans) began to gain rights, spokesmen (*tribunes*), and lawmaking power. The laws were also codified in the 5th and 4th centuries BC. The **Laws of the Twelve Tables** became known to all citizens. In 312 BC, plebeians were admitted to the Senate.

Although Rome's republican government was dominated by patricians and wealthy plebeians, it was both strong and stable while being flexible enough to deal with new challenges. The greatest challenges came as Rome expanded into the Mediterranean. Citizenship expanded, and there was great social mobility. As the republic evolved, it was the representatives of different groups in the Senate and Assembly who chose those who held executive and judicial power. Historically, this made the Roman constitution a more realistic model for later democratic republics than the small, often fractious governments of the Greek poleis. As Rome expanded, it came into direct competition with the era's other great power – the Phoenician city-state of Carthage in North Africa. A series of three **Punic Wars** followed.

These standards were symbols carried by the Roman Legions. "SPQR" means the Legions fought for "The Senate and the People of Rome.

PUNIC WARS	
War	**Result**
First Punic War (264-241 BC)	Rome took Sicily, but lost nearly 1/5th of its citizens
Second Punic War (218-201 BC)	After taking Sardinia and Corsica, Rome suffered heavy losses and destruction in Italy at the hands of Carthage's general, Hannibal; Rome finally invaded Carthage itself and subdued it. Carthage surrendered and a 50 year peace ensued.
Third Punic War (149-146 BC)	By 150 BC, Carthage rebuilt itself. Rome felt threatened and attacked. Rome destroyed Carthage's army and navy, totally demolished the city, ruined its land, and sold the inhabitants into slavery.

☆ CAPSULE – ROMAN EMPIRE: STRENGTHS & WEAKNESSES

EARLY STRENGTHS
- Centralized political authority
- Trained bureaucracy reported to Rome from every corner of the Empire
- Allowed local authorities to rule in local matters
- Deployed professional army with powerful navy for support and patrol
- Created order through traditions of law
- Established Latin as a universal language for commerce, law, government, and education
- Offered citizenship to people throughout the Empire
- Diffused Roman culture and absorbed other conquered cultures
- Financed a great connecting infrastructure of paved roads, plus aqueducts and public buildings
- Allowed religious diversity (at first, Christianity and Judaism persecuted)

LATER WEAKNESSES
- Diminished citizenship and constitutional institutions under a succession of absolutist emperors
- Compromised unity by dividing empire in two administrative units (Diocletian, r. 284-305 and Constantine, r. 306-337)
- Drained financial and natural resources by expansion, high military expenses, extravagancies
- Diluted power by giving provincial authority to barbarians in return for military service when citizens refused to live on frontiers
- Abandoned a Roman controlled army by heavy recruiting among barbarians
- Used skilled workers from the provinces to work in Rome, depleting provincial resources
- Failed to conserve natural resources and used wasteful agricultural practices

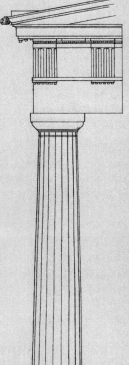

ENDURING LEGACY
- Codified Roman law became the basis for European law (except in Anglo-Saxon areas)
- Unified communications with Latin language which became the basis for most European languages, and the language of the Roman Catholic Church
- Preserved much Greek and Hellenistic learning
- Constructed public buildings that remained as basis for architectural design elements
- Engineered great connecting tissue of paved roads, plus aqueducts
- Legalized Christianity (4th century by the emperor Constantine. Later, became the official state religion.)
- Established the foundations of western culture (government, literature, technology, religion)

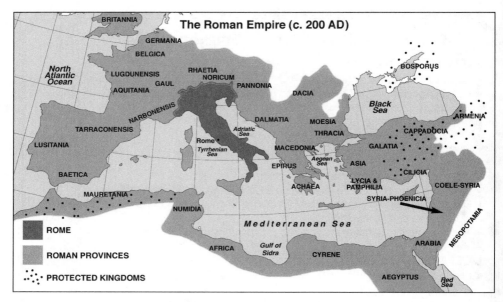

The Roman Empire (c. 200 AD)

In the 1st century BC, the constant wars against Carthage, and the campaigns in Spain, Gaul, and the Eastern Mediterranean took their toll. Rome's republican government and the economy destabilized. Taxes rose unfairly for many groups while others prospered, and unrest followed. Civil wars broke out in 130 BC and continued for nearly 80 years. Patricians and plebeians, reformers and dictators battled for power. Gaius **Marius** (r. 104-100 BC), Lucius **Sulla** (r. 88-70 BC), and finally Gnaeus **Pompey** and Julius **Caesar** (c. 49-44 BC) brought periods of calm.

Senate conspirators, fearing that Caesar would become dictator for life, assassinated him and started a final civil war (44-31 BC) which resulted in the end of the Roman Republic. In 27 BC, Caesar's nephew Octavian took the title **Imperator Caesar Augustus** (exalted emperor). He ended the civil wars, continued Caesar's reforms and purged corruption (see Age of Augustus on Golden Ages chart). After 27 BC, Augustus slowly changed the republic into a monarchy and empire that lasted 400 years (**Pax Romana**). However, the political power of Rome slowly declined in the 3rd, 4th, and 5th centuries under succession of emperors that shifted inconsistently between weakness and absolutism.

Augustus

SOCIAL DEVELOPMENTS IN THE ANCIENT WORLD

The cultural diffusion and blending of ancient civilizations was uneven. In some cases, it caused suffering and destruction as conquerors took resources by force and enslaved the vanquished. In most cases, an empire's economic enrichment led to prosperity and dominance of one group over another and the commerce that grew from the fusions.

Wars are vehicles for cultural diffusion. One example is the spreading of Greek or **Hellenistic Culture** eastward by Alexander the Great's conquests in the 4th century BC. The mixing and blending of culture followed his relentless march through Asia Minor, Egypt, and Persia to the Indus Valley.

In the classical era, varying stages of peace followed prolonged eras of war. These stable periods saw cultural advancement and intermixing. They sometimes led to periods called "**golden ages**" marked by extensive intellectual and creative achievements.

ALEXANDER & HELLENISTIC CULTURE

The Greeks called their land Hellas. Their ideas and culture traveled with their trade. Their colonies expanded and Hellenistic culture spread throughout the Mediterranean and into the Middle East. **Philip of Macedon** (359-338 BC) used revolutionary battle formations, cavalry attacks, bribery and his considerable wealth to conquer and unify all the divided Greek city-states as far as the Black Sea (except Sparta). Philip was preparing to challenge Persia for supremacy in the Middle East when he was assassinated. He was succeeded by his son, **Alexander the Great**, who completed his dream of a great empire with a Hellenistic culture. In his short 15 year reign, Alexander (r. 338-323 BC) unified Hellas and conquered territories from Asia Minor to Egypt and from Greece to the Indus River. Alexander's generals quarreled among themselves, and his empire disintegrated quickly after his death at age 33. Still, the interactions of culture that Alexander set in motion eventually spread Hellenistic arts, sciences, philosophy from the Mediterranean to Japan.

☆ CAPSULE – GOLDEN AGES OF THE ANCIENT WORLD

General Characteristics of Golden Ages
- Stability in political affairs leads to peace
- Development of notable architectural works
- Achievement in learning, literature, and arts
- Progress in transportation, communication, and trade
- Advancements in mathematics, science, technology

Greece: Age of Pericles (461-421 BC)
- Athens led the Delian League of seafaring poleis
- Philosophy of the Sophists and Socrates, Plato, and Aristotle influenced thinking
- Built the great buildings of Athens including the Parthenon
- Established classical sculpture of Myron, Phidias, Praxiteles
- Literature of Pindar, Sappho, Sophocles, Euripides, Aristophanes
- Scientific studies of Archimedes, Democritus, Hippocrates, Pythagoras

India: Age of Asoka (272-232 BC)
- Expanded borders of Maurya Empire
- "Rock Edicts" promulgated consistent legal system
- Protected missionaries to spread Buddhist belief system
- Developed infrastructure with road and messenger system
- Promoted architecture in public buildings, temples, dredging harbors for trade
- Developed primitive "Arabic" numerals, use of zero, and negative quantity theories in mathematics

Rome: Age of Augustus (27 BC-14 AD)
- Expanded, secured borders of the Empire
- Use of Latin language became widespread
- Maintained peace after decades of civil war
- Spread hybrid Roman / Hellenistic culture
- Expanded trade to Asia and Africa
- Tightened infrastructure with road and postal system
- Literature of Virgil, Ovid, Horace, Livy glorified Roman life
- Promoted architecture by rebuilding forums, baths, aqueducts
- Roman legal codes and judicial system spread throughout Europe

China: Han Dynasty (202 BC-220 AD)
- Helped build merchant class
- Redistributed land for peasants
- Spread Chinese as the imperial language
- Unified learning under Confucian principles
- Created civil service qualified by examinations
- Developed infrastructure with road and messenger system
- Secured borders with peasant army and fortifications (Great Wall begun)
- Ethnocentric exclusion of outside cultures and isolation from "barbarian' people

☆ CAPSULE – GLOBAL BELIEF SYSTEMS

Common Characteristics
- provided an organized form of spiritual worship
- unified the societies through cultural forces
- sought to give meaning to life
- gave understanding to the nature of the universe
- developed systems of ethical behavior

Judaism (1500-1000 BC)
(13.8 million estimated current adherents all divisions/sects*)
- **Organization**: autonomous congregations (synagogues) led by rabbi
- **Beliefs**: monotheism; seeks special relationship to God's mercy and a just and peaceful world order through prayer, a moral code (the *Ten Commandments*), family rituals, and public worship
- **Text(s)**: *Torah*, Hebrew Scripture (Biblical Old Testament)

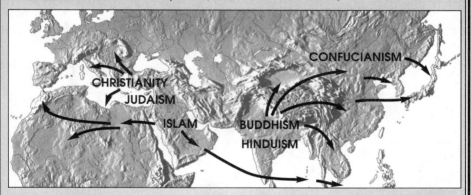

Hinduism (1500-500 BC)
(793 million estimated current adherents all divisions/sects*)
- **Organization**: autonomous temples where Brahmins preside over individual rituals
- **Beliefs**: polytheistic; commitment to an ideal life of ritual action to purify human acts so as to leave the material world (moksha) to become part of the eternal universal spirit of life (Brahman Nerguna)
- **Text(s)**: *Veda, Bhagavad Gita, Mahabharata, Ramayana*

Buddhism (566-486 BC)
(325 million estimated current adherents all divisions/sects*)
- **Organization**: independent sanghas – monastic orders – some sects have temples; some have rites, but mostly individual meditation
- **Beliefs**: Eightfold Path proper meditation, ethical behavior, and good deeds will help achieve Nirvana (ideal condition of rest, harmony, stability, or joy)
- **Text(s)**: *Tripitaka*, narrative scripture of Buddha's teaching; *Four Noble Truths* dogma

* Source for estimated adherents *World Almanac and Book of Facts*

☆ CAPSULE – GLOBAL BELIEF SYSTEMS (CONTINUED)

Confucian Philosophy (551-479 BC)
(150 million estimated current adherents all divisions/sects*)
- **Organization**: informal; gradually incorporated into China's traditional civil service & education systems
- **Beliefs**: social order stems from benevolence, traditional rituals, filial piety, loyalty and respect for superiors.
- **Text(s)**: *Analects* (Confucius' writing)

Daoist (Taoist) Philosophy (6th century BC)
(70 million estimated current adherents all divisions/sects*)
- **Organization**: independent monastic orders
- **Beliefs**: seek tranquil life, avoid aggression, act in harmony and balance with nature.
- **Text(s)**: *Daode Jing, Zuangzi* (writings attributed to Laozi (Lao-tsu) c. 4th century BC and Zhuangzi, c. 369-286 BC)

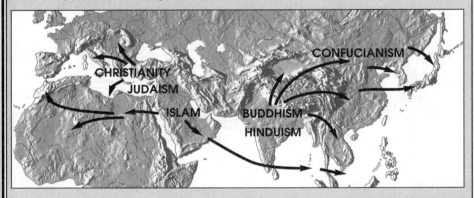

Christianity (1st Century BC/AD)
(1.9 billion estimated current adherents all divisions/sects*)
- **Organization**: many structures: Roman Catholic, Protestant sects, Orthodox Christians
- **Beliefs**: monotheism; divinity of Jesus, community of humankind, ethical behavior, and consistent ritual worship leads to reward in spiritual afterlife
- **Text(s)**: *Bible* (Old and New Testaments)

Islam (570-632 AD)
(1.1 billion estimated current adherents all divisions/sects*)
- **Organization**: combined civil and moral leadership under *Shari'a* rules sometimes on national level; also independent communities centered in local mosques
- **Beliefs**: community life governed by sacred teachings and the *Five Pillars* guiding ethical individual behavior and group worship and rituals
- **Text(s)**: *Qur'an, Sunna*

* Source for estimated adherents *World Almanac and Book of Facts*

LINKAGES

During the Neolithic Revolution 10,000 years ago, bands of hunter-gatherers began to form agricultural villages. In river valleys, certain villages grew, prospered, and produced broader cultures. The need for trade, protection, and irrigation moved groups to interact and pool resources into formative civilizations with cities and social institutions. As civilizations developed resources, they formed economic interdependencies, built great public works of architecture, organized spiritual beliefs into religions, and created bodies of literature and scientific and technical knowledge. By the Roman and Han Eras, civilizations interacted steadily and changed as they progressed. As new nomadic groups entered them – peaceably and forcibly – societies absorbed, remade, and diffused global cultures into great imperial systems.

QUESTIONS

1 One result of the Neolithic Revolution was
    1   an increase in the number of nomadic tribes
    2   a reliance on hunting and gathering for food
    3   the establishment of villages and the rise of governments
    4   a decrease in trade between cultural groups

2 In China, the development of ethnocentrism was most influenced by
    1   its historic reliance on foreign nations
    2   a long history of democratic government
    3   its geographic isolation
    4   a strong belief in Christianity

3 One similarity between the *Five Pillars of Islam* and the *Ten Commandments* of Judaism is that both
    1   support a belief in reincarnation
    2   promote learning as a means to salvation
    3   encourage the use of statues to symbolize God
    4   provide a guide to proper ethical and moral behavior

4 "If a seignior (noble) has knocked out the tooth of a seignior of his own rank, they shall knock out his tooth. But if he has knocked out a commoner's tooth, he shall pay one-third mina of silver" – *Code of Hammurabi*
Which idea of Babylonian society does this portion of the Hammurabi code of law reflect?
    1   All men were created equal under the law.
    2   Fines were preferable to corporal punishment.
    3   Divisions existed among social classes.
    4   Violence was always punished with violence.

5   One way the civilizations of the Sumerians, Egyptians, and Phoenicians were similar is that each
    1   developed an extensive system of writing
    2   emphasized equal education for all members of the society
    3   established monotheistic religions
    4   encouraged democratic participation in government affairs

6   A major contribution of the Roman Empire to Western Society is the development of
    1   gunpowder
    2   the principles of revolutionary socialism
    3   monotheism
    4   an effective legal system

7   The teachings of Confucius encouraged people to
    1   put their own interests first
    2   seek social order based on filial piety, loyalty, and respect for superiors
    3   live their lives focused on reincarnation
    4   follow a strict code of moral conduct

8   Which was a major role played by the Romans in the development of Western Civilization?
    1   preservers and adapters of other cultures
    2   creators of unique philosophical and religious systems
    3   defeat of the great invasions from Persia
    4   abolition of the institution of slavery

9   In river valley civilizations, permanent settlements were stable but were more vulnerable to attack and to acts of nature that ruined crops. This created a need for
    1   skilled hunters and gatherers of roots and wild edibles
    2   warriors to specialize in defenses and priests to intercede spiritually with nature
    3   nomadic tribal social structures
    4   democratically organized civil governments

10 "The Persians worshiped Ahura-Mazda; he was their great god, together with Mithra and the goddess Anahita; but the king acknowledged Amun-Ré in Egypt and Apollo at Delhi, whilst the Persian administration respected the cult of the Elamite god at Perseopolis." – *Harper Atlas of World History*
    Which idea is portrayed in this quotation?
    1   monotheism   3   infrastructure
    2   oligarchy   4   cultural diffusion

11 Which was a common reason for the successful administration of empires such as the Han in China, Maurya in India, and the Roman Empire in Mediterranean Europe?
1   The empires absorbed invasions by primitive nomads with little resistance.
2   Military and provincial governors coordinated efforts with a strong central government.
3   The Emperors all abolished slavery and offered land to all citizens who did military service.
4   The armed forces eradicated all conquered kingdoms and destroyed cities to halt opposition.

Base your answer to question 12 on the map below and your knowledge of social studies.

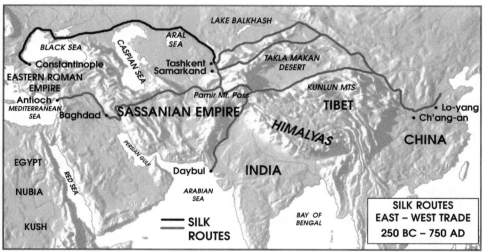

12 Which idea about the Silk Routes is best portrayed by the map above?
1   Land-locked countries are less prosperous than seafaring ones.
2   Natural routes are more successful than man-made ones.
3   Trade can be a method of cultural diffusion.
4   Trade reinforces ethnocentrism.

13 A study of the Indus, Nile, Hwang He, Tigris and Euphrates rivers would be most useful in understanding the
1   causes of decline of Mediterranean trade
2   role of geography in the development of early civilizations
3   reasons why nomadic tribes dominated prehistory
4   rise of Islam as a major cultural force in the Middle East

14 Which of the four suggested headings below (1 through 4) is the best heading for the outline below?

> I. _____
>   A. Stability in political affairs leads to peace
>   B. Development of notable architectural works
>   C. Achievement in learning, literature, and the arts
>   D. Progress in transportation, communication, trade
>   E. Advancements in mathematics, science, technology

    1   Silk Routes Spread Culture
    2   The Results of the Punic Wars
    3   The Causes of Neolithic Revolution
    4   Golden Ages of the Ancient World

15 Which conclusion can be drawn from a study of structures such as the Pyramids of Egypt, the Parthenon of Athens, and the Great Wall of China?
    1   Military victories are often commemorated by construction of great buildings.
    2   Architecture often reflects the values of a culture.
    3   River Valley civilizations needed irrigation systems.
    4   The labor of artisans and engineers was expensive.

THEMATIC ESSAY

Directions: Write a well-organized essay that includes an introduction, several paragraphs explaining your position, and a conclusion.

Theme: River valleys and early settlements

> Throughout ancient history, river valleys have played an important role in the development of regions.

Task:

> • Describe the spatial relationship of river valleys and human development.
> • Support your opinion by discussing the influence of two river valley civilizations.
> • Explain how each river valley shaped the culture and economic development of its region.

Suggestions: You may use examples from your study of global history and geography. Some suggestions you might wish to consider include the Huang He and Chinese Civilization, the Indus and early civilization in India, The Tigris-Euphrates and Mesopotamian Civilization, the Nile and Egyptian Civilization. **You are *not* limited to these suggestions.**

PRACTICE SKILLS FOR DBQ

Directions: The following task is based on the accompanying documents. The documents may have been edited for the purposes of this exercise. The task is designed to test your ability to work with historical documents. As you analyze the documents, take into account both the source of the document and the author's point of view.

Historical Context: Many forms of government evolved from the experiences of ancient civilizations. The documents below present differing views of how governments kept social order (social control).

Part A – Short Answer
The documents below relate to the process of governing in two poleis of Ancient Greece. Examine each document carefully, then answer the question that follows it.

Document 1

1   What characteristic of Athenian government does this scene portray?

_____

_____

_____

_____

_____

_____

_____

_____

Athenians Debate in the Ecclesia

Document 2

> "The citizen-soldiers of Sparta were the only inhabitants who held citizenship, and they made up the army. Their lives were ordered and controlled by the state. ... From age seven, the male Spartan was enrolled in a military group where his education consisted of rigorous gymnastic and military training. He was taught to read and write and practice the virtues of obedience and courage.
>
> "Public debate of issues was nearly unknown. The oligarchy of the five Ephors held supreme power and could veto the legislation of the 28-member council of elders – the gerusa."
>
> - Emerson Lavender, et. al., *A Thousand Ages*

2   How may the education of Spartans have influenced their role in government?

_____

_____

_____

_____

Part *B* – Essay Response
Task: Using only the information in the documents, write one or two paragraphs describing how the process of governing differed between Sparta and Athens.

State your thesis:

_____

_____

_____

_____

- Use only the information in the documents to support your thesis position
- Add your analysis of the documents
- Incorporate your answers to Part *A* scaffold questions

Additional Suggested Task:
From your knowledge of global history and geography, make a list of additional factors that could be used to show how the process of governing differed between Sparta and Athens.

500 TO 1200 AD

EXPANDING ZONES OF EXCHANGE AND ENCOUNTER

AD

500–

Byzantine Emperor Justinian
codifies Roman Law (528 AD)

600–

Li Yuan founds T'ang Dynasty (618)

Abu Bakr becomes first
Muslim Caliph (632)

700–

Muslims conquer Spain (718)

Umayyads overthrown
by Abbasids (750)

800–

Charlemagne crowned
Holy Roman Emperor (800)

900–

Zhao Guangyn founds
Song Dynasty (960)

1000–

Grand Duke Valdimir I of
Kiev converted to
Orthodox Christianity (988)

1100–

Pope Urban II launches
the First Crusade (1095)

1200–

Ibn Rushd (Averroes) preserves
work of Aristotle (1180)

Taking to the seas, the Vikings (among other sea-faring people), expanded the world through encounter and an exchange of goods.

INTRODUCTION

From 500 to 1200 AD great changes occurred causing more cultural diffusion. While the Roman Empire slowly decayed and Western Europe fragmented into disarray, other civilizations continued to reform, grow, and intermix at different rates. There was intensive interchange and cultural creativity. While the fall of old empires disrupted trade, merchants still carried goods and ideas among the regions. Knowledge of the great religions expanded as missionaries traveled to distant lands seeking converts. Invading nomadic tribes from the interior of Asia swept into Europe, India, and China. These encounters brought disruption, dislocation, and destruction. However, the encounters also brought new economic, social, and political exchanges to add to the foundations laid by older civilizations.

POLITICAL DEVELOPMENTS

REGIONAL EMPIRES

From 250 AD, nomadic peoples from the interior of Eurasia migrated toward the east, west, and south. These were nomads and pastoral people. They sought better lands, warmer climates, and were attracted to civilizations in China, India, Southwest Asia, and the Mediterranean. Desert expanses, open steppes, and mountain passes channeled a steady flow of migration and aggressive invasions.

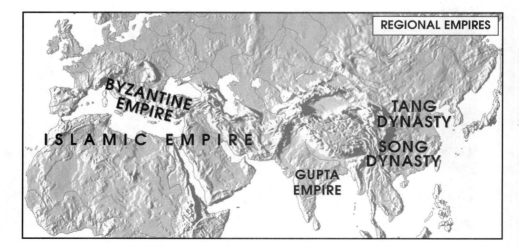

REGIONAL EMPIRES

BYZANTINE EMPIRE

ISLAMIC EMPIRE

TANG DYNASTY

SONG DYNASTY

GUPTA EMPIRE

☆ CAPSULE – REGIONAL EMPIRES

The T'ang Dynasty (618-902 AD)
- Claimed "Mandate of Heaven" (divine right) in chaos after Han collapse in 220 AD
- Expanded territory to north, west, and south
- Constructed canals and roads for internal trade
- Expanded trade throughout Asia
- Organized a complex legal system
- Redistributed land to peasants
- Set up a network of loyal, Confucian-trained civil servants (imperial bureaucracy)
- Made technical advances in printing, weaving, porcelain making, time keeping, gunpowder
- Produced literature and art: Li Bo, Du Fu, Wu Daozi
- Created new buildings: wooden palaces, temples, and pagodas
- Interacted with other cultures

The Gupta Empire (320-550 AD)
- Built roads for internal trade
- Expanded trade in silks, spices, and luxuries to Chinese, Sassanid Persians, Byzantines, and Romans
- Advanced mathematics (zero base), physics, and medicine (smallpox vaccine)
- Blended Sanskrit-Hindu-Buddhist languages and literature: Kalidasa's *Shakuntala*
- Constructed stupas (dome shaped Buddhist shrines), and elaborate carvings on Hindu temples (Madurai), cave temple murals revealed scenes of Gupta life
- Deepened caste system, sharply dividing the society, but adding stability and order

The Byzantine Empire (330-1453 AD)
- Preserved Roman laws. *Corpus Juris Civilis* (*Justinian's Code*) - became the model for European legal systems
- Served as a buffer for Western Europe against invasions from the east
- Strengthened power of the emperor for a nearly absolute, autocratic government
- Expanded trade in silks, spices, and luxuries to Chinese, Persians, and Western Europe
- Preserved and protected Eastern Orthodox Christian Church
- Blended Christian beliefs with Greek (Hellenistic) science, philosophy, art, and literature
- Preserved and adapted Roman architecture and engineering
- Produced mosaics and icons
- Spread culture and religion into Eastern Europe and Russia

THE PROCESS OF IMPERIAL DECLINE

As with the Roman and Han Empires, the energetic, golden ages experienced by the Gupta, T'ang, and Byzantine Empires eventually faded. Sustaining a vast political organization over a lengthy period is difficult. All of these empires showed similar patterns of decay and overextension.

Negative forces can make gains over time. As rule passes from generation to generation, it may lose momentum. The drive to make things better ebbs as problems are solved. Continuity and discipline weaken. Less vigilant and dedicated administrations open opportunities for bribery, corruption, and graft among entrenched officials. For example, provincial military commanders, if neglected by central monitors, can abuse their authority; sometimes they defy weak central authority, set up their own kingdoms, or even lead rebellions.

Groups that are conquered or peacefully migrate into the society are not always fully assimilated. Prejudice may keep them from participating fully as citizens. Their culture might conflict with the original society's common values. They do not always embrace rules and conventions that are not their own. While periods of reform take place, they are not always successful. As a result, once vibrant societies are drained trying to restore order and fall into decline.

Rome struggled to keep these groups at bay on its frontiers until the Empire weakened and fell to them. The Roman emperors retreated eastward, accepted Christianity, and reformed their besieged, shrunken realm into the Byzantine Empire. The barbarian attacks partially helped to unite India under the Gupta Dynasty and China under the T'ang Dynasty. The need to resist the invasions united various princes under central rule, and new regional empires emerged in Asia.

WESTERN EUROPE:
BARBARIAN KINGDOMS AND THE CHURCH

In the century after Diocletian divided the Roman Empire into eastern and western administrative sections, great numbers of people from the interior of Eurasia penetrated the once mighty frontier defenses. In 330, Emperor Constantine moved his capital to Byzantium (later called Constantinople). This eastern section reformed, strengthened, embraced Christianity, and slowly became the **Byzantine Empire**. The western section of the Empire fragmented into an ebb and flow of kingdoms ruled by Goths, Seubi, Vandals, Huns, Lombards, Franks, and others.

In the 4th and 5th centuries, the Mediterranean Basin saw a great intermixing and blending of cultures (Phoenician – Greek – Roman – Celtic – Germanic). The barbarian kingdoms rose and fell, colliding with each other, and with the Byzantines who, under Justinian, tried to reconquer the west. His great general, Belisarius, achieved some success, but Justinian's successors continued to lose

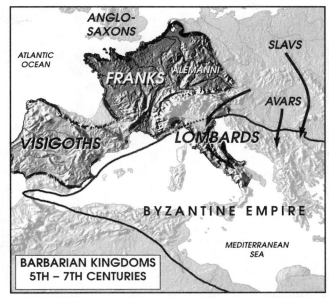

ground. In the meantime, the Christian Church slowly emerged as a unifying social and political force (see the ☆Capsule on next page).

FEUDALISM IN EUROPE

As the Roman Empire disintegrated, landholders along its frontier areas in Europe needed protection from invaders (Huns, Lombards, Goths and Vandals at first, then Vikings, Magyars, and Muslims). After barbarians repeatedly sacked cities, the inhabitants retreated to private strongholds. The European countryside was dotted with isolated, individual castles and fortresses surrounded by dependent farming communities. Wealthier individuals fortified their own homes (which evolved into castles in the later Middle Ages) and hired their own soldiers.

Eventually, as these landlords extended protection to the surrounding countryside, informal relationships with lesser landholders formalized. This organization became known as **feudalism**. The word is derived from Latin (*foedus* - agreement) and Old German (*fihu* - property). The basis of feudalism was mutual dependence. A **vassal** (lesser noble) was granted an estate (ɐ **fief**) by a noble or lord (dukes and counts) in exchange for produce, loyalty, and service. Vassals often had vassals of their own, so that everyone was involved in a social, political, and economic network – each owing allegiance to another. As time went on, these relationships grew more complex. The vassal needed the strength of an overlord for protection, and the overlord needed a collective of vassals to be strong.

☆ CAPSULE – THE MEDIEVAL CHRISTIAN CHURCH
A UNIFYING FORCE IN WESTERN EUROPE

Supplanting the Roman Empire (392-476 AD)
- Emperor Constantine's *Edict of Milan* (313 AD) ordered toleration of all religions
- Emperor Theodosius proclaimed Christianity the official religion of the Empire (392 AD)
- Emperors built churches enhancing and broadening the power of the clergy
- The emperors tried to rule from Constantinople, but Church leaders exerted control in the west
- Pope Leo I - not the emperor - persuaded Attila the Hun to spare Rome from sacking (452 AD)
- Roman Church organization (network of bishops under Pope) similar to imperial Rome's

Converting the Barbarians (496-768 AD)
- Conversion of barbarian kings to Christianity enhanced influence of the Church
- Leaders of barbarian kingdoms relied on clergy to administer their realms and set up laws
- Church teachings were used to restrain barbarians' excesses
- The separation of power between church and state blurred
- The kingdom of the Franks became the central staging area for conversions (Clovis to Pepin)
- Political support of the Church legitimized the barbarian kings' authority

Dominating Medieval Society (496-768 AD)
- Church synods (meetings) oversaw rules and regulations of ordinary life and regulated wealth through compulsory tithes (required contributions)
- Church leaders approved marriages among nobles to ensure harmony
- Charlemagne (r. 768-814 AD) used counts and bishops to administer the provinces (counties)
- Charlemagne defended the Pope and his lands against Lombards, Saxons, Muslims
- Church receiving 1/10th of the conquered lands' produce (farm goods)
- Pope Leo III crowned Charlemagne Holy Roman Emperor (800 AD) snubbing the Byzantine Emperor; Charlemagne accepted religious authority over political rule.

During the **Early Medieval Period** (500-1000 AD), the feudal relationships became permanent and hereditary, interlocking families and whole regions. Even Church lands became entwined in the system, so that bishops and abbots were often lords to some and vassals of others. Also, merchants and artisans paid allegiance to lords in the forms of service, money, or produce. Land was power and allowed one person to control another. New conquests from frequent feudal wars meant an overlord could grant new fiefs and control more vassals.

☆ CAPSULE – FEUDAL RELATIONSHIPS

Overlord Provided Vassals with
- Landed estates (fief)
- Armed forces
- Roads, bridges, dams
- Justice in disputes among vassals (trials by combat)

Vassal Provided Overlord with
- Allegiance (homage, fealty)
- Tributary money or goods
- Military service and fighting men when summoned
- Ceremonial duty
- Three feudal dues: ransom, dowry, knighthood
- Hospitality and entertainment on visits

ARUNDEL CASTLE
England
Built in the 11th century by Norman Richard Fizalan overlooking the Arun river.
©PhotoDisc, Inc 1994

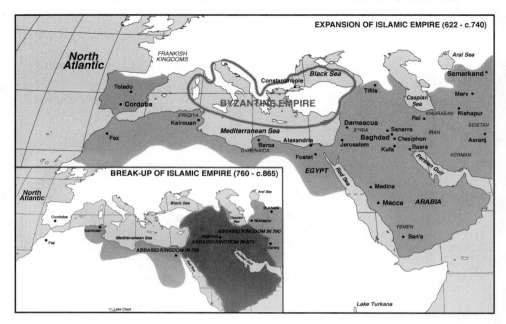

ARAB CONQUESTS BUILD AN ISLAMIC EMPIRE

After Muhammad's flight to Medina in 622 AD (*Hegira*), the Prophet and his Muslim followers launched a series of campaigns that brought him back to Mecca in victory (624 AD). When Muhammad died in 632, western Arabia was under Muslim control. His successor, **Abu Bakr**, the first caliph, launched zealous ***jihads*** (crusades to spread the new faith). The Arab armies' military momentum made many converts, but the faith itself attracted many, too. People confused by polytheism and the complexities of Christianity were drawn to the simplicity of Muhammad's new religion. Numbers were also a factor. Spreading the faith was not in the hands of a small group of clergy. All Muslims in the army considered themselves missionaries conquering for Allah. Jews and Christians were generally accepted, because they shared monotheistic revelations of the Bible.

Over the next century, the Prophet's successors (**caliphs**) led an incredible series of Arab conquests. Bold use of horse cavalry and aggressive tactics enabled them to unseat the Sassanians in Persia (644-656 AD), cross the Indus (712 AD), separate Egypt (640 AD) and Syria (657 AD) from the Byzantine Empire, drive across North Africa (643-711 AD), and push into Spain to threaten the Frankish Kingdoms (732 AD).

☆ CAPSULE – ISLAMIC EMPIRE

Military Conquest to Imperial Rule (c. 632-750 AD)

- Internal conflicts: separated into two sects: Sunn'i followed the 1st four caliphs and Shi'ite followed Muhammad's son-in-law, Ali
- Warriors became rich by sharing in the spoils of conquered territories
- Military garrisons collected tribute from conquered peoples
- Umayyad Caliphs' (660-749) administrators directed conversion of conquered peoples to Islam

DOME OF THE ROCK MOSQUE
Jerusalem, Built in Umayyad times.
©PhotoDisc, Inc 1994

- Converts to Islam joined the army and received administrative posts
- Arabic mandated as official language
- Uniform coinage used, making transactions and distant trade easier

A Golden Age (c. 750-850 AD)

- Umayyad caliphs overthrown by Abbasids (749-1258) who moved the capital to Baghdad
- Abbasid caliphs shared power among Arabs (religion), Persians (administration), Turks (military)
- Tribute and taxes funneled to major urban centers (Baghdad, Damascus, Kufa, Basra, Fustat)
- Construction of mosques, palaces, canals accelerated
- Classical works of the Greek translated, adapted, and advanced in astronomy, navigation, philosophy, science, mathematics, and medicine (Ibn Sina, <u>Canon of Medicine</u>, c. 900 AD)
- Art and architecture blended Greco-Roman and Byzantine styles with Persian
- Legal system of the *Shari'a* advanced a combined spiritual and temporal law
- Imperial security expanded trade and travel connecting Asia, Africa, and the Mediterranean

Fragmentation (after 865 AD)

- Internal struggles over religious dogma and interpretation of law
- Rival caliphs arose, rebellions sparked large regions to break with Abbasids
- Provincial centers became strong, governors challenged Baghdad for more power and independence.
- Series of outside invasions weakened the Abbasid rule (Seljuk Turks - beginning c. 900, Christian Crusades - beginning c. 1050, Mongols - beginning c. 1216)

CHRISTIAN CRUSADES IN THE MIDDLE EAST

By 1000 AD, many of the divided kingdoms of Western Europe were growing stable and wealthy. However, the Byzantine Empire – which had protected Europe from Muslim and many barbarian invasions – was weakening and under siege from the **Seljuk Turks**. By the end of the 11th century, the Turks had taken most of the eastern Mediterranean states and much of Asia Minor. In 1095, the Byzantine Emperor appealed to the Pope for help. Pope Urban II organized an expedition of European knights to rescue Jerusalem in the **Holy Land** (Palestine). For the next 200 years, seven more expeditions invaded the eastern shores of the Mediterranean.

Marred by petty jealousies of European nobles, the **Crusades** (from the Spanish *cruzada* – marked by a cross) generally failed. In some cases, frustrated crusaders took to massacring Jews and Byzantine Christians. Only briefly did the crusades free the Holy Land from the Turks, but they did create a legacy of hatred and suspicion between the two great religions. The disruption of European life and the loss of many nobles began an undermining of the feudal system that led to political upheavals. The increase in trade and travel also led to greater mobility in Europe, further upsetting the stagnancy of feudalism.

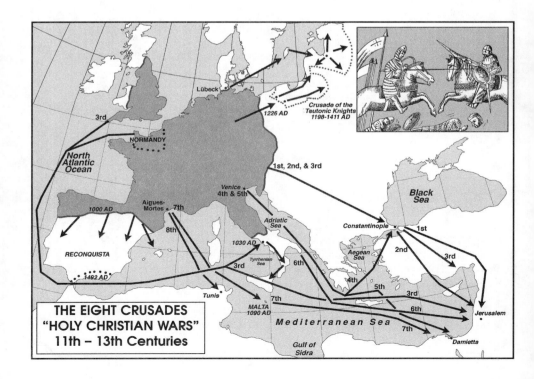

THE EIGHT CRUSADES
"HOLY CHRISTIAN WARS"
11th – 13th Centuries

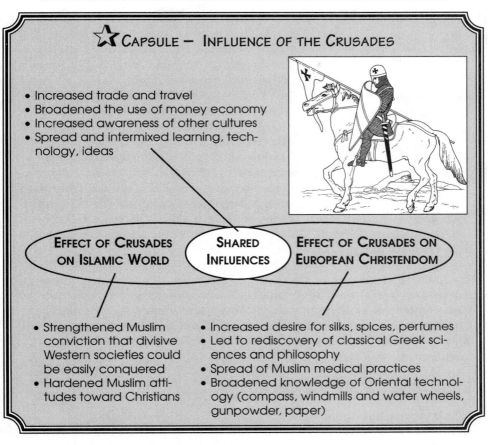

★CAPSULE – INFLUENCE OF THE CRUSADES

- Increased trade and travel
- Broadened the use of money economy
- Increased awareness of other cultures
- Spread and intermixed learning, technology, ideas

EFFECT OF CRUSADES ON ISLAMIC WORLD — **SHARED INFLUENCES** — **EFFECT OF CRUSADES ON EUROPEAN CHRISTENDOM**

- Strengthened Muslim conviction that divisive Western societies could be easily conquered
- Hardened Muslim attitudes toward Christians

- Increased desire for silks, spices, perfumes
- Led to rediscovery of classical Greek sciences and philosophy
- Spread of Muslim medical practices
- Broadened knowledge of Oriental technology (compass, windmills and water wheels, gunpowder, paper)

SOCIAL DEVELOPMENTS

In the seven centuries between 500 and 1200 AD, cultural diffusion proliferated. The regional empires interacted with surrounding people and a great intermixing of language and ideas took place. Buddhism, Christianity, Hinduism, and Islam spread far and wide beyond the lands of their origins. Christian Europe was only on the far western edge of the dense centers of population, growing production, and burgeoning urban life of Eurasia. Yet the developments of the early Middle Ages in Europe made possible the rise of a new and powerful civilization in the next era. China, Byzantium, Islam, and Christianity left lasting marks far beyond their cultural centers.

CHINESE INFLUENCE ON KOREA, JAPAN, AND VIETNAM

The **Yamato** of southern Honshu, Japan's first great governing clan, formed alliances and unified the country by the 4th century. Early in their ascendancy, the Yamato sent emissaries to China's Han Court (57 AD).

From that point, scholarly pilgrims journeyed to China and returned to spread Chinese script and Buddhist teachings. These became blended with native Shinto beliefs and oral traditions.

The Korean Peninsula acted as a cultural bridge between Japan and China. In the 4th century, the Yamato traded along the Korean coast and colonized Mimana on the southern tip. On the Peninsula, their mixture of Japanese and Han culture interacted with Mongolian and older Chinese influences to form a unique Korean culture. In the 7th century, China's T'ang empress supported the attempts of the Silla Dynasty to unify the whole peninsula.

Later, the armies of the T'ang Dynasty made tributary states of Korea and Vietnam. They remained independent but recognized the T'ang emperors as their protectors. They sent regular payments to the Chinese. In the process, the influence of Chinese culture grew, with the client states becoming aware of Chinese philosophies, technology, art, architecture, and literature.

BYZANTINE INFLUENCE ON RUSSIA

Orthodox missionaries were sent by Byzantine emperors into Eastern Europe and the steppes in the 8th century. They transmitted Byzantine culture to the Slavs, Khazars, Bulgars, and Avars. They developed the cyrillic alphabet for the Slavic language. By the 9th century, the inhabitants were conquered by Norse Vikings called **Varangians** who slowly absorbed the Slavic-Byzantine language and culture. In the 10th century, the Varangians north-south trade with Constantinople influenced the conversion of Grand Duke Vladimir I to Orthodox Christianity. This made Kiev a cultural center that influenced what eventually became the Russian Empire.

Eastern Orthodox Catholic churches are easily identified by their "onion" shaped (often gold) domes.   *©PhotoDisc, Inc 1994*

ISLAMIC INFLUENCE ON MIDDLE EAST SOCIETY

In the 7th century, the Eastern Hemisphere was encompassed by the dramatic rise of Islam as both a new world religion and a civilized tradition. In one hundred years, Islamic forces conquered more territory than the Romans had in eight hundred. The **Abbasid Caliphate** established an Islamic Empire that became a center for the exchange of goods, ideas, and technology from South Asia across the Middle East and North Africa to Spain.

The great urban centers (Baghdad, Damascus, Kufa, Fustat, Kairouan) developed commercial power and became seats of learning. The *Shari'a* (Islamic code) not only outlined the pathways of religious beliefs and ritual, but the rules of conduct and individual rights as well. There were no castes or rigid feudal structures as in other societies. Individuals could rise in status through their own actions. Education was open to boys of all classes because reading the *Qur'an* was important, but higher education was a province of the rich.

Slavery was common in the Islamic Empire. The *Qur'an* spoke of humane treatment for slaves. Muslims could not be taken as slaves, but the jihads of the 7th and 8th centuries produced many slaves from conquered lands.

Men were allowed more than one wife, and women's roles were traditional (wife, mother, caregiver, household manager). A woman could own and inherit property, attend mosque services, and was allowed to read and write. But, all other power in the society was reserved for males.

CHRISTIAN CHURCH INFLUENCE ON WESTERN EUROPE

Christianity became the cultural foundation of a new civilization in Western Europe. Besides holding political power and struggling with kings and feudal lords for power, the Roman Catholic Church dominated daily life. A bureaucracy of archbishops, bishops, and abbots (most of whom were also land holding nobles), administered both the Church and secular (worldly) rules of behavior. Most Christians feared eternal damnation more than worldly punishments. Taking the sacraments and obeying Church laws avoided excommunication – a fate worse than death, for it meant an eternity in Hell.

Peasants and nobles alike had to be baptized and married in the local church. They all had to pay a **tithe** (1/10th of their income) to the Church. Attending Mass was a social event where news was shared. The local priests often conducted schools and ministered to the sick and poor.

The Medieval Church had a double standard for women. Women could join a religious order as nuns, but there was no way to achieve equality in the Church for women. They could not hold office or be priests. The Church created many rules governing marriage, and there were protections against exploitation by men. Women were largely restricted to the home. Rarely were they admitted to schools or allowed access to higher learning. Women could not hold or inherit property although they often managed the estates while their husbands were off on military expeditions.

The Church established monasteries where monks or nuns lived and worked in isolated spiritual communities. Some monasteries interacted with the society. Some specialized in care of the sick and developed medical facilities and regional hospitals. Others copied and illustrated manuscripts to preserve important documents and ancient literary works. They first became Europe's archives and libraries then centers of learning. Some evolved into universities where the monks did scholarly research. Some monks and nuns joined preaching or missionary orders to spread the Faith throughout Europe. Examples include Saint Augustine and Saint Patrick spreading the Faith to the British Isles.

HINDU CASTE SYSTEM INSTITUTION IN INDIA

Hinduism flowered in India under the Guptas and spread to the courts of Southeast Asia. According to the traditions of the sacred *Veda*, Hindu society was divided into the four main **varna** or classes: **Brahmins** (priests), **Ksatriya** (warriors and political leaders), **Vaisya** (wealth producers: farmers, craftsmen, merchants), **Sudra** (servants of the other three varna). From within these four classes evolved hundreds of complex hierarchal social groupings called **jati** (castes). The Hindu law of **karma** (fate) determined caste membership and had to be accepted. Religiously, certain castes were deemed holier than others. All castes developed rules of behavior that kept them from associations with other, less pure castes. Economic position and social identity became closely linked to these human divisions. **Dharma** (duty or conduct) required fulfillment of the social expectations of the caste. The system strictly divided the society. It affected the entire interaction among individuals. The castes depended on each other for basic needs, but the rules made exchange difficult and inefficient. The rigid rules kept the society stable and harmonious, but slowed the acceptance of change and made progress difficult. It also made Indian society less flexible to meet challenges from foreign societies.

ECONOMIC DEVELOPMENT

MANORIALISM IN MEDIEVAL EUROPE

Manorialism was the relationship between those who held the land (lords, nobles, Church hierarchy) and the peasants or serfs who worked on it. The system evolved as the Roman Empire disintegrated in the 4th century. With invasions more frequent, small farmers found themselves in need of protection from their wealthier neighbors. It evolved into a system where the strong dominated the weak. Over time, the land of peasant farmers was absorbed into the wealthy landholder's estate, or manor. The peasants gradually became tenants or perhaps **serfs** (legally

☆ CAPSULE – MEDIEVAL MANORIAL RELATIONSHIPS

Peasant / Serf Provided
- Payments in kind for use of arable land
- Labor to the lord for tasks such as building roads, bridges and dams
- Help in defending the castle in case of attacks
- Labor on the land farmed for the lord's household (lord's demesne, property)

Landlord Provided
- Land to support the peasant's and / or serf's livelihood
- Military protection against invasion
- Economic security against crop failure
- Justice in a local court

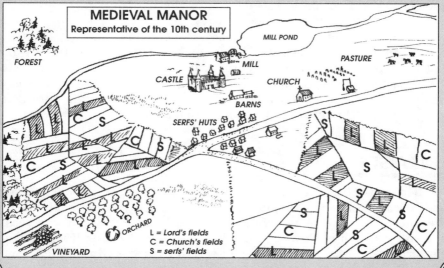

MEDIEVAL MANOR
Representative of the 10th century

MILL POND

FOREST

MILL

CASTLE

PASTURE

CHURCH

BARNS

SERFS' HUTS

ORCHARD

VINEYARD

L = Lord's fields
C = Church's fields
S = serfs' fields

bound to the lord in a near slave status). They became bound by duty and law to work the lord's lands and to aid in time of peril. In exchange, they were granted small subsistence plots and protection.

BARTER IN EUROPE

In the Early Medieval Period, travel was unsafe. The brisk money trade of the Roman Empire shriveled to nothing. There was little surplus to trade in the isolated, subsistence economies of the manors. The localized manorial and feudal relationships became the basis for a barter economy. **Barter** is the direct exchange of goods and services of equal value without the use of money. It became the basic system of allocating resources on isolated manors. Goods from outside were rare, but the few traveling merchants often took other goods (jewels, weapons, cloth) in return for their wares. In the later Middle Ages, invasions slowed and travel became safer. Knowledge of the world, enhanced by the Crusades, created new demands. Long-distance trade was renewed, and desires for a broader array of products from far off made it lucrative. Eventually, an easier, less clumsy money system re-emerged in Europe.

CIVILIZATIONS LINKED BY TRADE

Trade provided the one viable link that kept ideas and global awareness alive. The large regions linked by powerful religious and other cultural factors often remained apart from each other in the period from 500 to 1200. Political differences made open interaction difficult. Life was still primarily agricultural, and technological change was slow. Interdependence was not yet a crucial factor in global affairs.

However, communication trickled among civilizations via the trade that occurred. On the edges of these regional civilizations, trade sometimes acted as a bridge for cultural diffusion. The Silk Road connected China to the Middle East, but awareness of China came secondhand to Mediterranean traders such as the Christian Venetians who interacted with Byzantine merchants who bought from Muslims.

LINKAGES

Between 500 and 1200 AD, new empires were born as older, classical ones decayed. The rise of the Gupta and T'ang Dynasties brought new life to civilization in Asia, while the fall of Rome left a political, social, and cultural void in Europe. The division of the Christian Church into a western Latin (Roman) branch and Eastern Orthodox (Byzantine) branch

broke down cultural unity. As the Byzantine Empire struggled to preserve classical culture, Islam arose. In Europe, manorialism led to an isolated economic order, while feudalism created a stratified social and
political order. Both brought stability, but at the price of a stagnant,
unprogressive society.

New social institutions, such as the great religions, brought cultural
unity to some regions. They also spread to new areas causing cultural
diffusion. Buddhism, Christianity, and Islam reached great heights of
influence over vast, new areas. Intellectual and scientific discoveries
crossed cultures with the journeys of religious missionaries as well as
merchants, diplomats, and scholars. The Islamic jihads and the Christian
Crusades also caused civilization to widen in scope. In the rapid spread
of its beliefs, Islam reorganized, revitalized, and diffused Arab culture
from India to Spain. In the midst of Teutonic, Viking, and Central Asian
invasions of Western Europe, the Christian Church slowly became the
preserver and unifier of European culture.

QUESTIONS

**Base your answer to questions 1 and 2 on the speakers' state-
ments below and your knowledge of social studies**

Speaker A: We base the affairs of our community on the *Shari'a.* It is
the code based on Allah's revelations in the *Qur'an,* Muhammad's
thoughts, and the historic consensus of our community. It gives us
guidance on marriage, divorce, contracts, and commerce.

Speaker B: There can be no interpretation of God's will by ordinary
individuals. Only the Holy See in Rome can say what is the true
meaning of sacred scripture. Once proclaimed, all must accept it as
dogma.

Speaker C: Our rules of life flow from our caste. Our social groups
dictate how we live, eat, dress, and earn our livelihood. We treat each
other as our caste prescribes. Our society has order because each person knows his/her place.

Speaker D: Each person has a duty to others. If we do our duty and
afford respect to our parents and rulers we will have peace and the
society will have order and harmony.

1   Which speaker's statement best reflects the control of the Medieval
     Christian Church?

     1   A   3   C
     2   B   4   D

2   Speaker *D* reflects the ideal of
     1   India's *jati* class structures
     2   centralized authority
     3   Confucian order
     4   Islamic *ummah* (religious community life)

3   Since the 8th century AD, a major source of disunity among Muslims
     has been
     1   use of the human figure in art
     2   the establishment of quotas for oil production
     3   differences in the religious teachings of Shi'ites and Sunnis
     4   the spread of the Islamic Faith through invasion and trade

4   Rome during the Pax Romana and the Christian Church in Medieval
     Europe are examples of
     1   constitutional monarchies   3   feudal governments
     2   centralized powers   4   democratic states

5   In Western Europe during the Early Medieval Period, education
     declined as a direct result of the
     1   rise of absolute monarchs
     2   fall of the Roman Empire
     3   loss of power of the Christian Church
     4   rediscovery of classical Greek civilization

6   A major feature of the Golden Age of Muslim culture was the
     1   development of the foundations of modern science and mathe-
          matics
     2   political and economic isolation of the Arab world
     3   adoption of democratic government
     4   persecution of Christians and Jews

7   An important long-term result of the Crusades in the Middle East
     was the
     1   destruction of Muslim military power
     2   restoration of the Byzantine Empire
     3   creation of a large Christian state on the Red Sea
     4   spread of Middle Eastern culture and technology to Europe

8   The *Hejira*, Muhammad's journey from Mecca to Medina in 622 AD,
     is important to Muslims because the journey
     1   resulted in Muhammad's death
     2   signified the establishment of the Islamic faith
     3   established Byzantine rule throughout the region
     4   ended Muhammad's attempts to spread Islam throughout Arabia

9   The caste system (*jati*) influenced traditional rural Indian society by
     1   promoting political instability
     2   reducing the power of landowners
     3   limiting social and economic progress
     4   contributing to greater social mobility

10   Charlemagne's Empire was similar to that of Alexander the Great because both were
     1   located in Central Europe
     2   models of democratic rule
     3   quickly divided by successors after their deaths
     4   united under one central religious belief system

11   Judaism, Islam, and Christianity share a belief in
     1   the central authority of the Pope
     2   a prohibition on the consumption of pork
     3   reincarnation and the Four Noble Truths
     4   monotheism and ethical conduct

12   In European feudal society, an individual's social status was generally determined by
     1   birth   3   individual abilities
     2   education and training   4   marriage

Base your answer to question 13 on the diagram below and your knowledge of social studies

13   Which idea about the reality of Medieval manor life is best portrayed by the diagram above?
     1   Interdependence was critical.
     2   Religious ritual restrained progress.
     3   Prosperity was in the hands of the few.
     4   Freedom was the key determinant of life.

14 One similarity between the cultures of traditional China and traditional Japan was that
1   religion played a minor role in society
2   the educated class was held in high esteem
3   social mobility was encouraged
4   the people elected the political leaders

15 The growth of feudalism in Europe during the Middle Ages was primarily caused by the
1   rivalry over colonial empires
2   long-term decrease in trade
3   decline of the Roman Catholic Church
4   collapse of strong central government

16 "The emperor is equal to all men in the nature of his body, but in the authority of his rank, he is similar to God, who rules all."
                              – a 4th century visitor to Constantinople, *Byzantine Splendor.*
Which idea of Byzantine government society does this quotation reflect?
1   The sole ruler is endowed with absolute power.
2   Authority must be shared as it is in nature.
3   All men were created equal under the law.
4   Certain classes have higher privileges.

THEMATIC ESSAY

Directions: Write a well-organized essay that includes an introduction, several paragraphs explaining your position, and a conclusion.

Theme: invasions

> Throughout ancient history, invasions have had both
> negative and positive effects on the development of regions.

Task:

> • Describe the effect of invasions by outsiders on a settled
>   society.
> • Support your opinion by discussing the influence of *two*
>   invasions on civilizations.

Suggestions: You may use examples from your study of global history and geography. Some suggestions you might wish to consider include the invasions of: the Hsiung-Nu on China, Alexander the Great on Persia and Egypt, the Franks on France, the Lombards on Italy, the Varangians on what became Russia, Islamic jihads in Spain, the Arya on India. **You are *not* limited to these suggestions.**

PRACTICE SKILLS FOR DBQ

Directions: The following task is based on the accompanying documents. The documents may have been edited for the purposes of this exercise. The task is designed to test your ability to work with historical documents. As you analyze the documents, take into account both the source of the document and the author's point of view.

Historical Context: The keys to successful government evolved from the experiences of ancient civilizations. The documents below present different views of success in governing.

Part *A* – Short Answer

The documents below relate to *the behavior of rulers* in early China and Japan. Examine each document carefully, then answer the question that follows it.

Document 1

1   What characteristic does Confucius feel is most important for a ruler to have?

> "If a ruler is upright, all will go well without orders. But if he himself is not upright, even though he gives orders, they will not be obeyed."
>
> – Confucius, *The Analects*, c. 500 BC

_____

_____

_____

_____

Document 2

2   What kind of relationships are necessary for successful government?

> "...some disobey their lords and fathers and keep up feuds with their neighbors. But when the superiors are in harmony with each other and inferiors are friendly, then affairs are discussed quietly and the right view of the matter prevails. "
>
> – Prince Shotoku of Japan, c. 600 AD

_____

_____

_____

_____

Part *B* – Essay Response

Task: Using only the information in the documents, write a one or two paragraph discussion of factors contributing to success in government.

State your thesis:

_____

_____

_____

_____

_____

_____

- Use only the information in the documents to support your thesis position
- Add your analysis of the documents
- Incorporate your answers to Part *A* scaffold questions

_____

Additional Suggested Task:

From your knowledge of global history and geography, make a list of additional factors that help governments succeed.

_____

_____

_____

_____

_____

_____

_____

_____

_____

_____

_____

1200 TO 1650 AD

BC

3000– Yayoi people move into Japan
from Asia (3000)

AD

600– Japan's Classical Heian Period (604)

GLOBAL INTERACTIONS

AD

1100–

1200– Minamoto Yoritomo becomes
Shogun (1180)
Genghis Khan launches the
Mongol invasions (1206)

1300–

Black Death sweeps
through Europe (1348)

1400–

Renaissance takes hold in Europe (1400)

Zheng He's expeditions to South
Asian and Africa (1405)

Turks capture Constantinople (1453)

1500–

Vasco DaGama arrives in India (1498)

Protestant Reformation begins –
Luther posts *95 Theses* (1517)

1600–

British East India Company founded (1600)

INTRODUCTION

As they approached the new millennium of 1000 AD, civilizations in East Asia and Europe went through political and social upheavals. Yet, the disruptions led to new interactions in the next few centuries. In Asia, physical isolation helped Japan emerged as a unique civilization. Mongol conquerors from Central Asia swept through China, India, the Middle East, and into Eastern Europe. After the conquests came a peace that revived between Europe and Asia. During and after Mongol dominance, China regrouped into a formidable power. In Europe, commerce began to revive and spread after the Crusades. Commercial interactions undermined the stagnant feudal life of Europe. In the 1200 to 1600 period, new patterns of mobility began challenging the basic economic, social, and political institutions of global civilizations.

POLITICAL DEVELOPMENTS

JAPAN: EMPERORS AND SHOGUNS

Gradually, the Yamato clan chieftains had exerted influence in the southern regions of Japan and even sent expeditions to Korea by the 4th century AD. Contact with China led to the adaptation of Chinese-style script, cuisine, dress, rituals, and a unique blending of Buddhism with native Shinto beliefs.

☆ CAPSULE – TRADITIONAL RULE IN JAPAN

- **7th century: Shotoku Taishi** established the power of the emperors, their city-based power declined by the 11th century.

- **12th century:** Shogun **Minamoto Yoritomo** (c.1192) unified the **daimyo** and their samurai into a strong, feudal bureaucratic alliance.

- **17th century:** Shogun **Tokugawa Ieyasu** (1639) strengthened the shogunate, tightened control, imposed strict order, and isolated the country from outside influences.

In 604 AD, contact with China's T'ang Dynasty led Prince Regent **Shotoku Taishi** to create a central authority based on Buddhist / Confucian ideals and a bureaucratic administrative network. Subsequent emperors redistributed land to overcome the power of local aristocrats. They ruled first from Nara and later from Heian where Japan's culture blossomed from the 9th to the 11th centuries. Gradually, the emperors' city-based power shrank as the **daimyo** (feudal lords) exerted power in the countryside. The warrior daimyo commanded groups of vassal knights called **samurai** and most pledged allegiance to the strongest military leader, the **shogun**.

MONGOLS: IMPACT OF CONQUESTS

In the great Eurasian land mass, between the forests of the north and the mountains and deserts of the south are the steppes. They are an enormous band of grassy, treeless plains that stretch from northern China to eastern Europe. From the 4th to the 13th centuries, fierce nomadic cavalries swept out of the Central Asian steppes to form the largest empire ever known. First came the Huns, then the Seljuk Turks, and finally, the

Mongols. In the early 13th century, one charismatic leader, Temujin (1167-1227), better known as **Genghis Khan** (or Jenghiz) united the main tribes to become the Mongols' "universal leader." His conquest of northern China in 1215 compromised the Song Dynasty. In 1219, Genghis Khan sent his "mounted thunder" westward, taking the central Asian trading cities of Tashkent and Samarkand, and pressing into the territory of the Abbasid Caliphs and the Kievan Rus (early Russia).

After Genghis Khan's death, khanates (kingdoms) founded by his sons and grandsons asserted independence. The western khanates became Islamic in character. Under his grandson, **Kublai Khan** (1215-1294), China experienced its first period of "foreign rule." Kublai Khan claimed the "Mandate of Heaven" and organized the **Yuan Dynasty** (1279-1368) where the Mongols' fierce loyalty and respect for age blended with Confucian traditions. Mongol legal codes meshed with the traditional Chinese legalism. Kublai Khan placed Mongols in the highest positions of his Empire, but wisely retained a Chinese bureaucracy and civil service. Well enforced, his rule led to a period of peace and prosperity. Because of burgeoning trade, the splendor of the Great Khan's China became known from Asia to Europe. Although it weakened and fell in less than a century, the Yuan Dynasty welcomed outside cultures and spread its influence into Southeast Asia.

★ CAPSULE – MONGOL EMPIRES (SEE MAP AT RIGHT)

China: Yuan Dynasty (1279-1368)
- Became first foreign group to rule all of China.
- Created capital at Beijing ("northern capital").
- Directed military expeditions against Japan, Indochina, Burma, and the island of Java, Malaya.
- Adopted Buddhism.
- Opened China to many contacts with outside world.

India: Mughal Dynasty (1526-1707)
- Set up by Muslim invader **Babur** (descendent of Genghis Khan and Tamerlane)
- Demonstrated tolerance toward Hindus and Buddhists.
- Great Rulers included **Akbar** (r. 1556-1605), **Jahangir** (r. 1605-1627), **Shah Jahn** (r. 1627-1658).
- Magnificent Persian/Mughal art and architecture (Taj Mahal) influenced Indian style.

Southwest and Central Asia: Hulegu and Jagati Dynasties (1258-1385)
- Hulegu (also called Ilkhans, 1258-1353) assimilated Islamic culture of Persia, Iran, Iraq, Syria; sacked, then rebuilt Baghdad.
- Jagati (also called Chagatei, 1270-1385) assimilated Turkic culture and adapted Islam.
- Created law codes built on loyalty to khans.
- Learning and trade flourished.

Russia: Khanate of the Golden Horde* (1240-1400)
- Mongols merged with the Tatars and adopted Turkic language and Islam.
- Batu Khan destroyed Kiev, the most important Russian state, in 1240.
- Conquest caused Kiev to decline into one of the most backward European nations.
- Russian princes became Mongol vassals and required to pay heavy tribute.
- Internal divisions enabled Moscow nobles to defeat the Mongols at Kulikovo in 1380.
- Broke up into separate khanates of Astrakhan, Crimea, and Kazan

(*Name derived from the colorful tents of the Mongol encampments)

AFRICA: SUB SAHARAN KINGDOMS

Africa is the second largest continent. Its natural environment shaped its development. The three million square mile expanse of the Sahara Desert separated Medieval African civilizations to the south from the civilizations farther north. The seas were a barrier too. Ancient Egypt, Nubia, and Carthage used the Mediterranean as a trade route to the world, but interior societies had limited access. Not until after 1000 AD was there much north-south contact. In the 9th and 10th centuries, Arab traders began to cross the Sahara in search of the legendary kingdoms of west Africa. They found prosperous cities where merchants oversaw the exchange of coastal gold for inland salt. Under rulers such as

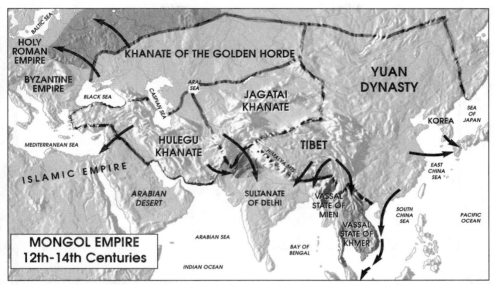

MONGOL EMPIRE
12th-14th Centuries

Mali's great **Mansa Musa** (c. 1330), cities such as Timbuktu had organized governments, university centers, and highly developed architecture and art.

Cultural diffusion began between the west Africans and the Arab traders of the north. Islam began to spread. Its diversity allowed it to merge with traditional religious beliefs. Islam's community rule blended well with traditional order and the religion spread rapidly, creating a broad, common bond in the region.

The kingdoms of west Africa were loose unions of trading centers connected by alliances made by military strongmen. The alliances were fragile and civil wars made them more so. Traditional life did not adapt to newer technologies – especially weapons – as readily as it had to Islam. Demand for

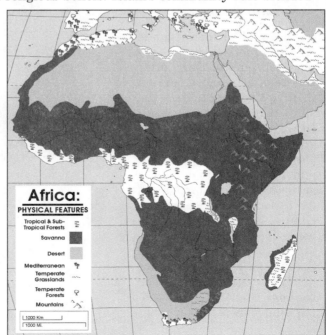

Africa:
PHYSICAL FEATURES

Tropical & Sub-Tropical Forests
Savanna
Desert
Mediterranean
Temperate Grasslands
Temperate Forests
Mountains

1000 Km
1000 Mi.

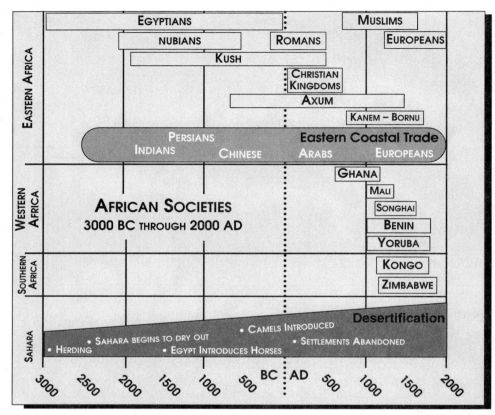

Arab and European goods led to an increase in the taking of slaves especially after the 16th century. Common in Africa for centuries, the slave trade caused societies to war on each other constantly. The colonization of the Americas in the 15th and 16th centuries created a surge of demand for slaves. As time went on, Senegal, Ghana, Nigeria, and Angola were frequented by slave merchants from Portugal, Spain, and Holland. Pursuit of slaves tore West Africa asunder, and the great trading kingdoms disintegrated.

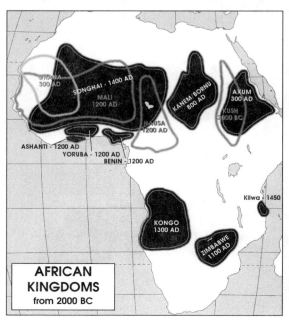

AFRICAN KINGDOMS
from 2000 BC

EUROPE: THE RISE OF ROYAL POWER

AND THE GROWTH OF NATION-STATES

Slowly, a powerful tide of economic and social changes flowed through Europe in the 13th and 14th centuries. The general peace of the era aided the growth of trade and towns. This led to greater exchange of goods, but also saw the movement of ideas amid the questioning spirit of the Renaissance.

Even as negative a force, as the **Black Death**, contributed to wide-spread change. The bubonic plague took 75 million lives, but it also deci-mated the economic life of the manors and upset the system that bonded people and land. With their estates and realms disintegrating, nobles tried to restrict people by imposing new taxes, but the peasants resisted, wandered off, and in some cases launched rebellions. Local nobles lost the support of the growing middle classes in the towns, too. The burghers allied themselves with kings. National monarchs could give them protec-tion on a larger scale and demanded less from them in taxation.

Even the most powerful institution of Europe could not maintain tra-dition: the Church lost many clerical leaders to the plague and its inter-nal schisms hastened the break down of the old Medieval order. After the Protestant Reformation, the resulting religious wars accelerated change even more.

In the midst of all of this change, national monarchs began to exert more power. The struggles of the French and English in the **Hundred Years War** (1337-1453) to decide land claims ended in the French expelling the English. More important, both countries had finally united behind their respective monarchs and endowed them with formidable armies. The Spanish had united behind their monarchs (Ferdinand and Isabella) in the 1470s to expel the Moors (Muslims) and complete the 700-year *Reconquista*.

fleur d'lis
emblem of the
Bourbon Kings
of France

The large standing armies of these campaigns became the source of power for the monarchs, making them "emperors within their own kingdoms" and formidable powers outside. They claimed to speak and act for their entire nation. The command of broad military power allowed them to overcome challenges from rival nobles. The bureau-cratic structures they built (somewhat like those of the Chinese) allowed them to enforce laws, provide equitable justice, and collect taxes efficiently. The monarchs exerted **divine right** – they claimed their power was absolute and came from God and that they were responsible to no one but God.

The centralization of power and use of shrewd ministers enabled the French kings such as Francis I, and Henry IV to withstand the religious upheavals of the Protestant Reformation (Wars of Religion). This strength allowed them to defy the power of the Habsburg Holy Roman Emperors and assert their national sovereignty. This strength grew as clever ministers such as **Cardinal Richelieu** (1585-1642) made the dynasties – like the Bourbons – formidable.

In England, monarchs such as **William I** (William the Conqueror, r. 1066-1087) and lawgivers such as **Henry II** (r. 1154-1189) moved toward divine right absolutism. However, their power was limited by strong traditions that made them share power with the nobles. From the time of the *Magna Carta* (1215), English nobles claimed certain liberties for all free men so that all might be defended from royal whim. The *Magna Carta* assured supremacy of the law as opposed to absolute power for monarchs. It set the precedent that certain taxes were not to be levied without the common consent of the **Parliament**. Originally a council of landholders and clergy, the Parliament emerged in the 13th century to exert control over treasury funds (**revenue**) of the kingdom. For more than 500 years English monarchs struggled over money with the **bicameral** legislative body (two houses: Lords and Commons).

After a series of civil wars in the mid 15th century, the Tudor Dynasty strengthened the English monarchy and saw it through the religious struggles of the Reformation and positioned England as a major power offsetting the rising power of Spain and France.

TUDOR MONARCHS OF ENGLAND	
Monarch	**Events**
Henry VII (r. 1485-1509)	united the kingdom after dynastic civil war (War of the Roses); rebuilt wealth; financed first voyages of discovery; aided development of naval force
Henry VIII (r. 1509-1547)	broke with Rome and set up the Anglican Church; patronized art and literature
Edward VI (r. 1547-1553)	regents continued Protestant reforms (died at age 16)
Mary I (r. 1553-1558)	tried to restore Catholicism; executed and exiled Protestants; allied with Spain through marriage
Elizabeth I (r. 1558-1603)	restored Protestantism, but gave tolerance to Catholics; fought in Wars of Religion against France; aided Dutch Protestant rebellion against Spain; defeated the Spanish Armada; began settlement of English colonies in America

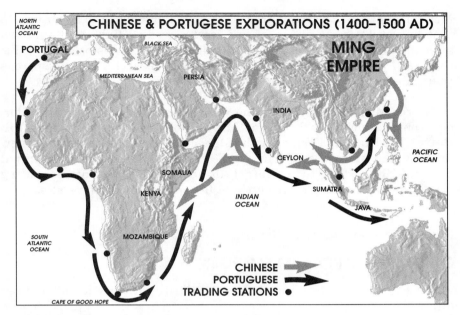

CHINESE & PORTUGESE EXPLORATIONS (1400–1500 AD)

ECONOMIC DEVELOPMENTS

NEW TRADE AND GLOBAL INTERACTIONS

As the Mongol invasions subsided in the 13th century, Asian khanates were strictly ruled, but the strictness worked in favor of commerce. The tight military control of the Mongol khans brought enough security to the vast region from the Pacific Ocean to the eastern

GLOBAL TRADE CENTERS	
Cities	**Connections**
Canton, China (now Guangzhou)	Asian goods traded for Indian, Persian, and European goods; foreign merchants confined to enclave outside city walls
Cairo, Egypt (formerly Fustat)	Arab goods traded for eastern and sub-Saharan African goods, then exchanged for European, Indian, and Asian goods; expanded under the Fatimid Dynasty and Saladin (Salah ad-Din); declined after 1400 due to Turkish invasions and plagues
Constantinople, Turkey	Asian goods traded for European goods; battered by Crusaders and Venice, it was still a terminus of the Silk Route until it fell to the Turks in 1453
Venice, Italy	European goods traded for Middle Eastern, African, Asian goods. Independent of the Holy Roman Empire, Venice created large naval force for defense and protection of Mediterranean merchant fleets

Mediterranean Sea to make trade and travel safe for over a century. In that hundred year period, east and west recreated links that survived after the Mongol khanates disintegrated. (Note: Some historians call this era the "**Pax Mongolia**," comparing it to the peaceful and prosperous years of early Roman Empire – the Pax Romana.)

In the Mongol Era, Yuan China was opened to a steady stream of foreign contacts including the Italian **Marco Polo** (1270s) and the Arab **Ibn Battua** (mid 1300s). Even after the Mongol rule was overthrown, the new dynasty, the **Mings**, authorized the fantastic voyages of the intrepid Admiral **Zheng He**. In the late 14th and early 15th centuries, Ming China was reputed to have a merchant fleet exceeding 6,000 vessels.

FAIRS, TOWNS, AND GUILDS:

EUROPEAN CAPITALISM EMERGES

In Europe, the new knowledge and desire for luxuries introduced during the Crusades outlasted the holy wars. Trade grew in the Mediterranean, spearheaded by the Italian cities (Venice, Genoa, Pisa). They became staging points for the movement of goods through Western Europe where life had become more peaceful. Commercial activity started first with movable fairs, then led to the growth of more permanent towns such as Lyon, Paris, and Bruges.

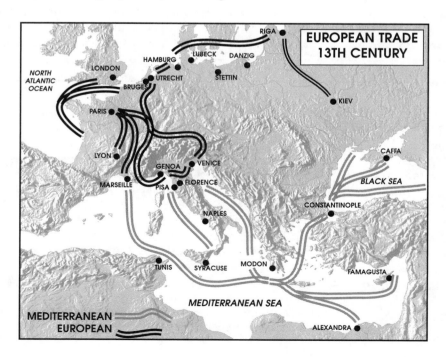

European towns also grew because climate and farm techniques improved grain production. Not as many workers were needed on the manors and some became involved in trading and transporting surplus produce. Seasonal trade fairs grew into more permanent trading centers. With an improved diet (an increase in the quantity and quality of food), the population increased. Between the 10th and 13th centuries, Europe's population doubled to 60 million.

In the towns, lords charged fees to the new merchant class for land and for protection. This new "middle class" (between the peasants and the nobles) grew wealthier and was able to afford its own protection. Slowly, the middle-class grew less dependent on the local nobles. In many cases, its allegiance (and taxes) went to national monarchs because they could offer broader protection for growing trade. Some commercial centers became independent city-states (e.g., Venice, Milan, Hamburg). In larger cities, merchants and craftsmen joined into **guilds** to:

- defend or police their towns and to secure liberties against nobles
- regulate trade and industry (limit businesses, control supply and price)
- provide professional education (train apprentices, certify journeymen and master craftsmen)
- support members in sickness (early insurance)
- ensure economic stability in the community

Town life grew complex and merchants needed to move goods quickly. The cumbersome barter system yielded to a resurrection of **money**. Coinage, of course, had been around since ancient times, but went out of

use in the isolated manorial life of early Medieval Europe. After 1100 AD, the commercial revival demanded a more universal medium of exchange. What emerged were networks of goldsmiths who stored supplies of gold (for a fee) and issued letters of credit (for a fee) that could be carried by merchants and then exchanged for gold by other goldsmiths (for a fee). All these fees meant there was great wealth made in the exchanging process. Gradually, **banking houses** grew from these rudimentary beginnings.

Merchants and bankers pooled their resources to extend commerce beyond their towns and even their kingdoms. When they joined forces to send out protected caravans, convoys, and long-range trading expeditions, merchants and bankers gave birth to a new economic structure – **capitalism**. They were doing what seemed natural: investing their personal private **capital** (wealth) to expand **supply** in response to perceived consumer markets (**demand**). Trade groups sprang up all over Europe. An example is the **Hanseatic League**'s 14th century alliance of merchants that grew to a commercial network of 200 towns along Europe's Baltic Seacoast. Such early alliance models later grew into joint stock companies such as the British and Dutch East India Companies that would sponsor explorations of new trade routes and establish colonies.

This "commercial revolution" triggered a larger global vision. In 14th and 15th century Europe, Portugal's attempts to push the Muslims back to Africa's north coast led **Prince Henry the Navigator** (1394-1460) to found a center (Cape St. Vincent) for research and launching expeditions down Africa's west coast seeking an eastward passage to Asia.

SOCIAL DEVELOPMENTS

JAPANESE SOCIETY

The natural environment shaped Japan's development. As an **archipelago** (large group of islands) off the eastern shore of Asia, the seas sheltered Japan from conquest. The separation allowed Japan to accept or reject outside influences. The islands' rugged terrain and limited farmland made travel and social interaction difficult and led to the predominance of isolated clan (*uji*) cultures. By the 4th century AD, the **Yamato** clan chieftains slowly exerted influence in the southern regions and even sent expeditions to Korea. Contact with China led to the cultural diffusion of Chinese-style script, cuisine, dress, rituals, and a unique blending of Buddhism with native Shinto beliefs.

China's Buddhist / Confucian ideals were absorbed in the 7th to 11th centuries during the Nara and Heian periods when the poetry of **Sei Shonagon** and writings of **Murasaki Shikibu** emerged. Later, the emperors' power shrank and the shogun's power rose, and the military tone of life made the society more rigid and ordered. Under the **Tokgugawa Shogunate** (1603-1867), Japan's culture

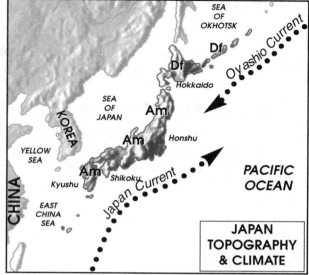

became isolated and static. However, the peace brought some cultural advancements such as the **Noh** theatre with its Zen Buddhist themes, the **kabuki** comedies and dramas, and **haiku** poetry.

The Japanese feudal system was similar to the Medieval European system in that samurai vassals lived in strongholds, served an overlord, and were bound by ritual oaths and codes. Like the European knights'

☆ CAPSULE – FEUDAL JAPANESE SOCIAL CLASSES

SHOGUN & DAIMYO

SAMURAI

PEASANTS & TRADESMEN

code of chivalry, the code of **bushido** stressed honor, self-discipline, bravery and simple living, but it also included Zen Buddhist beliefs. Unlike European feudalism, the peasants were not serfs (near slaves) bound to the lord and the land. Of course, European feudalism eroded slowly between 1200 and 1500, Japanese feudalism lasted until the modern era, and its military culture was a strong social force until after World War II.

★CAPSULE – BLACK DEATH – BUBONIC PLAGUE

In the late Middle Ages, poor sanitation in rapidly growing, tightly packed towns led to frequent plagues and epidemics. Between 1348-1353, bubonic plague wiped out nearly one-third of Europe's population. Known among the Mongols, it appears to have been carried by rats on ships traveling from Black Sea ports into the Mediterranean. In six years, it swept across Europe like a tidal wave, killing millions from Sicily to Scotland.

Death toll estimates in 14th century Europe, Asia, and Africa exceeded 100 million. It took two centuries to bring the population back to 1347 levels. Bubonic plague is caused by a bacterium transmitted by fleas that have fed on the blood of infected rats. It is commonly transmitted by breathing air exhaled by infected persons. It spreads through the bloodstream and the lymphatic system. In untreated cases, death occurs within a few days – and unlike today, there was no cure in the 1300s.

The Black Death disrupted Asian trade routes and brought Europe's revival to a standstill. It triggered crop shortages and famines since few were left to tend the farms. Guilds and crafts suffered as master craftsmen were lost. Knowledge of the law declined as jurists perished, and universities closed for lack of staff. Serfs and peasants rebelled or ran off when lords demanded pre-plague rate they could not pay. In some areas, loss of serfs meant lords had to begin paying wages to laborers.

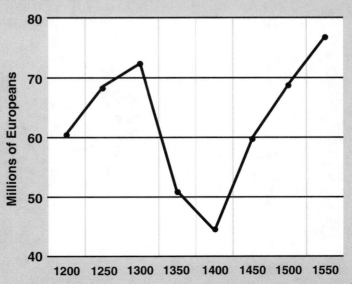

RENAISSANCE – A NEW, QUESTIONING SPIRIT

The steady economic and political changes in Europe after 1100 AD, especially the enlivened trade of the Mediterranean, spurred cultural change. The struggle between the Church and the growing power of national monarchs caused a questioning of accepted values. Interaction with Arab and Byzantine preservers of Greco-Roman legacies reawakened interest in ancient classical thought and culture.

Western Europe's view of the world shifted from a narrowly religious one to a broader secular (worldly) view. This rebirth of interest in the world was later termed the **Renaissance**. Thinkers and artists celebrated a growing confidence in individual human accomplishment called **humanism**. Greek and Roman influences permeated art, architecture, and philosophy. Intellectual focus shifted from concern for the spiritual afterlife to improving the present human condition.

RENAISSANCE ACHIEVEMENTS		
LITERATURE		
Person	**Work**	**Key Ideas**
Dante Alighieri (Florence, 1265-1321)	*The Divine Comedy*	epic allegory in Italian vernacular describes a journey through hell, purgatory and paradise
Geoffery Chaucer (England, 1340-1400)	*Canterbury Tales*	pilgrims tell tales of Medieval life in vernacular English
Desiderius Erasmus (Netherlands, 1466-1536)	*Praise of Folly*	used teachings of the Bible, early Christianity, and ancient pagan thinkers to ridicule the corruption of officials and the clergy
Thomas More (England, c. 1478-1535)	*Utopia*	lashed into the unjust social and economic corruption in England; describes an imaginary state based on humanist reason
Miguel de Cervantes (Spain, 1547-1616)	*Don Quixote*	intended to poke fun at the Spanish romances of chivalry and to analyze the value of idealism
ITALIAN ART AND ARCHITECTURE		
Leonardo DaVinci (1452-1519)	*Mona Lisa, Last Supper*	model "Renaissance Man" – experimented in the arts, mechanics, science; constructed fountains, fortifications, churches; experimented in manned flight, war machines
Michelangelo Buonarotti (1475-1564)	*Moses, David,* Sistine Chapel ceiling, dome of St. Peter's	Biblical and classical figures of athletic prowess and dynamic action; painting, sculpture, and architecture
Raphael (Rafaello Sanzio, 1483-1520)	*Disputa, Sistine Madonna*	classical forms, allegories, madonnas, and subjects from antiquity

RENAISSANCE ACHIEVEMENTS (CONTINUED)		
POLITICAL SCIENCE		
Person	**Work**	**Key Ideas**
Nicolo Machiavelli (Florence, 1469-1527)	*The Prince, Discourses*	advice on increasing and holding power; recommended that absolute monarchs preserve power pragmatically (use violence carefully, respecting subjects and their property and preserve prosperity); claimed political actions have consequences that cannot be fully controlled, and the ruler must sometimes accept that "the end justifies the means;" called for Italian unity and an end to foreign intervention
TECHNICAL INNOVATION		
Johann Gutenberg (Germany, 1398-1468)	movable type, printing ink, letter press process	invented printing using movable type in Europe (already being done in China from the 8th century); supplied the needs for more and cheaper reading matter and expanded learning and communication

Although the cultural renewal spread to all corners of Europe, artists and philosophers gravitated to the city-states of Northern Italy. Their wealth and interaction in the world, plus their independence from monarchs and the papacy, made them natural cradles for humanistic growth.

PROTESTANT REFORMATION

The sweep of the great political and economic changes that percolated in Europe in the late Middle Ages, along with the new Renaissance attitudes about life, art, architecture, and literature, affected all its institutions. Finally, it shook the foundations of the major institution – the Roman Catholic Church. From the 1300s, power struggles among kings, emperors, and popes had undermined the Church's authority. Many of the faithful were bewildered at the Church's inabili-

EUROPEAN RELIGIONS
Mid-Sixteenth Century

NORTH ATLANTIC OCEAN

CALVINIST

NORTH SEA

BALTIC SEA

EASTERN ORTHODOX

CHURCH OF ENGLAND

CALVINIST

CALVINIST

LUTHERAN

ROMAN CATHOLIC

ADRIATIC SEA

BLACK SEA

ISLAM

MEDITERRANEAN SEA

ty to combat the Black Death, and the plague took the lives of many Church leaders. As political power funneled into the hands of powerful monarchs, the Church's authority was being questioned more and more. The Renaissance spirit of questioning revealed and broadcast Church corruption and eroded its traditional authority. Well known scholars such as Erasmus and Thomas More urged the Church to reform itself, but the warnings went unheeded by the complacent hierarchy.

Martin Luther protesting Church practices by posting his grievances on the door of the Wittenberg Cathedral.

In the first quarter of the 16th century, reformers became numerous and militant. They had many different criticisms and differences among themselves, but **Protestant** reformers such as **Martin Luther**, **John Calvin**, **Ulrich Zwingli**, and **John Knox** promoted several common ideas:

- acceptance of the Bible as the key source of revelation
- salvation of the soul by faith alone
- universal priesthood of all believers
- self-interpretation of the Bible
- questioning of traditional rituals and some of the sacraments

The call for reform swept through Europe. The use of Gutenberg's moveable type made books plentiful and reading became more common. Protestant theses and pamphlets spread the call like wildfire. In some places reformers wanted more radical cures than the reform of the Church that the followers of Luther or Calvin demanded. Numerous sects rejected any connection between church and state. Many wanted a return to the the simple beliefs of the first Christians. In England, Henry VIII argued with the Pope over annulment of his marriage and then created the Church of England (Anglican Church) with himself as head.

Europe was torn asunder by the Reformation. The Church excommunicated Luther and other reformers, but it did not attempt any internal reform. Late in the 16th century (after the Council of Trent, 1545-1563), the Roman Catholic Church finally launched the **Counter-Reformation**. The movement intensified missionary work, investigated and persecuted heretics, funded military actions against Protestants, and even persecuted Jews. Yet, the Church had delayed too long. Europe fragmented into scores of religious and political splinters.

By the late 1500s, Northern Europe (England, Scotland, Scandinavia, German states) developed national churches. Monarchs joined them to defy the authority of the Church and the Holy Roman Emperor. Religious wars and massacres erupted lasting well into the 17th century; among them:

- The Peasants' War (1524-1526) in Germany saw 100,000 killed.
- The Wars of Religion (1562-1598) in France spread into the Netherlands.
- The Thirty Years War (1618-1648) in Germany and Poland began the breakup of the Holy Roman Empire.

LINKAGES

The global interactions of the 13th to 17th centuries resulted in bringing different civilizations into closer contact. The way people lived, worked, and thought all changed. The great stimulus for change was trade. It led to a commercial revolution. The rulers of China and Japan strengthened traditional culture. Yet, they struggled with the impact of increasing commercial contacts with other global regions. In Asia and the Middle East, the Mongols' rule created a stability. Their successors, the Turks, strengthened, but isolated the Muslim world.

In Western Europe, revitalized trade was a powerful force in opening society. Population began to increase rapidly as a result of better food production and health practices. Capitalism emerged and accelerated commerce even more. It changed the way production and labor were organized. It undermined manorialism and gave rise to towns that grew into cities. It made education necessary.

Urban cultural interactions produced the Renaissance – the rebirth of interest in the classics and human achievement. The merchants of Italian city-states and Portuguese navigators unleashed a drive for sea routes to obtain the spices and luxuries of Asia – a drive that eventually led to the European awareness of previously unknown continents.

Also in European society, amidst a great purging and revival of spirit, the Reformation focused a new interest in spreading Christianity. The Reformation also fragmented European society. The key forces that forged the "modern world" emerged from all this change and interaction and set the scene for the global interdependence of the modern era.

QUESTIONS

Base your answer to questions 1 and 2 on the illustration below and your knowledge of global history and geography.

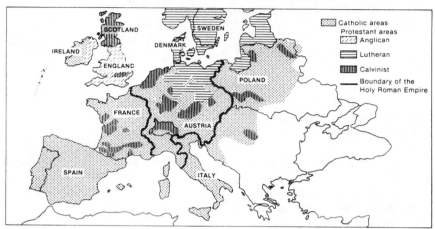

1   Which statement about the Holy Roman Empire is supported by the map?
   1   The religion of the people in the Holy Roman Empire was either Lutheran or Catholic.
   2   The Holy Roman Empire had fewer Protestant areas than the rest of Europe did.
   3   Calvinism was dominant throughout the Holy Roman Empire.
   4   Protestant influences were strongest in the northern areas of the Holy Roman Empire.

2   Which title would be most appropriate for this map?
   1   "The Impact of the Protestant Reformation"
   2   "The Catholic Counter-Reformation"
   3   "The Fall of the Holy Roman Empire"
   4   "European Religious Unity"

3   "Unless I am convinced by Scripture and plain reason ... my conscience is captive to the Word of God. I cannot and I will not recant anything, for to go against conscience is neither right nor safe. Here I stand, I cannot do otherwise" – Martin Luther, *Diet of Worms* (1517)
   When Martin Luther said, "...my conscience is captive to the Word of God," he was referring to belief in
   1   the supremacy of the Bible over Church policies
   2   imprisoning those who disagreed with Church teachings
   3   maintaining the unity of the Church
   4   the need for nepotism

4   In Europe during the Middle Ages, increases in trade and commerce resulted in
   1   lower living standards for industrial workers
   2   decreased economic rivalry among kings
   3   increased political power for the clergy
   4   development of towns and cities

5   During the Age of Absolutism (1600s and 1700s), European monarchies sought to
   1   increase human rights for their citizens
   2   centralize political power in their nations
   3   develop better relations with Islamic rulers
   4   encourage the growth of manorialism

6   Which geographic factor has helped China remain isolated for many centuries?
   1   many natural harbors
   2   navigable river systems
   3   severe climate
   4   northern and western mountain ranges

Base your answer to question 7 on the illustration at the right and your knowledge of global history and geography.

7   This illustration reflects a traditional Japanese theme of
   1   the desire to control the forces of nature
   2   reliance on the sea for food
   3   the Emperor's arrival from the sea
   4   respect for the power and beauty of nature

8   One way in which the Seljuk Turks, Mongols, and Crusaders were similar is that they all
   1   invaded the Middle East and affected its culture
   2   succeeded in bringing democracy to the Middle East
   3   moved through the Middle east as nomads
   4   established extensive, permanent empires in the Middle East

9 Which is a major characteristic of the Renaissance?
  1 conformity   3 mysticism
  2 humanism   4 obedience

10 Which statement describes the situation in Russia during the 200 years when the Mongols ruled?
  1 Russia experienced a cultural Renaissance.
  2 Russia was isolated and paid tribute to the Khans.
  3 Westernization and industrialization began in Russia.
  4 Democratic reforms were encouraged in Russian society.

11 Africa's geography is characterized by
  1 an absence of rain forests
  2 an irregular coastline and excellent harbors
  3 a diversity of topography
  4 a lack of major river systems

Base your answer to questions 12 on the illustration at the right and your knowledge of global history and geography.

12 Which of the following was the basis for Mongol rule?
  1 the resemblance of the Mongol cavalry to the Pax Romana legions of the Roman Empire
  2 the ease of trade and travel made security easier to maintain
  3 the assimilation of Islamic dogma into the Mongol belief system
  4 the intensity of military organization and collection of tribute

13 A major purpose for the guilds that formed in European towns in the late Medieval Era was to
  1 provide financial support for local nobles
  2 regulate trade and industry
  3 defend the Church against Protestant heresies
  4 protect against barbarian invasion

14 England's Tudor rulers, unlike the absolute monarchs of Spain and France, were required to
1   share power with a representative body
2   remain firmly supportive of the Pope
3   strengthen the feudal system
4   follow the "mandate of heaven"

15 Prince Henry the Navigator, Admiral Zeng He, Mansa Musa, and Marco Polo characterized the Age of Global Interaction (1200-1650) because they
1   ruled by divine right as absolute monarchs
2   helped to integrate the major religions
3   were active in promoting naval and commercial enterprises
4   revolutionized the military tactics of their cultures

THEMATIC ESSAY

Directions: Write a well-organized essay that includes an introduction, several paragraphs explaining your position, and a conclusion.

Theme: Geographic influences on human affairs.

> Throughout history, geographic factors have altered the economic, political, and social development of cultures.

Task:

> Choose *two* cultures from the Age of Global Interaction (1200-1650) and identify *two* geographic features which influenced the cultures.
> For *each* culture
> • Describe the *two* geographic features related to that culture.
> • Explain how the specific geographic features had a positive or negative influence on that culture.

Suggestions:
You may use any geographic and cultural relationship from your study of global history and geography. Some suggestions you might wish to consider include Japan's island locale, Korea's peninsula location, the Mongols and the Eurasian steppes, the Sahara and early African Kingdoms, Venice's location on the Mediterranean Sea, China and the Himalayas, Tien Shan, and Kunlun Mountains. **You are *not* limited to these suggestions.**

PRACTICE SKILLS FOR DBQ

Directions: The following task is based on the accompanying documents. The documents may have been edited for the purposes of this exercise. The task is designed to test your ability to work with historical documents. As you analyze the documents, take into account both the source of the document and the author's point of view.

Historical Context: For centuries, the arts have often been outward signs of change within a society. The documents below present examples of art in the Middle Ages and in the Renaissance.

Part A – Short Answer
The documents below relate to art in the Middle Ages and in the Renaissance. Examine each document carefully, then answer the question that follows it.

Document 1

1   Describe the depiction of the horse in the above detail of the Middle Ages' Bayeux Tapestry (11th century).

_____

_____

_____

_____

_____

_____

Document 2

> "Il Caballo" a horse sculpture
> designed in 1505 by Leonardo
> DaVinci for the Duke of Milan
> but never completed; from a
> recent rendition by the Tallix
> Foundary, Beacon, NY
> - photo by Diane Galante, 1999

2   How was Leonardo Da Vinci's approach to
    art different from that of Medieval artists?

    _____

    _____

    _____

    _____

    _____

    _____

    _____

Part *B* – Essay Response

Task: Using only the information in the documents, write one or two
paragraphs on how art in the Renaissance differed from that of the
Middle Ages.

State your thesis:

    _____

    _____

    _____

    _____

- Use only the information in the documents to support your the-
  sis position
- Add your analysis of the documents
- Incorporate your answers to Part *A* scaffold questions

_____

Additional Suggested Task:

From your knowledge of global history and geography, make a list of
additional examples that could be used to show how art changed from the
Middle Ages to the Renaissance.

1450 TO 1770 AD

THE
FIRST
GLOBAL
AGE

AD

1400–

Zeng He explores Indian
Ocean for the Mings (1425)

Mehemed II conquers
Constantinople (1453)

1500– Islamic Songhai Kingdom in West Africa (1500)

Cortés conquers the Aztecs (1521)

Ottoman westward expansion blocked at Battle of Lepanto (1571)
English fleet defeats Spain's Armada (1588)
Akbar unites Northern India (1590)

1600–

Romanov Dynasty
begins in Russia (1613)

Spain conquers Peru (1632)

Puritans dethrone
Charles I (1646)

England's Glorious
Revolution (1688)

1700–

Peter the Great begins con-
structing St. Petersburg (1703)

INTRODUCTION

In this First Global Age, civilizations of Asia and Europe actively engaged civilizations in Africa, the Americas, and the Pacific Rim. European encounters and exploration grew out of the quest for trade, wealth, and knowledge begun in the Commercial Revolution and Renaissance of the 13th, 14th, and 15th centuries.

Aztecs built cities such as Tenochtitlan with pyramid temples to gods, plazas, aqueducts, and causeways.

ECONOMIC DEVELOPMENT

EUROPEANS EXPAND TRADE

TO ASIA, AFRICA, AND THE AMERICAS

The 15th century is one of those turning points in history; it laid the groundwork for capitalism and the world market. Western Europeans circumnavigated Africa and its gold fell into their hands.

In South Asian commerce, European merchant fleets became more prominent as Chinese regional activity declined. After the magnificent fleets of **Zheng He** retreated from the Indian Ocean in the mid 1400s, Portuguese navigators (e.g., da Gama, de Almeida, de Albuquerque) rounded Africa's Cape of Good Hope and moved European trade into India, Indonesia, Indochina, and finally, China itself. The Portuguese even man-

EARLY VOYAGES OF DISCOVERY		
YEAR	EXPLORER (COUNTRY)	AREA
1487-1488	Dias (Portugal)	West coast of Africa, Cape of Good Hope
1492-1502	Columbus (Spain)	West Indies, Caribbean
1497-1499	da Gama (Portugal)	east coast of Africa, India
1497	Cabot (England)	Canada, No. America
1513	Balboa (Spain)	Central America, Pacific
1519-1522	Magellan (Spain)	Circumnavigates globe
1534-1535	Cartier (France)	Canada - St. Lawrence R.
1608	Champlain (France)	Eastern Canada, northern U.S.
1609	Hudson (Netherlands)	Arctic Ocean, North America

aged to establish a trading station in Japan despite the Tokugawa Shoguns' seclusion policies.

In the 16th century, the Portuguese were Europe's leading dealers in products to East Asia. After **Pedro Cabral** claimed Brazil in 1497, Portuguese trading stations in West Africa became the staging grounds for the growing slave trade to America's colonial plantations. The government did not actively manage trade as did the other mercantilist states of Europe. Little of Portugal's great wealth was reinvested in new fleets or home manufacturing. As a result, Portugal's leadership in trade declined, and it lost many of its colonial posessions to the intense competition of the Spanish, Dutch, and English.

MERCANTILISM

In this First Global Age, the quest for wealth and national commercial power shifted rapidly from Italy, Portugal, and Spain to Germany and finally to the Netherlands, France, and England. National monarchs rose in political importance and worked to overcome the power of the nobles and the Church. Kings tried to produce common loyalty among their subjects – especially cultivating the **burgesses**, **burghers**, or **bourgeoisie** (the new merchant middle class). The monarchs needed a system to finance their activities. Under deft finance ministers such as France's **Jean Baptiste Colbert** (c. 1670s), mercantilism emerged. Through tax policies and trade regulations, **mercantilism** aimed at accumulating gold in national treasuries to purchase military supplies and maintain a formidable national army and navy (e.g. Philip II's grand Spanish Armada).

Mercantilist ministers encouraged private voyages of discovery and colonial enterprises (via joint stock companies) with monopoly charters to generate wealth. Having colonies meant the government could exert control over trade and prices for the raw materials needed for manufacturing as opposed to buying such goods from other countries. Supposedly, this would keep wealth within the nation.

Mercantilists sought a **"favorable balance of trade."** This meant that in international trade, the country made money. As far as other countries were concerned, the national accounts had to show that **exports** (goods sold to others) exceeded **imports** (goods bought from others).

Theoretically, colonies contributed to the favorable balance. Besides being a cheap source of raw material, they were supposed to provide closed, controllable markets for home industries. Mercantilists set up

☆ CAPSULE – "GOD, GOLD, AND GLORY"
EUROPEAN COLONIAL EXPANSION (1487-1609)

Causes
- Growth of urban population and wealth generated markets
- Desire for spices and luxury goods (silks, jewels)
- Need for sea routes to Asia (Ottomans and Turks blocked overland routes)
- Development of better navigational techniques
- Development of better geographic knowledge and maps
- National monarchs needed wealth to consolidate power and compete with other powers
- Desire to spread Christian faith

Nations adopted mercantilist* economic philosophy escalating expansionism

(*accumulating bullion, establishing colonies and a merchant marine, and developing industry and mining to attain a favorable balance of trade)

Effects
- Europeans exploited the wealth of the Americas, Africa, India, Southeast Asia
- Colonial empires and political competition grew
- Slavery and the slave trade spread globally
- Forced labor systems emerged on colonial plantations in the Americas and Southeast Asia
- Mesoamerican civilizations destroyed (Aztec, Inca)
- European diseases killed many indigenous people
- Cultural diffusion accelerated
- Capitalism expanded
- Large numbers of Europeans migrated to other regions (especially the Western Hemisphere)

rules that forbade certain types of manufacturing in colonies, forcing colonists to buy from home markets. This practice led to smuggling or flagrant breaking of mercantilist regulations. In reality, national governments followed a policy of **benevolent neglect**. Mercantilist governments spent little on enforcement of the rules in the colonies as long as revenues were produced for their national treasuries.

☆ CAPSULE – SPAIN BUILDS A NEW WORLD EMPIRE

Explorers

- Christopher Columbus (Caribbean, Honduras, 1492-1502)
- Ponce de Leon (Puerto Rico, Florida, Venezuela, Colombia, c. 1513)
- Vasco Balboa (Panama, Pacific Ocean, c. 1513)
- Francisco Cordoba (Mexico, c. 1517)
- Fernando Magellan (South America, Philippines, 1519-1522)

Conquistadores

- Diego Velazquez de Cuellar, c. 1514 (Cuba & Caribbean)
- Hernando Cortés, c. 1521 (Mexico)
- Francisco Pizarro, c. 1534 (Peru)

Viceroys

- The Spanish monarchs set up a near feudal administration for the New World. They appointed Spanish nobles as **viceroys** (regional governors) with almost absolute power to oversee the royally chartered **encomiendas** (plantations) and mining operations granted to **peninsulares** (lesser nobles) usually administered by **criollos** (American-born children of peninsulares).

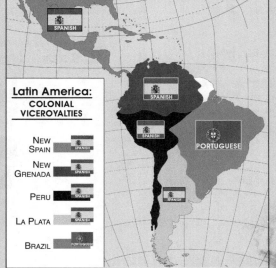

Latin America:
COLONIAL VICEROYALTIES

NEW SPAIN	SPANISH
NEW GRENADA	SPANISH
PERU	SPANISH
LA PLATA	SPANISH
BRAZIL	PORTUGUESE

☆ CAPSULE – SPAIN'S IMPERIAL SOCIETY

Social Structure

A social class system emerged in the Spanish colonies based on birth and intermixing of the races. *Peninsulares*, lesser nobles from Spain received vast land grants from the crown and were responsible to the viceroys to produce wealth and keep order. *Criollos*, American-born children of peninsulares often managed the encomiendas. Soldiers, merchants, and overseers intermarried with Native Americans producing a class called *mestizos* who made up the peasants and independent farmers. Amerindians, *mulattos*, and African slaves made up the lower classes.

PENINSULARES
Iberian Aristocrats

CRIOLLOS
Decendents of Peninsulares

MESTIZOS
Caucasian & Amerindian

MULATTOS
Caucasian & African

AFRICAN SLAVES

AMERINDIANS

LATIN AMERICAN
COLONIAL CLASS STRUCTURE

CULTURAL DIFFUSION

To Spain:	To the Americas:
ores, tobacco, sugar, corn, potatoes, beans, chocolate, tomatoes, squash	diseases (smallpox, influenza, cholera), domestic animals (horses, ...), technology (plows, guns, wagons), Spanish language, Catholic religion, governmental organization, class structures, slavery

Slavery

Spain and Portugal were never able to attract a large enough work force to their colonies. The Europeans decimated the Native American population through conquest, imported diseases, and by over-working them on the encomiendas. By the mid-1600s, Spain and Portugal were importing tens of thousands of slaves from Africa annually.

Settlement

Early military bases and administrative centers began functioning as ports for exports from the **encomiendas**. They grew into colonial towns and cities and a merchant class evolved. Church activity spawned towns, too, as missionaries built churches, schools, and hospitals to minister to settlers and Native American converts.

SLAVES BROUGHT TO THE NEW WORLD COLONIES
COLONIAL MOTHER COUNTRY WITH % OF TOTAL

FRANCE 3%
NETHERLANDS 2.8%
SPAIN 25%
ENGLAND 32%
PORTUGAL 37%

0   5   10   15
Millions of Slaves Imported

SOCIAL DEVELOPMENTS

AMERICAN CIVILIZATIONS 1400 BC - 1570 AD

The two great landmasses of the Western Hemisphere stretch 12,500 miles and encompass nearly 16 million square miles from the the Arctic to the Antarctic. Both the Pacific and Atlantic coasts have narrow plains rising into highland plateaus and mountains. Both the North and South American continents have central basins drained by great rivers (Missouri-Mississippi and the Amazon, respectively).

Geography influenced early settlement. Once through the passes of the Rocky-Sierra Madre Cordillera, early inhabitants of North America found it easy to migrate from west to east because of the open plains. Early inhabitants of South America found it hard to migrate from west to east because of the high barrier of the Andes and the thick vegetation of the Amazon rain forest. These were the Native Americans, or Amerindians, as they are sometimes called today. The early settlers lived as nomads some 10,000 to 30,000 years ago. In the Neolithic Age, around 5,000 to 9,000 years ago, they developed agricultural techniques and became more settled with religious beliefs and commercial and military activities.

On most of North America, perhaps because of the abundance of game and ease of migration, cultures remained

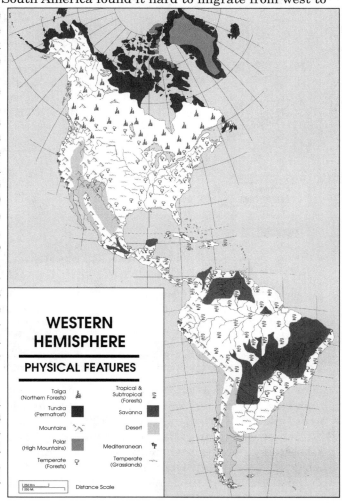

WESTERN HEMISPHERE

PHYSICAL FEATURES

Taiga (Northern Forests)		Tropical & Subtropical (Forests)	
Tundra (Permafrost)		Savanna	
Mountains		Desert	
Polar (High Mountains)		Mediterranean	
Temperate (Forests)		Temperate (Grasslands)	

Distance Scale

☆ CAPSULE – MESOAMERICAN CIVILIZATIONS
1400 BC - 1500 AD

STRENGTHS

legal codes
fortress cities
writing systems
accounting systems
traveling bureaucrats
astronomical calendars
adaptations to vertical climates
zero-based mathematics
mythology & religious rituals
monarchy-theocracy governments
imperial road & communication systems

WEAKNESSES

FALL TO
SPANISH CONQUISTADORES
1535 AD

- Frequent warfare within the civilizations weakened them by the 16th c.
- Lack of horses, wagons, and gunpowder technology of Europeans
- Empires were fragile alliances of rival groups Spanish troops introduced unknown diseases

Latin America:
ANCIENT
CIVILIZATIONS

AZTEC
1200 AD – 1500 AD

MAYAN
1500 BC – 1500 AD

INCA
1200 AD – 1500 AD

more nomadic for a longer period. In Central and South America, perhaps because the terrain was more rugged and less hospitable, settlements grew into urban cultures by 1000 BC. These were the forerunners of the Mesoamerican cultures encountered by the Europeans in the Age of Discovery. While these civilizations were highly developed, their technology and weaponry were less sophisticated than that of the Spanish conquistadores who subdued them in the 1520s and 1530s.

POLITICAL DEVELOPMENT

Many rulers of the nation-states and empires that emerged from the late Medieval Era embraced **absolutism** – the concentration of power in the hands of one person or a small elite ruling group. Many monarchs claimed their power came from God by divine right, and they were not responsible to any group or institution for their actions.

All over the globe, absolute monarchs built power controlling the independence of the old landed nobles and ignoring representative councils and assemblies. With the exception of isolated Japan, this also meant building power on the new wealth generated from global trade and the economic reorganization it caused. In Europe, absolute monarchs tried to overcome the waning power of the Roman Church, working with new religious situations, and cultivating relationships with burghers, burgesses, or bourgeoisie. Many European monarchs solidified their absolutist power by adopting mercantile financial policies and encouraging trade ventures involving establishment of colonies.

The wealth that was produced often went to building national armies and launching military adventures aimed at defeating rival monarchs and acquiring new territories. Often, such military actions squandered the new wealth. Few monarchs were forward-thinking enough to invest in merchant fleets or build better ports and transportation systems to aid economic growth. Eventually, this weakened the monarchies. Portugal and Spain lost their edge to the Dutch and English by the mid-1600s. Technically under the Holy Roman Emperor, the Dutch fended off several invasions by outside monarchs and built a remarkable trading empire by reinvesting and modernizing their fleets and ports. Aided by a war between Spain and England, the Dutch revolted in the late 16th century and won independence from Spanish Habsburg rule in 1648 (*Peace of Westphalia*).

The rise of national power and the building of global empires were intoxicating, not just to the monarchs, but to the the new middle class, whose expanding wealth and influence made them loyal to the kings. Their financial aid allowed the monarchs to check opposition from the landed nobles. In ***Leviathan***, philosopher Thomas Hobbes (English, 1588-1679) felt absolutism was part of "natural law." He indicated that freedom had to be subjected to the order and security provided by strong, absolute monarchs. While freedom can be chaotic, Hobbes' view naively assumed that monarchs were fair and honest and that their ministers were above corruption and deceit.

☆ CAPSULE – ABSOLUTISM 1450-1750
GLOBAL PERSPECTIVE

England: Parliament struggling with absolutist rule of the Stuart Dynasty

Spain: Absolutist Rule of Philip II

France: Absolutist Rule of Louis XIV

Central Europe: Holy Roman Empire of Charles V

Russia: Expansion & absolutist rule of Peter I (the Great)

Japan: Isolationist absolutism of the Tokugawa Shoguns

China: Ming Dynasty Restores Ethnic Chinese Rule 1368-1644 AD

Ottoman Empire: Golden Era under Suleiman I (the Magnificent)

Safavid Empire: Shi'ites revive the culture of ancient Persia (Iran)

India: Golden Era of Mughal Rule / Absolutist rule of Akbar

The Western Hemisphere was largely under the control of European powers at this time - see "God, Gold, and Glory" (Star Capsule, p. 130)

England:
Evolution of English Parliamentary Government (see p. 139)

Spain
In 1556, **Philip II** inherited the Spanish, Dutch, and Portuguese Habsburg domains of his father (Holy Roman Emperor Charles V) as well as their trade empires. He "micromanaged" affairs, kept decisions away from the nobles, and relied on a very few trusted advisors. In constant wars, Philip squandered much of Spain's wealth. He defeated the French and the Ottomans and quelled a rebellion in the Netherlands. However, he lost the northern provinces of the Netherlands, and In 1588, in an attempt to restore power to the Catholic Church, his great armada failed to conquer England's forces.

France
The most prominent of the absolutists, **Louis XIV** (r. 1643-1715) declared that he himself was the state ("L'etat, c'est moi."). He had crafty, machiavellian ministers (Mazarin, Colbert) to insulate him from the nobles. To watch them and their affairs, Louis required extravagant and impoverishing court life at Versailles. He put down revolts viciously, and replaced most nobles who challenged him with loyal middle class civil servants. Like other absolute monarchs, Louis tried to enhance power through conquests, but failed at most of his wars and drained the national treasury, weakening France's colonial empire.

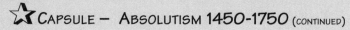 ★ CAPSULE – ABSOLUTISM 1450-1750 (CONTINUED)

Central Europe

Holy Roman Emperor **Charles V** (r. 1519-1556) dominated the Netherlands, Spain, Spanish dependencies in Italy (Sicily, Sardinia, Naples) and in the New World, and the Habsburg possessions in Germany, Austria, and Hungary. He defended Christian Europe against the invasions of the Muslim Turks (Ottoman Empire), and the Catholic Church against Lutheran and Calvinist Protestantism. Charles gave monopolies to large merchant firms in exchange for loans for arms and military expeditions. He brought trusted Castilian (Spanish) advisors to administer the Empire to overcome opposition in Germany and Hungary.

Russia

Russian Tsars followed an absolutist example set by **Ivan IV** (the Terrible, r. 1533-1584) who turned against his council and created a secret police to watch the nobility and other officials. Internal revolts and outside invasions kept Russia backward until the 17th century. **Peter I** (the Great, r. 1682) developed a civil service, diluted the nobles' authority, and brought the Orthodox Church and its wealth under his control. Peter tried to reform the country by bringing in western ideas, and new forms of education. He adoped military and manufacturing technology, and a new form of mer-cantilism, but allowed serfdom to continue.

Ottoman Empire

Suleiman I (the Magnificent, r. 1520 to 1566) emphasized fair systems of legis-lation, justice, and taxation and provided strong financial management. The empire reached its height of power and grandeur under his reign, and its arts flourished. Suleiman concentrated most on military campaigns against the Habsburgs of Austria and the Safavids. By 1535, the Ottomans had con-quered North Africa and Mesopotamia. Their powerful eastern fleet safe-guarded old trade routes and revived the economic prosperity of the Arab provinces. The Ottoman control of the Mediterranean pushed the Europeans into reliance on Atlantic trade routes.

Safavid Empire (Persia / Iran)

A group of Islamic (Shi'ite) mystics came to dominate Persia in the 16th and 17th centuries. The Safavid Dynasty kept absolute power as shahs by divid-ing power. They kept Persians in the bureaucracy but had northern Iranians (Turkomans) to control the military. The Safavids were finally defeated by the rival Ottomans in 1736.

India

Akbar (the Great, r. 1556-1605) solidified Mughal rule by defeating Afghan challengers and conquering most of the Indian subcontinent. As an abso-lutist, he broke up the landed aristocracy, brought Hindu chiefs into the gov-ernment and set up a loyal bureaucracy, brutally crushing any opposition. Akbar set up fair tax system, built roads for communication and official trav-el, standardized weights and measures, encouraged the arts, and allowed religious tolerance toward non-Muslims.

☆ CAPSULE – ABSOLUTISM 1450-1750 (CONTINUED)

China

In 1368, a peasant rebellion overthrew the Mongol Dynasty. Its leader became **Hong Wu**, founder of the Ming Dynasty that restored ethnic Chinese rule from 1368-1644. In true absolutist fashion, Hong Wu relied on a small, loyal palace guard and reduced the role of the civil service to concentrate his power. Early Ming rulers rebuilt Beijing (Peking), expanded overland trade with central Asia, set up tributary relations with Japan and several Southeast Asian kingdoms. The early Mings sent Zheng He on his famous maritime expeditions which ranged as far as the eastern coast of Africa. Later Ming emperors developed a cultural dominance by cutting down on trade and relations with the outside world. Their ethnocentrism perpetuated the ancient belief that China was "the middle kingdom" between heaven and earth, superior to all foreign culture. The later Mings minimized outside influences.

Japan

Tokugawa Shoguns controlled the political life of Japan from 1603-1867. From Edo (modern Tokyo), they dominated as national rulers and checked the power of daimyo (feudal lords). They built tight administrations around a restricted bureaucracy of loyal vassals. They avoided subversive conspiracies with outside powers and kept the government stable by enforcing a strict seclusion that virtually isolated Japan from the world for two centuries.

RESPONSE TO ABSOLUTISM:

LIMITING THE MONARCHY IN ENGLAND

Patterns of absolutism vary. Some absolute rulers such as Russia's Catherine the Great, Maria Theresa of Austria, and Frederick the Great are classified as **enlightened despots** – acting for the benefit and advancement of the society (see page 150). Most of the time, however, absolutists ignore individual and group rights when power becomes so centralized. The ruler or ruling group becomes isolated and distant from those ruled. Unlike most countries, England had a long history of tempering the power of the monarchs. At the same time that absolutism and divine right were on the rise globally, political forces resulted in the legislative representatives of various groups (Parliament) exerting supreme power over the monarchy.

Cromwell   Charles I

☆ CAPSULE – EVOLUTION OF ENGLISH PARLIAMENTARY GOVERNMENT

PARLIAMENT

- *Magna Carta* (1215)*

- **Model Parliament** (1295) gained control of revenues granted to monarch

- **Houses of Lords** and **Commons** emerge as representation expands

- *Petition of Right* (1628)*

- **English Civil Wars** (Puritan Revolution, 1642-1649) forces of Parliament, aided by the Scots, fight those of King Charles I

- **Execution of King Charles I** by Parliament (1649)

MONARCHY

William I, "the Conqueror" (r. 1066-1087): set up strong new ruling class of nobles and tightly knit feudal system

Plantagenet Dynasty (r. 1154-1399)
Henry II (r. 1154-1189) laid basis for royal courts clashing with nobles over jury system and English common law and royal finances

Tudor Dynasty (r. 1485-1603)
Henry VII, Henry VIII, and Elizabeth I strengthened monarchy, increased nationalist spirit, created national church, had occasional disputes with Parliament

Stuart Dynasty (r. 1603-1714)
James I, Charles I - tried to reign as absolute monarchs, largely ignoring and undermining Parliament

- **Commonwealth Government** (1649-1659): ruled by military council under the dictatorship of Lord Protector Oliver **Cromwell**

- Restoration of Monarchy
- *Habeas Corpus Act* (1670)*

Charles II accepted sharing power with Parliament

- **Glorious Revolution** (1688): Parliament overthrew James II for favoring Catholicism and installed new monarchs: William and Mary

- *Bill of Rights* (1689)*

Hanover Dynasty (r. 1714-1901)

Windsor Dynasty (r. 1901-)

Parliament Supreme: England continues to evolve into a constitutional monarchy with representative democracy and individual rights growing and absolute monarchy restricted.

*see Chart on p. 140

DOCUMENTS OF ENGLISH RIGHTS	
Document	**Ideas**
Magna Carta (1215)	English barons rebelled against King John's high taxes and military failures and forced him to sign the **Magna Carta**. It strengthened due process by requiring both a proper trial and lawful judgment in royal courts before levying a sentence.
Petition of Right (1628)	Charles I's extravagances and foreign wars required a Parliamentary session, and a clash forced an important compromise. The **Petition of Right** restricted the monarch's power to collect taxes, quarter troops in private homes, declare martial law, imprison individuals without just cause (habeas corpus concept), and insured jury trials.
Habeas Corpus Act (1670)	During Charles II's reign, Parliament settled religious toleration controversies and passed the **Habeas Corpus Act** – arrested individuals were guaranteed a statement of charges against them, opportunity for bail, and a speedy trial.
Bill of Rights (1689)	Under William and Mary, Parliament forbade taxation without its consent, and broadened due process rights to include protection from cruel and unusual punishments and excessive bail and fines.

LINKAGES

This First Global Age was one of transformation. Political, social, and economic forces present in our own times emerged in this age. Beginning in the 15th century and into the 18th century, this First Global Age saw a new and influential interaction of the civilizations of Asia and Europe with civilizations in Africa, the Americas, and the Pacific Rim.

By force of arms, the Ming, Ottoman, and Mughal Empires dominated Asia and North Africa. They unified diverse populations politically, culturally, and economically. In Europe, absolute monarchs, employing the divine right theory, attempted to eliminate opposition and unify their kingdoms. European encounters and exploration of the Western Hemisphere grew out of the quest for trade, wealth, and knowledge that intensified in the Renaissance.

From the second half of the 15th century, Europe's population grew. As it did, a number of other forces merged to bring the West out of the isolation of the late Medieval Period. The advent of colonialism, the emergence of national monarchies, the concentration of wealth in the hands of a few merchant houses, and the appearance of state and private monopolies created the conditions for economic expansion of the West. The retreat of China and Japan from global activities and their near isolation took them from the forefront of economic progress into stagnation, allowing the West to become dominant in global affairs.

QUESTIONS

Base your answer to questions 1 and 2 on the speakers' statements below and your knowledge of social studies

Speaker A: Any good ruler knows it is better to be loved than feared.

Speaker B: The king commands the army, but the legislators are more powerful – they control the purse strings of the realm.

Speaker C: Plots and assassinations cannot be anticipated by preventive murder and preventive confiscation.

Speaker D: I ordered the four secretaries of state to sign nothing without speaking to me of it.

1   Which speaker's statement best reflects absolutism?
    1   A   3   C
    2   B   4   D

2   Speaker *B* reflects the idea of
    1   divine right   3   limited power
    2   centralized authority   4   bureaucracy

3   Which idea was shared by the ancient Maya, Aztec, and Inca civilizations?
    1   practicing rituals to please the gods
    2   equality among social classes
    3   direct democracy
    4   nomadic life style

4   One effect that mountain ranges, rain forests, and river systems have had on Latin America has been to
    1   encourage cultural diffusion
    2   limit the development of transportation and communication systems
    3   permit nations in the area to use a single form of government
    4   allow the development of large amounts of arable land

5   One principle in the theory of mercantilism is that colonies should be
    1   granted independence as soon as possible
    2   considered an economic burden for the colonial power
    3   encouraged to develop their own industries
    4   acquired as markets and sources of raw materials

6 The *Magna Carta* and the English *Bill of Rights* are documents that
   1 limited the power of the monarch
   2 established England as an independent state
   3 intensified the conflict between church and state
   4 decreased the wealth of the nobles

7 During the commercial revolution, the joint stock company was developed to meet the needs of
   1 communism   3 socialism
   2 mercantilism   4 feudalism

8 One behavior common among absolutist monarchs in the First Global Age was that they
   1 supported nationalist movements within their empires
   2 ended feudalism and improved the lives of the peasants
   3 engaged in military conquests to raise personal and national prestige
   4 instituted important reforms that gave most citizens an active voice in the government

9 A major result of the European Age of Discovery was
   1 a long period of peace and prosperity for the nations of Europe
   2 extensive migration of people from the Western Hemisphere to Europe and Asia
   3 the fall of European national monarchies and an end to the power of the Catholic Church
   4 the end of regional isolation and the beginning of a period of European global domination

10 During the 16th century, the encomienda system of agriculture implemented by the Spanish in Latin America and the plantation system established by other European nations in southeast Asia were similar in that both
   1 produced multicrop economies
   2 redistributed land to the peasants
   3 diminished the power of the military
   4 depended on a system of forced labor

11 Both Japan and China decided to limit trade with Europe during much of the 16th and 17th centuries because the Japanese and the Chinese
   1 had few products to sell to the Europeans
   2 held religious beliefs that prohibited contact with foreigners
   3 thought European technology would hinder any effort to modernize
   4 believed they would receive no benefit from increased contact with the Europeans

12 As a result of the Glorious Revolution and the English *Bill of Rights*
    of 1689, government in Great Britain gradually became a
    1   theocracy   3   direct democracy
    2   limited monarchy   4   socialist republic

13 A lasting impact of the pre-Columbian civilizations of Latin America
    was that these cultures
    1   influenced art and architecture of later societies
    2   encouraged social mobility through education
    3   developed a complex system of trade with Europe
    4   developed the first representative democracies in Latin America

**Base your answer to
question 14 on the
photograph and cap-
tion at the right and
your knowledge of
social studies**

Large cannon built during Peter the Great's reorganization
of the Russian military resulting from his study of Western
technology.   © Sue Ann Kime 1997

14 The cannon in the picture is symbolic of a mixed legacy left by Peter
    the Great of Russia. Which statement best sums up that legacy?
    1   Peter substituted warfare for economic growth.
    2   Peter's reforms could not overcome the military power of the
        Mongols.
    3   Peter built great cities, but destroyed his country's religion in
        the process.
    4   Western technology accelerated progress, but did not reform the
        culture.

15 During the Middle Ages, Europeans did not eat potatoes or corn
    because these vegetables
    1   were forbidden by the Catholic Church for religious reasons
    2   had not yet been introduced to Europe from the New World
    3   were believed to be poisonous
    4   were too expensive to import from China

THEMATIC ESSAY

Directions: Write a well-organized essay that includes an introduction, several paragraphs explaining your position, and a conclusion.

Theme: absolutism

> During the First Global Age (1450-1750) rulers sought to centralize their power, and in the process, they changed the world in many ways.

Task:

> - Select *three* absolutist leaders or groups of leaders from the First Global Age.
> - Discuss their influence on their country and those around them.
> - Argue whether their influence was generally positive or negative.

Suggestions:
You may use any *three* leaders or groups of leaders from your knowledge of global history and geography. Some suggestions from the First Global Age that you might wish to consider include the Ottoman Empire's Sultan Suleiman I (the Magnificent), the Tokugawa Shoguns of Japan, England's Stuart Dynasty, Spain's Philip II, Ming China's Emperor Hong Wu, France's Louis XIV, Holy Roman Emperor Charles V, Russia's Ivan I (the Terrible), India's Akbar (the Great), Russia's Peter I (the Great). **You are not limited to these suggestions**.

PRACTICE SKILLS FOR DBQ

Directions: The following task is based on the accompanying documents. The documents may have been edited for the purposes of this exercise. The task is designed to test your ability to work with historical documents. As you analyze the documents, take into account both the source of the document and the author's point of view.

Historical Context: While distant trade and travel were common from ancient times, the drive in Europe to discover new lands in the 15th-17th centuries became intense.

Part A – Short Answer
The documents that follow present views of the European Age of Discovery. Examine each document carefully, then answer the question that follows it.

Document 1

"There was a special quality about the needs, the skills, and the imaginations of Europeans in this age that sent them searching the globe. Renaissance Europe needed precious metals and spices. While individual merchants sought gold and silk, pepper and cloves in the Far East during the Middle Ages, it was only in the 15th century that governments joined the search. This was not due merely to greed. Europe was genuinely desperate for metal to make into coin: its own gold deposits, such as those in Ireland, were exhausted ... bullion was not just wealth, but the means of obtaining wealth."

– John R. Hale, The Age of Exploration, 1966

1　Why did European nations become involved in the "Age of Discovery" (15th-17th centuries)?

_____

_____

_____

Document 2

"...Our principal intention, in soliciting from Pope Alexander VI the concession of the lands discovered and to be discovered, was to convert their peoples to our holy Catholic faith... I beg the King my lord very affectionately, I order and command the Princess my daughter and the Prince my son, to execute and accomplish this intention.

Let it be their principal end, and let them apply all their diligence to it. Let them not permit, or be the cause, that the Indians inhabiting the said islands and mainland suffer any damage in their persons or their property. They shall be vigilant, on the contrary, to see that these peoples be treated with justice and kindness. And if they receive any prejudice, let this prejudice be repaired..."

– as quoted in Readings in Medieval and Early Modern History,
James Hanssom, et. al

2　What was Queen Isabella's order trying to accomplish?

_____

_____

_____

_____

_____

Part *B* – Essay Response

Task: Using only the information in the documents, write a one or two paragraph explanation of why European nations became so involved in exploration in the 15th to 17th centuries.

State your thesis:

_____

_____

_____

_____

_____

_____

- Use only the information in the documents to support your thesis position
- Add your analysis of the documents
- Incorporate your answers to Part *A* scaffold questions

_____

Additional Suggested Task:

From your knowledge of global history and geography, make a list of additional factors that could be used to show why European nations became so involved in exploration in the 15th to 17th centuries.

_____

_____

_____

_____

_____

_____

_____

_____

_____

1750 TO 1914 AD

AN AGE
OF
REVOLUTIONS

AD

1750–

Wealth of Nations published (1776)

French Revolution begins (1789)

L'Overture begins Haitian revolt (1791)

1800–

Congress of Vienna meets (1814)

Great Reform Bill in Britain (1832)

Communist Manifesto published (1848)

1850–

Opening of Japan (1853)

Sepoy Mutiny (1857)

Emancipation Edict in Russia (1861)

Berlin Conference (1885)

1900–

Boxer Rebellion (1899)

INTRODUCTION

The Age of Revolutions did much to shape life in the 20th century and continued to affect events entering the 21st century. The Scientific and Intellectual Revolutions began movements which influenced social, political, and economic events for many years. The political revolutions in France, the United States, and Latin America owed much to the ideas of the Enlightenment *philosophes* (thinkers). Nationalism – an emotional dedication to the

Nelson

Napoleon

independent interests or culture of a particular nation – emerged as a powerful force in Europe. It later on diffused to areas such as India, Palestine, and Turkey. The vigorous nationalism that emerged in this period can be traced to some of the *philosophes* who believed that natural law called for men to live in nation-states. The inquiring mindset established in the Scientific Revolution had economic effects too. It can be seen in the Agrarian and Industrial Revolutions. Some of these key developments led to other events and movements such as imperialism which had considerable global impacts.

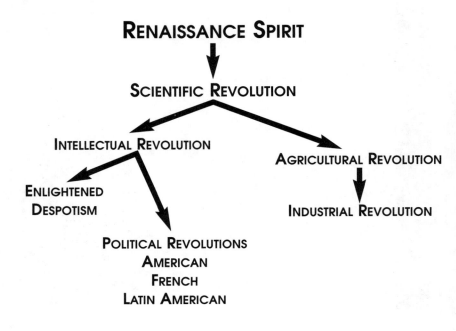

RENAISSANCE SPIRIT

↓

SCIENTIFIC REVOLUTION

INTELLECTUAL REVOLUTION

AGRICULTURAL REVOLUTION

↓

ENLIGHTENED DESPOTISM

INDUSTRIAL REVOLUTION

POLITICAL REVOLUTIONS
AMERICAN
FRENCH
LATIN AMERICAN

SIR ISSAC NEWTON
(1643-1727)

Work: – **Principia**
- discovered universal law of gravitation
- co-invented calculus

Impact:
- led to search for natural laws governing relations among men
- improved navigation
- increased knowledge of solar system
- ability to determine trajectories increased use of artillery

SOCIAL DEVELOPMENTS
SCIENTIFIC REVOLUTION

The **Scientific Revolution** (16-17th centuries) was an outgrowth of the Renaissance characteristics of questioning formerly accepted authority and striving for progress. Observation and experimentation became the basis for conclusions. Some of the key people in the world of science such as Copernicus and Galileo can be considered Renaissance men. Their work influenced that of Newton and many others.

INTELLECTUAL REVOLUTION
(ENLIGHTENMENT OR AGE OF REASON)

The **Intellectual Revolution** (also called the Enlightenment and the Age of Reason) of the 17th and 18th centuries began in England and

THE INTELLECTUAL REVOLUTION

John Locke (1632-1704) **Two Treatises of Government**
Men have natural rights of life, liberty, property
Men have right of revolution if government fails to protect rights

Voltaire (1694-1778) **Letters on the English**
Admired relative freedom of speech, press, religion in England

Montesquieu (1689-1755) **The Spirit of the Laws**
Believed in separation of powers
Wanted balance of power among branches of government

Rousseau (1712-1778) **Social Contract**
"Man is born free, yet everywhere he is in chains"
Men give power to government (General Will) to act for good of people

moved to France and the United States. The *philosophes* (Enlightenment intellectuals, especially in France) used reason to try to establish laws of nature that governed the activities of men. Many of them were optimists and believed that humans could be a force for good and that their actions would lead to progress. However, it is important to note that the *philosophes* had important areas of disagreement. Voltaire supported control by enlightened absolute rulers (despots), while Locke and Rousseau believed that power should rest with the people.

POLITICAL DEVELOPMENTS
THE FRENCH REVOLUTION

Supported by the ideas of Voltaire, enlightened despots such as **Maria Theresa** of Austria (1740-1780), **Frederick the Great** of Prussia (1740-1786), and **Catherine the Great** of Russia (1762-1796) claimed to use their power for the benefit of the people. As a group, the enlightened despots ruled as absolutists and were sometimes brutal and ruthless, but also used their powers in beneficial ways:

• codified laws
• built schools and hospitals
• limited church power
• modified serfdom

The enlightened despots' attempts at reform had limited success. Conditions did improve in the countries they ruled, but often the challenges, protests, and revolts that the reforms triggered were suppressed by the very same monarchs for fear of compromising their power.

The **French Revolution** (1789-1799) brought more sweeping and radical political change than individual despots. The ideas of Locke and Rousseau supported the actions of the French people in their overthrow of Louis XVI and his wife, Marie Antoinette. Up to the Revolution, the privileges of the monarch and the First and Second Estates (clergy and nobles) left few opportunities for the Third Estate (commoners) which paid most of the taxes. The failure to tax the first two Estates left the government short of funds and on the verge of bankruptcy. The bourgeoisie of the Third Estate was frustrated by the Old Regime system (absolute monarchy, over-privileged aristocracy, corrupt and inefficient bureaucracy, and rigid social structure).

To deal with the agricultural and financial crisis in 1789, Louis XVI called the **Estates-General** into session for the first time in 175 years. The resulting election campaign spread the ideas of the *philosophes* and strengthened the determination of the people to change the government.

A pattern of revolutionary power shifts emerged as various groups struggled to further their interests. This pattern, with modifications, appeared in some later revolutions.

The chaos resulting from frequent government changes and violence left the French situation ripe for a strong leader, **Napoleon Bonaparte**. First among the three-person Consulate that overthrew the Directory late in 1799, Napoleon concentrated power in his own hands as he enacted many revolutionary reforms. In 1804, he crowned himself emperor of France.

Historically well known for his military victories against Austria, Prussia, and Russia, Napoleon also enacted a series of reforms that benefitted the French people. As his armies marched across Europe, they

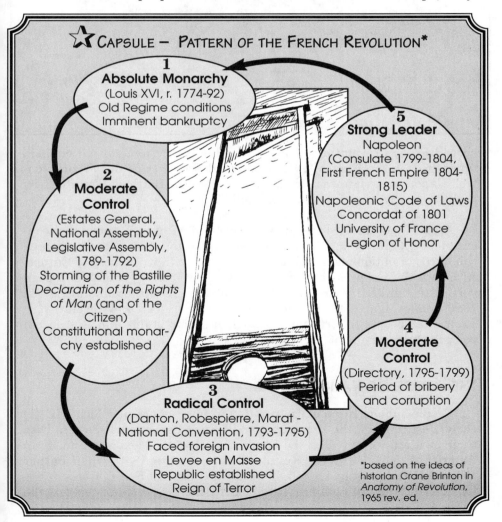

★ CAPSULE – PATTERN OF THE FRENCH REVOLUTION*

1
Absolute Monarchy
(Louis XVI, r. 1774-92)
Old Regime conditions
Imminent bankruptcy

2
Moderate Control
(Estates General,
National Assembly,
Legislative Assembly,
1789-1792)
Storming of the Bastille
*Declaration of the Rights
of Man* (and of the
Citizen)
Constitutional monarchy established

3
Radical Control
(Danton, Robespierre, Marat -
National Convention, 1793-1795)
Faced foreign invasion
Levee en Masse
Republic established
Reign of Terror

4
Moderate Control
(Directory, 1795-1799)
Period of bribery
and corruption

5
Strong Leader
Napoleon
(Consulate 1799-1804,
First French Empire 1804-1815)
Napoleonic Code of Laws
Concordat of 1801
University of France
Legion of Honor

*based on the ideas of
historian Crane Brinton in
Anatomy of Revolution,
1965 rev. ed.

EUROPE
c.1812 – BEFORE THE CONGRESS OF VIENNA

spread French revolutionary ideas. Gradually, the force of nationalism unleashed by the French led to conquered people resisting French control. Napoleon's reign was ultimately ended at the Battle of Waterloo by a coalition led by England's Duke of Wellington.

After Napoleon's defeat, the **Congress of Vienna** – under the leadership of the Austrian, Prince **Metternich**, restored absolutism, ignored the forces of nationalism and democracy, and redrew the map of Europe. Although the Congress of Vienna's actions avoided a general European war for a hundred years, a series of revolutions did occur during the 1820s, 1830s, and 1848. The democratic forces triggered by revolution in France led people to struggle to establish nation states and to secure a voice in the government.

THE FORCE OF NATIONALISM

People outside Europe also revolted in favor of the new ideas. In the early 19th century, the preoccupation of European colonial powers with their own affairs provided the opportunity for the Mexicans and Latin Americans. The **Mexican Revolution** started in 1810, when Father **Miguel Hidalgo** issued a call for revolution against Spain. Class differences and "iron triangle alliances" led by the land-holding nobles, the

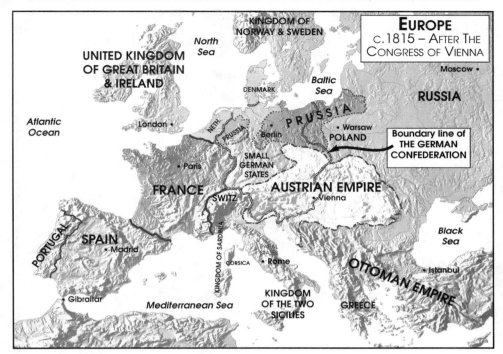

military, and the Roman Catholic Church often frustrated the interests of the mestizos and the indigenous population. After independence, these problems persisted and were made worse by periods of foreign involvement. The instability led to periods of dictatorship by a series of **caudillos** (strong men). Some leaders, such as **Benito Juarez**, tried to decrease the power of the Church and the landlords, but others, such as **Porfirio Diaz**, seized Native American lands. During the 1920s, government stabilized, and the Institutional Revolutionary Party (PRI) established a one party approach.

To some extent, modern **nationalism** can be viewed as an outgrowth of the Intellectual Revolution. Many *philosophes* declared that nature decreed that men of similar characteristics should live together. This idea inspired people to want their own homelands. In some cases, nationalism worked to pull people together as in the cases of the Italian and German unifications. In other instances, nationalism resulted in fragmentation of existing countries. This was true for the Austro-Hungarian Empire after World War I, the Soviet Union at the end of the Cold War, and the former Yugoslavia today. **Chauvinism**, an extreme form of nationalism, can result in tremendous evil as seen in Hitler's Germany.

There are many similarities between the German and Italian **unification movements** as well as an important difference: the Italians used

☆ CAPSULE – LATIN AMERICAN REVOLUTIONS
LATE 18TH – EARLY 19TH CENTURIES

CAUSE:
Inspiration of intellectual revolutionary writings of Locke, Rousseau, Voltaire, Jefferson, Paine, etc.

CAUSE:
Inspiration of American and French Revolutions.

CAUSE:
Preoccupation of Spain and Portugal with fighting Napoleon in Europe

RESULT:
Portuguese royal family escaped Napoleon by fleeing to Brazil. Pedro I set up new independent kingdom in 1821 when his father returned to Portugal. Pedro II assumed full power after Pedro I's abdication.

RESULT:
By the mid-1820s, L'Overture, Bolívar, San Martín, O'Higgins led revolts that created Haiti, Paraguay, Argentina, Chile, Uruguay, Peru, Bolivia, the United Provinces of Central America, and Gran Colombia

RESULT:
By 1830s, geographic factors (mountains, Amazon) plus cultural differences defeated attempts at unification (e.g., Gran Colombia, United Provinces of Central America)

MEXICO 1821
GULF OF MEXICO
CUBA 1898
HAITI 1804
DOMICAN REP 1844
CARIBBEAN SEA
UNITED PROVINCES 1823-1839
VENEZUELA 1821
GUYANA 1966
SURINAME 1975
FRENCH GUIANA
COLOMBIA 1819
GRAN COLOMBIA
ECUADOR 1822
BRAZILIAN EMPIRE 1822
PERU 1824
BOLIVIA 1825
PARAGUAY 1811
CHILE 1816
URUGUAY 1823
ARGENTINA 1816

democratic plebiscites in addition to wars, the Germans relied on wars alone. Once Germany unification was complete, the balance of power in Europe was upset. This led to a series of actions by Germany and France that helped to cause World War I.

ITALIAN AND GERMAN UNIFICATION

Italian Unification
Austro-Sardinian War
Plebiscites
(votes on issues)
Cavour - political
Garibaldi - military
Mazzini - inspiration

BOTH
Austro-Prussian War
Franco-Prussian War

German Unification
Danish War
Zollverein
(Customs union)
Bismarck - political
von Moltke - military
Fichte - inspiration

As Europeans spread their control to less developed areas in the late 19th century, they also spread their ideas of nationalism. Since people in these areas had few common characteristics, nationalism often took a negative form - uniting them in opposition to the colonial power. For example, in India, the **Hindu Indian National Congress** and the **All-India Moslem League** opposed British control, but their religious divisions made forming a national independence movement difficult. Turkey's strategic location on the Dardanelles and Bosporus invited foreign intervention. The Turks, like the Chinese, were humiliated by concessions (capitulations) forced on them by foreigners that compromised their sovereignty. The nationalist Young Turks, eventually led by **Kemal Ataturk**, struggled to make reforms, but gained little until the Turkish Republic was proclaimed in 1923.

ECONOMIC DEVELOPMENT

REVOLUTIONS IN FARMING AND INDUSTRY

Although many revolutions are violent, it is also possible to bring about major change peacefully. The Scientific and Intellectual Revolutions are examples. The **Agrarian** and **Industrial Revolutions** owe much to the spirit of the Scientific and Intellectual Revolutions which encouraged questioning and the scientific method. Both of these economic movements were also largely non-violent, but they brought dramatic differences in the way that people lived.

In Europe, the shift from the medieval three-field approach to more modern farming first appeared in England where *Enclosure Acts* from the 16th to the 19th centuries led to consolidation of land tracts more suitable for machinery. The work of **Jethro Tull** (seed drill), **Charles "Turnip" Townshend** (rotation of crops), and **Robert Bakewell** (scientific breeding of cattle) accelerated mechanized farming. On the continent of Europe, fragmentation of land made progress slower but no less dramatic. As new inventions and approaches to farming made their appearances, per capita production increased. This made more goods available for manufacturing and freed laborers to work in the factories.

Like the Agrarian Revolution, the Industrial Revolution appeared first in England. Since many of the inventions were made by people involved in the **domestic system**, it is not surprising that the textile industry was the first to be affected. The increasing demand of the global market stimulated by English commercial interests led people to look for ways to improve per capita production.

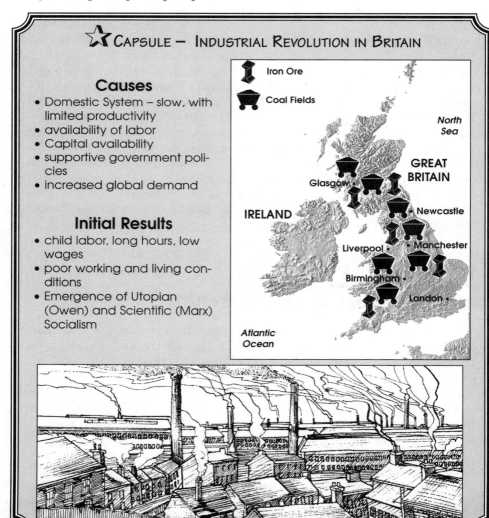

☆ CAPSULE – INDUSTRIAL REVOLUTION IN BRITAIN

Causes
- Domestic System – slow, with limited productivity
- availability of labor
- Capital availability
- supportive government policies
- increased global demand

Initial Results
- child labor, long hours, low wages
- poor working and living conditions
- Emergence of Utopian (Owen) and Scientific (Marx) Socialism

Iron Ore

Coal Fields

North Sea

GREAT BRITAIN

Glasgow

IRELAND

Newcastle

Liverpool

Manchester

Birmingham

London

Atlantic Ocean

TECHNOLOGICAL MILESTONES OF THE INDUSTRIAL REVOLUTION

	Inventor	Invention	Effect
TEXTILES	John Kay (1704-1764)	Flying Shuttle	Doubled speed of weavers
	James Hargreaves (1730-1778)	Spinning Jenny	Could spin 8-20 threads at once
	Richard Arkwright (1732-1792)	Water Frame	Used water power; factories developed; could spin 48-300 threads at once
	Samuel Crompton (1753-1827)	Spinning Mule	Combined jenny and water frame; could spin fine thread
	Edmund Cartwright (1743-1823)	Power Loom	1st application of power to weaving
TRANSPORTATION	James Watt (1736-1819)	Steam Engine	New source of power allowed many applications and the location of factories in many different places
	George Stephenson (1781-1848)	Steam Locomotive	Faster land transportation
	Thomas Telford (1757-1783) & John McAdam (1756-1836)	Hard Surfaced Roads	Faster land transportation in all kinds of weather

The social and political problems resulting from the economic upheaval of the Industrial Revolution led many to blame the laissez-faire ideas of **Adam Smith** (*Wealth of Nations*, 1776). Smith believed that government should keep its hands off business, and he supported free trade. Many critics felt that his ideas also meant that the government should not protect the workers. Utopian socialists such as **Robert Owen**, Count de **Saint Simon**, and **Charles Fourier** developed different ideas to alleviate the factory and mine problems. However, the work of scientific socialists such as **Karl Marx** and **Frederick Engels** (*The Communist Manifesto*, 1848) presented the greatest challenge to laissez-faire capitalism. Ironically, their writings prompted governments to carry out reforms that may have prevented some of the revolutions of the proletariat that they predicted.

KARL MARX

<u>Works</u>: *Communist Manifesto, Das Kapital*
• founder of modern communism
• believed in class struggle, surplus value theory, economic interpretation of history, inevitability of socialism

<u>Impact</u>: influenced thinking of Lenin and others, revolutions and establishment of dictatorships and command economic systems in the Russia, Cuba, North Korea, Eastern Europe

THE ECONOMICS OF IMPERIALISM

The new methods of production diffused gradually from England to continental Europe and the United States. After 1870, the pace of industrial change quickened. By 1914, Germany, France, and the United States rivaled England. The increase in demand for raw materials and markets led to renewed imperialism toward the end of the 19th century.

Between 1841 and 1851, Ireland's population fell from 8.2 million to 6.6 million through starvation, disease, and emigration – especially to the United States.

Economic concerns and the desire to keep Ireland as a producer of raw materials and importer of manufactured goods influenced British policy during the **Great Hunger** of the 1840s. A potato blight struck the main food crop of the Irish, and many died from hunger. Yet, the British refused to modify their *Corn Laws* to allow more importation of grain, and absentee landlords continued to demand their rents. Eventually, Britain did provide for relief and changed the laws, but hundreds of thousands died and many more emigrated. British-Irish relations were further poisoned.

COMMODORE PERRY'S GOALS
- protect shipwrecked sailors
- secure refueling stations
- open Japan to foreign trade

The opening of Japan in 1853 by Commodore **Matthew Perry** can be viewed as part of imperialism. However, the Japanese responded differently from other targets of imperialism. They forced the shogun to abdicate and restored the emperor to power (**Meiji Restoration**). Then they began a program of modernization which involved borrowing many of the ideas of the westerners. This made rapid progress possible. The **Sino-Japanese War** (1894-1895) and the **Russo-Japanese War** (1904-1905) marked the emergence of Japan as a major power. However, Japanese economic development helped to increase nationalism and led to imperialist expansion in the 20th century.

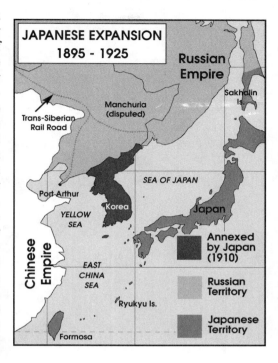

However, Africa, the last, vast, unclaimed area was the major target of late 19th century imperialism. Although the coastal areas were explored and claimed as the early Portuguese explorers struggled to find an all-water route to the Far East, the deserts, rain forests, diseases, and few navigable rivers into the interior limited inland exploration. However, the demands of the Industrial Revolution and the increasing nationalism of European powers intensified interest in the area. After the **Berlin Conference** (1885) called by Bismarck established some rules for claiming African land, a "Scramble for Africa" broke out. This led to disputes among the European powers (British and French at Fashoda) and between the Europeans and Africans (Europeans and the Zulu leader, Shaka). Nevertheless, by 1900, only Liberia and Ethiopia remained independent.

The European approach to China was somewhat different. Problems developed from the trade imbalance between the two areas. The Europeans wanted Chinese tea, silk, porcelains, and other products, but the Chinese wanted few European products. This led to the introduction of opium. Chinese attempts to abolish the drug sale in the mid 19th century led to the **Opium Wars** and the unequal Treaties of Nanking and Tientsin. The results allowed European nations and the United States more privileges in China. Resentment against the foreigners increased,

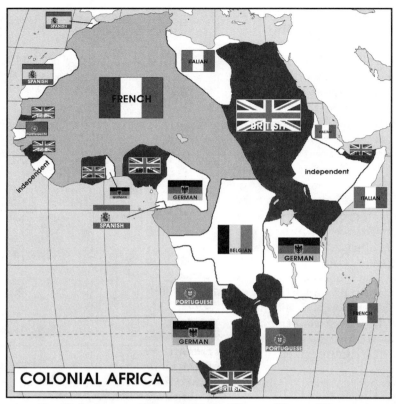

COLONIAL AFRICA

triggering the **Taiping** and **Boxer Rebellions**. The military strength of the foreigners brought defeat and further humiliation for the Chinese. After 1900, revolutionaries under the leadership of **Sun Yixian** agitated against the foreigners and the Chinese government.

Imperialism had positive and negative results on both the imperialist powers and the conquered peoples. European nations clashed and their disputes helped to cause both World Wars. While industrial nations became dependent on their empires for raw materials and markets, they also enriched their cultures with art, food, clothes design, and anthropological finds.

SOME EFFECTS OF IMPERIALISM ON CONQUERED PEOPLE	
Positive Effects	**Negative Effects**
Infrastructure improved	People with common culture separated
Education improved	Natural resources exploited
Access to medical care increased	Native cultures damaged
Food supply increased	Economic self-sufficiency lost
Economic development stimulated	Cash crops overemphasized
Internal conflicts decreased	Family life disrupted
	Native life expectancy diminished

SUN YIXIAN

Work: *The Three Principles of the People*
- leader of Chinese Revolt against Q'ing Dynasty in 1911
- helped found Chinese Republic, served as its president
- believed in three principles of democracy, nationalism, people's livelihood

Impact:
- regarded as founder of modern China
- urged modernization to meet challenge of West

LINKAGES

The changes that occurred during the Age of Revolutions provided much of the framework of the social, political, and economic developments of the 20th century. The time period saw the developed world move away from the influences of the Middle Ages and toward a modern society. It also saw the beginning of cultural diffusion on a global basis - a diffusion which was to lead in the direction of one global culture as the 21st century approached.

QUESTIONS

1   "The proletariat of industrialized nations will revolt because of the evils of capitalism." This quotation reflects the ideas of
   1   Adam Smith   3   Karl Marx
   2   Robert Owen   4   John Locke

2   "Whenever law ends, tyranny begins, if the law be transgressed to another's harm, and whosoever in authority exceeds the power given him by the law and makes use of the force he has under his command. . .which the law allows not, ceases in that to be a magistrate, and [since he is] acting without authority, may be opposed."

                                          – John Locke

   In this quotation, John Locke supports the right of
   1   opposition to those who abuse authority
   2   magistrates to make the laws
   3   the military to take command
   4   the tyrant to rule without laws

3   Otto von Bismarck is to the German states as which of the following is to the Italian states?
   1   Joseph Mazzini   3   Guiseppe Garibaldi
   2   Camillo di Cavour   4   Pope Leo X

4   The American, French, and Latin American Revolutions of the 18th and early 19th century are similar in that all three
1   resulted in a return to autocratic rule
2   were influenced by the ideas of the *philosophes*
3   were opposed to colonial control
4   led to an economic decline

5   A major result of the wars of the Napoleonic Era was the
1   end of British supremacy on the seas
2   immediate unification of the Italian and German states
3   spread of the ideas of nationalism and democracy
4   end of feudalism in Eastern Europe

6   The failure of Simón Bolívar's dream of a united South America is largely attributed to
1   opposition of the United States
2   regional differences within the area
3   Spanish attempts at reconquest
4   British refusal to honor the *Monroe Doctrine*

7   Although the Congress of Vienna largely ignored the forces of nationalism and democracy when making its decisions, it might be regarded as a success because
1   there were no revolutions against its decisions
2   the Holy Alliance worked well to preserve the peace
3   it eliminated most continental monarchies
4   no major all-Europe war occurred for about 100 years

8   Unification of the German States had a major impact on global history because it
1   led to German domination of the sea routes
2   upset the balance of power in Europe
3   led Russia to seek a war of revenge
4   seriously weakened the Germany economy

9   When the Turkish Republic was established in 1923,
1   Russia gained control of the Dardanelles and Bosporus
2   women were forced to wear traditional dress
3   only traditional methods of production could be used
4   separation of church and state occurred

10 A major result of the Industrial Revolution in Western Europe was that
1   mercantilism became the dominant economic system
2   the middle class was strengthened politically
3   people moved from urban to rural areas
4   traditional ways increased in importance

11 The Sepoy Mutiny, the Boer War, and the Boxer Rebellion are similar in that all three
1   resulted in independence for the areas involved
2   were won by the colonial peoples
3   resulted in economic gains for the indigenous people
4   were revolts against foreign influence or control

12 The need for raw materials and markets, nationalism, and the concept of the "White Man's Burden" led to
1   the Crimean War   3   imperialism
2   socialism   4   industrialization

13 Japan became a model for modernization and technological development because
1   the people quickly assimilated western culture
2   the government played no role in bringing about change
3   it rapidly emerged as a developed and powerful nation
4   it achieved its goal without involvement in foreign trade

Base your answer to question 14 on the graph below and your knowledge of social studies.

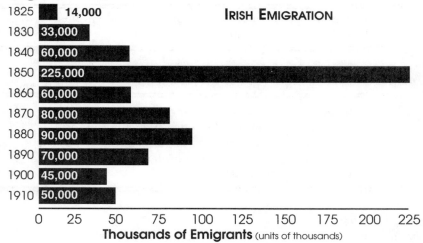

IRISH EMIGRATION

Year	Thousands of Emigrants
1825	14,000
1830	33,000
1840	60,000
1850	225,000
1860	60,000
1870	80,000
1880	90,000
1890	70,000
1900	45,000
1910	50,000

0   25   50   75   100   125   150   175   200   225
Thousands of Emigrants (units of thousands)

14 Which is a valid conclusion based on the information on the graph and your knowledge of global history and geography?
1   Religious persecution caused many to emigrate from Ireland.
2   The end of the British draft after the Napoleonic Wars in 1825 led to a decrease in Irish emigration.
3   The Great Hunger around 1845 eventually led many Irish to flee from the resulting famine.
4   Large bonuses paid for Irish laborers in Australia were a factor in emigration around 1845.

15 "...the Chinese people have only family and clan solidarity; they do
     not have national spirit. Therefore even though we have ... people
     gathered together in one China, in reality they are just a heap of
     loose sand."

                                             – Sun Yixian, 1911

In this quotation, Sun Yixian is saying that the Chinese people
1   are locally oriented
2   have many cultural differences
3   only act in their individual interest
4   like grains of sand, are easily swept away

THEMATIC ESSAY

Directions: Write a well-organized essay that includes an introduction,
several paragraphs explaining your position, and a conclusion.

Theme: nationalism

> Throughout modern global history, nationalism has
> played both positive and negative roles.

Task:

> • Select *one* positive and *one* negative example of the
>   way in which nationalism has impacted history.
> • For *each* example, discuss the forces that led to the
>   development of the example selected and discuss its
>   impact on later history.

Suggestions:
You may use any example of nationalism from your study of global
history and geography. You might wish to consider nationalism in France
during the French Revolution (1789-1799), in the Balkans in the late
20th century, in Hitler's Germany, in the Italian or German States in the
late 19th century, in the former Soviet Union after the end of
communism, in 20th century India prior to 1947, in the Zionist
Movement, among Palestinian Arabs. **You are *not* limited to these
suggestions.**

PRACTICE SKILLS FOR DBQ

Directions: The following task is based on the accompanying documents. The documents may have been edited for the purposes of this exercise. The task is designed to test your ability to work with historical documents. As you analyze the documents, take into account both the source of the document and the author's point of view.

Historical Context: Imperialism significantly altered the areas that were subject to colonial rule.

Part A – Short Answer
The documents below relate to British imperialism in India. Examine each document carefully, then answer the question that follows it.

Document 1

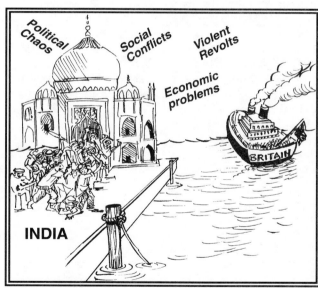

1   What problems did the British leave behind when they left India?

_____

_____

_____

_____

_____

_____

Document 2

2   What benefits does Bonnerji acknowledge from British rule?

> "… It is under the civilizing rule of the Queen and the people of England that we meet here together. …Were it not for these blessings of British rule I could not have come here … without the least hesitation and without the least fear that my children might be robbed and killed in my absence; nor could you have come from every corner of the land, having performed, within a few days, journeys which in former days would have occupied months. …It is to British rule that we owe the education we possess; the people of England were sincere in the declaration made more than half a century ago that India was a sacred charge entrusted to their care by Providence.
> – W.C. Bonnerji, President, Indian National Congress (first meeting of the Indian National Congress, 1885)

_____

_____

_____

Part *B* – Essay Response

Task: Using only the information in the documents, write one or two paragraphs evaluating the positive and negative aspects of British colonial rule on India.

State your thesis:

_____

_____

_____

_____

_____

- Use only the information in the documents to support your thesis position
- Add your analysis of the documents
- Incorporate your answers to Part *A* scaffold questions

Additional Suggested Task:

From your knowledge of global history and geography, make a list of additional factors that could be used to show the impact of British colonial rule in India.

1900 TO 1950 AD

A HALF CENTURY OF CRISIS AND ACHIEVEMENT

AD

1900–

Triple Entente
completed
(1907)

1910–

Archduke Franz Ferdinand
assassinated (1914)

Russian Revolutions (1917)

Treaty of Versailles signed (1919)

1920–

Republic of Turkey established (1923)

Universal suffrage in Britain (1928)

Great Depression begins (1929)

1930–

Hitler becomes German
Chancellor (1933)

Long March begins
in China (1934)

Nazi-Soviet Nonaggression
Pact (1939)

1940–

Yalta Summit Conference (1945)

Prototypes of Advanced P-51 Fighter-Bombers used by allies as WW II ended.

INTRODUCTION

The half century between 1900 and 1945 saw social progress in the fields of science, medicine, technology, and women's suffrage. Unfortunately, it also witnessed disastrous political events: two world wars, the rise of totalitarian governments, and modern genocide. Economically, governments faced two depressions, one after World War I, and the much more serious Great Depression that began in 1929. After the end of World War II, the world saw the decline of colonialism, the emergence of a multitude of new nations, and the development of the Cold War between the **superpowers**, the United States and the Soviet Union.

The developments in science, medicine, and technology began about the mid-point of the 19th century. The innovators often based their work on that of predecessors and made corrections or adjustments. Their work produced such different results as weapons of mass destruction, vaccinations, and improvement in nursing care.

EMPIRES IN CRISIS:

WORLD WAR I

As World War I (1914-1918) approached, Eastern Europe was organized into three autocratic and large **multinational empires**: the Russian, the German, and the Austro-Hungarian. In each of these empires, there were sizable minority groups whose nationalism led them to desire independence. Also in Eastern Europe, there were some small countries such as Serbia and Greece whose independent status served as role models. However, in Western Europe, most people were organized in largely homogeneous, democratic nation-states.

SCIENTIFIC INNOVATORS

Pierre (1859-1905) and **Marie Curie** (1867-1934) – Proved that atoms could be split

Albert Einstein (1879-1955) – *Theory of Relativity* ($E=MC^2$); unified field theory

Sigmund Freud (1856-1939) – Role of unconscious in emotional problems; use of dreams to unlock it

Louis Pasteur (1822-1895) – Bacteria's role in causing disease; vaccine for rabies

Florence Nightingale (1820-1910) – Founded modern nursing; battlefield nursing during Crimean War

The causes of World War I are complicated, and the relationships among the major European powers (Britain, France, Germany, Russia, and Austria-Hungary) were critical. Their economic and political rivalries combined with a lack of an international forum for discussion of issues made it difficult to avoid war. After the assassination of **Archduke Franz Ferdinand** and his wife by Gavrilo Princip – a member of a Bosnian Serb group desiring union with Serbia, Austria sent a harsh ultimatum to Serbia. This was backed unconditionally (carte blanche) by Germany. When Serbia refused to accept one provision, the downward spiral toward war preparations and declarations began.

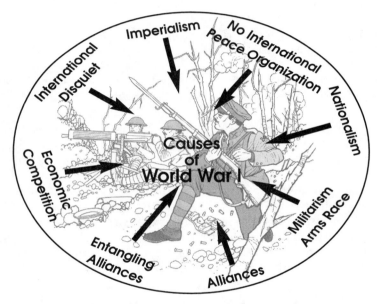

The War was largely a defensive war fought using systems of trenches, dugouts, and attempts to cross "no-man's land." Tremendous loss of life occurred for just yards of territory. However, the technological developments of the war such as airplanes, tanks, and long-range artillery were predictors of the coming offensive nature of World War II. The United States entered World War I after German actions, including unrestricted submarine warfare, cost American lives. America's entry brought supplies and an infusion of soldiers and helped to turn the tide in favor of the Allies.

A TROUBLED PEACE

The results of World War I were far-reaching and their repercussions are still being felt. Approximately ten million died and another twenty million were injured. In some European countries, a serious imbalance between the number of males and females in the population occurred. Other results included:

- **Women's suffrage** – many countries extended the right to vote to women in recognition of their contributions to the war effort.
- **Governmental powers increased** – command economies necessary for war, censorship, and propaganda provided examples for totalitarian governments.
- **Rise of developing economies** – India, Brazil, Argentina, and others developed their industries to rival Europe.
- **Armenian Massacres** – genocide of up to 1 million Christian Armenians were killed or died during deportation by Moslem Ottoman Turks who feared their independence movement and possible treason.
- *Treaty of Versailles* – German war guilt clause; reparations; new or reestablished nations; German loss of all colonies; limits on German military; provisions for a League of Nations.

However, the decisions made at the **Paris Peace Conference** (Versailles, 1919) also had long term effects. U.S. President Woodrow Wilson proposed his *Fourteen Points* as the basis for the peace settlement. He pushed hard to create the **League of Nations**, urged self-determination for nations, and an equitable adjustment of colonial claims. However, British leader, **David Lloyd-George** wanted more colonies and reparations. French leader **Georges Clemenceau** was most concerned about obtaining French security, weakening Germany, and gaining reparations. As a consequence, Wilson's idealistic *Fourteen Points* were largely ignored in the **Treaty of Versailles**.

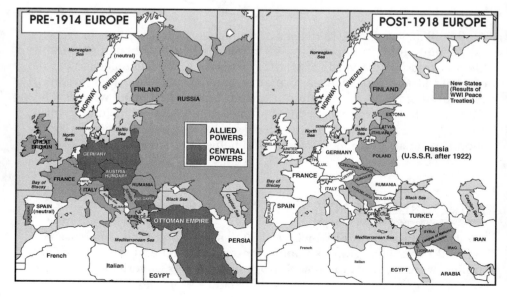

CAUSES OF THE RUSSIAN REVOLUTIONS, 1917

- Tsarist policies: "orthodoxy, autocracy, nationalism"

  - Russification, purges, secret police
  - Modernization and contact with the West
  - Urban working and living conditions
  - Weak response to Revolution of 1905
  - World War I losses
  - Reliance on advice of Rasputin

RUSSIA IN CRISIS

In 1917, in the midst of World War I, two revolutions occurred in Russia, one in March and one in November. The causes of these revolutions are complex and many go back to 19th century events.

The March Revolution brought the abdication of Tsar Nicholas II. A liberal, western-oriented Provisional Government came into power. The inability of this government to win the War on the eastern front and the increasing casualty rate led to more dissatisfaction. Also, it did not deal adequately with the people's demands for **"Peace** (end the War), **Land** (immediate land reform), **and Bread** (improve food supply)." These weaknesses made it possible for the radical socialists or **Bolsheviks** under the leadership of **V.I. Lenin** to win support. This led to the second revolution in November. It resulted in the overthrow the provincial government, the emergence of a Communist-Bolshevik government, and the forming of the U.S.S.R. (Union of Soviet Socialists Republics).

During most of the the period of Lenin's rule (r. 1917-1924), a civil war raged. The **Reds** (Bolsheviks) defeated the **Whites** (a combination of opposition groups) in a brutal civil war. During this time, the royal family was assassinated on Bolshevik orders. The Bolsheviks also followed "War Communism," a harsh economic policy. By the time the civil war appeared to be over (1921), Russian production had fallen by 50% compared to 1914 figures. Subsequently, Lenin introduced the **New Economic Policy** (NEP, 1921-1927) which permitted elements of capitalism. Lenin also agreed to sign the *Treaty of Brest-Litvosk* with Germany and end Russian participation in World War I even though Russia would lose large land areas.

JOSEF STALIN

- established totalitarian government
- introduced Five Year Plans (1928), command economy
- purges of 1930s against military, party, government
- use of Russification

Impact:
- thousands killed or exiled to Siberian gulags
- rapid industrialization
- Kylak opposition to forced collectivization led to "terror famine"
- signed Nazi-Soviet Non-Aggression Pact with Hitler
- gained important Eastern European concessions in wartime conferences

After Lenin's death in 1924, a power struggle between **Josef Stalin** and **Leon Trotsky** led to Stalin's emergence as the new leader in the totalitarian government of the Soviet Union.

POLITICAL CRISIS: TOTALITARIANISM ON THE RISE

Totalitarianism also appeared in Western Europe in the aftermath of World War I. The communist dictatorship was on the extreme left side of the political spectrum, but the emerging fascism was on the extreme right. These groups were often rivals. The communists supported the proletariat and the fascists advocated for landowners, industrialists, and the lower middle class.

In Italy, the problems associated with World War I (war debts, unemployment, land seizures, strikes, unsatisfied territorial demands, and a weak government) helped the fascist **Benito Mussolini** to win support. In the midst of this chaos, Mussolini and his Blackshirt followers organized the "March on Rome." After Mussolini's promise of support for the monarchy, King Victor Emmanuel III appointed him premier. A fascist government assumed power legally.

BASIC ECONOMIC SYSTEMS		
Questions	**Market Systems**	**Command Systems**
• Who makes the economic decisions?	• Individual consumers and producers	• Government planners
• How are the decisions carried out?	• Privately owned industries	• Government owned industries
• Who gets the profits?	• Individual producers	• Government

During the 1920s, the German **Weimar Republic** (1919-1933) faced many of the same problems seen in Italy. However, its position was further complicated by its super democratic structure which led to ineffective and fragmented coalition governments.

> ### COMMON FASCIST IDEAS
> - democracy was weak and strict obedience to authority was necessary
> - violence, a useful means to an end
> - suppression of opposition through terror and censorship
> - chauvinism was a requirement for a strong state

The continuation of conservatives in government, judicial, and military offices; and the burdensome reparations were also issues. It was impossible for Germany to pay the $35 billion in war reparations owed to the allies under the *Treaty of Versailles*. After the 1923 **Ruhr Crisis**, the *Dawes* and *Young Plans* reduced the yearly payments and helped to stabilize the situation. When Germany became a signatory of the *Locarno Pact* (1926) and the *Kellogg-Briand Pact* (1928), it rejoined the international family of nations.

ECONOMIC CRISIS: THE GREAT DEPRESSION

At the end of World War I, most countries experienced a postwar depression as the difficult conversion to peacetime production occurred. By 1924, the global economy began to improve, and during the last part of the 1920s, it appeared that prosperity had returned. However, underlying weaknesses including overproduction, increasing unemployment, high tariffs, and a tremendous rise in the stock market forecast trouble. On "Black Friday" in October 1929, stock prices on the New York Stock Exchange plummeted. Economic problems moved rapidly to almost all areas of the global economy – the **Great Depression** began.

The tremendous decrease in production and the corresponding rise in unemployment led to different governmental reactions. Economic nationalism and tariffs increased. Some nations (Britain and France) began to reduce spending in order to balance their budgets as government revenue decreased. In the U.S., President **Franklin Roosevelt** (1933-1945) began a program of activist deficit spending ("prime the pump") with the introduction of the New Deal. Under deficit spending, the government sponsored work programs for the unemployed and pensions for the elderly to seed money into the economy and artificially generate demand. This approach was supported by the ideas of an English economist, **John Maynard Keynes**.

In Germany, Hitler stimulated the economy by injecting massive government spending on military production. The Great Depression seriously hindered the democracies' response to the rising totalitarian tide during the 1930s; and, the depression really did not end until the outbreak of World War II.

POLITICAL CRISIS: NATIONALISM v. COLONIALISM

Colonies were also very dissatisfied with the outcome of World War I. European countries continued to dominate them – often using the cover of League of Nations mandates. This was true in Palestine where both Arabs and Jews felt that their war efforts should be rewarded with independence. The **Zionist Movement** campaigned for a Jewish state and actively encouraged Jewish migration to Palestine. The Arabs feared displacement. The British *White Paper of 1939* suggested limiting Jewish immigration, but was never implemented.

Reza Khan of Persia (Iran) overthrew the Shah, forced the withdrawal of Soviet troops, and won concessions from British oil interests. He pursued a program of internal reform and modernization very similar

Mohandas Gandhi
- Hindu leader of Congress Party
- encouraged use of passive resistance, civil disobedience, boycotts, and nonviolence against British
  - Salt March to defy British monopoly on salt sale
  - against mistreatment of untouchables and women
- favored Indian production of homespun textiles

Impact:
- leadership led to independence of India
- beginning of changes in treatment of untouchables and women
- others began to follow nonviolent approach worldwide

to that of Ataturk in Turkey. However, he encountered the opposition of religious leaders and sparked the struggle between modernization and traditionalism that continues today.

In China, continued chaos after the death of Sun Yixian in 1925 led to the rise of **Jiang Jieshi** (Chiang Kai-Shek) as leader of Guomindang, Sun's Nationalist Party. He was able to gain some concessions from the Western Powers and won the support of landowners and merchants. However, Jiang opposed the emerging communists led by **Mao Zedong**. A resulting civil war led the communists to undertake the **Long March** (1934-1935) to the mountainous border near the U.S.S.R. Here the communists worked to gain peasant support with promises of land reform.

POLITICAL CRISIS: NAZISM ON THE RISE

Adolf Hitler's rise to power in Germany in 1933 marked the establishment of the second fascist-totalitarian government in Europe. As in the case of Mussolini, he was able to play on people's economic concerns (Great Depression), hatred of the Paris peace settlement, and willingness to use the Jews as scapegoats for Germany's problems. His "Big Lie"

⭐ CAPSULE – ESTABLISHMENT OF TOTALITARIAN GOVERNMENT IN GERMANY

Social Policies
- Genocide against 6,000,000 Jews in Holocaust, plus 6 million non-Nazis
- Women expected to be mothers and homemakers
- Art, literature, music to serve goals of government
- Book burnings

Political Policies
- Censorship of media
- Elimination of political opposition
- Use of Gestapo
- Nazi Youth Movement

Economic Policies
- Private ownership of property with government control
- Government control of hours and wages
- Use of forced labor, concentration camps
- Public works programs such as autobahns

technique led him to promise "all things to all people." After the elections gave the Nazis the largest number (but not a majority) of seats in the Reichstag, ailing German President von Hindenburg asked Hitler to form a government. Thus, the second fascist government achieved power legally.

JEWISH LOSSES IN WORLD WAR II			
Nation	Jewish Population Sept. 1939	Jewish Losses	Percentage of Jewish Losses
Poland	3,300,000	2,800,000	85.0
U.S.S.R. (Nazi occupied)	2,100,000	1,500,000	71.4
Czechoslovakia	315,000	260,000	82.5
France	300,000	90,000	30.0
Austria	60,000	40,000	66.6
Italy	57,000	15,000	26.3

Source: Holocaust Museum, Washington, D.C.

GLOBAL CRISIS: THE WORLD AT WAR...AGAIN

The prelude to World War II began with the problems and dissatisfactions arising out of the *Treaty of Versailles*. Japan emerged from World War I stronger economically and politically. Attempts to limit Japanese expansionist and militarist ambitions at the **Washington Conference** (1921-1922 – *Four-Power Treaty, Five-Power Naval Armaments Treaty, Nine-Power Treaty*) were only temporarily successful. The League of Nations was also ineffective in dealing with major powers, because of its requirement for unanimous votes and an unwillingness of the democracies to take firm stands against aggressors. Problems of dealing with the Great Depression led the democracies to adopt neutrality and appeasement to avoid confrontation. Therefore, fascist Japan, Italy, and Germany challenged the democracies through their **Rome-Berlin-Tokyo Axis** (alliance) in a series of crises which led to World War II. Temporarily neutralizing a threat from Stalin and the U.S.S.R., by signing of the **Nazi-Soviet Non-Aggression Pact** in August, 1939, Hitler's stormtroopers invaded Poland and began World War II.

World War II (1939-1945) was an offensive war which used the airplanes, tanks, and motorized vehicles developed during World War I to move quickly. The German commanders used the term "blitzkrieg" to describe the lightning speed of this strategy. The development of radar and sonar helped the Allies to counter the Axis threat. The development of the V-1 and V-2 jet-propelled bombs by the Germans and the atomic bomb by the U.S. heralded a new type of warfare. However, the decision by U.S. President **Harry Truman** to use the atomic bomb twice against the Japanese in August 1945 caused much subsequent controversy because of the high number of civilian casualties and long term health damage.

ROAD TO GLOBAL WAR	
Aggressors / Crisis	**Actions/Results**
Japan Manchurian Crisis (1931)	A suspicious minor bombing of Japan's South Manchurian Railroad created an excuse to spread forces throughout Manchuria and create the puppet state of Manchukuo. The League of Nations condemned Japan's actions. Japan then withdrew from the League.
Italy Ethiopian Invasion (1935)	Italy attacked from its colonies in Eritrea and Somaliland. Conquest created a large Italian East Africa province and heightened Italian nationalism for Mussolini's fascism. League imposed weak sanctions and later cancelled them.
Italy and Germany Spanish Civil War (1936-1939)	German and Italian armies tested their weapons and tactics. Fascist victory brought Generalissimo Francisco Franco (1892-1975) to power. Destruction in Spain kept it out of World War II.
Germany Austrian *Anschluss* (1938)	Hitler forced the Austrian leaders to accept Nazis in the government, then invaded, and forced it into union (*Anschluss*) with Germany.
Germany Sudeten Appeasement Czechoslovakia (1938)	Hitler demanded rule over the predominantly German-speaking Sudetenland in western Czechoslovakia. At the international **Munich Conference**, France and Britain **appeased** Hitler (gave in to avoid war).

During World War II, a series of international conferences did much to shape the postwar world. The North Atlantic meeting (1941) between President Franklin Roosevelt and British Prime Minister **Winston Churchill** resulted in the *Atlantic Charter*, a document whose idealist goals resembled the *Fourteen Points* of Woodrow Wilson. Later conferences provided a more concrete basis for the peace.

February 1945
Yalta Conference Leaders:
Churchill, Roosevelt,
and Stalin.

source – UPI

ENDING OF WORLD WAR II – CONFERENCES

Teheran Conference (1943) – Churchill, Roosevelt, Stalin
- Normandy invasion confirmed
- Plans made for international organization to replace League of Nations

Yalta Conference (1945) – Churchill, Roosevelt, Stalin
- Decisions on Eastern Europe
- German division into zones of occupation
- Russian entrance into War against Japan

Potsdam Conference (1945) – Churchill (replaced by Clement Attlee), Truman, Stalin
- Disarmament, demilitarization, denazification of Germany
- Decision to hold war crimes trials (Nuremberg Trials)
- Reparations from occupied Germany for Soviet war damages

World War II caused over 40 million deaths and cost in excess of a trillion dollars. The Western European nations were so weakened that the colonial peoples moved to gain independence, and the world was left with two superpowers, the United States and the Soviet Union. This led to the **Cold War** which dominated international politics for the next forty years.

LINKAGES

In the half century of crisis and achievement from 1900 to 1950, the world underwent remarkable and chilling changes. The progress made in medicine and methods of treating the ill improved life-expectancy. Many scientific breakthroughs came in methods of fighting wars such as the development of airplanes and radar, but they ultimately improved civilian life.

Totalitarian governments in Russia, Germany, and Italy sacrificed civil and human rights to increase the power of dictators. These same governments controlled the economies to promote economic advancement and build their military power. Thousands of people lost their lives in Stalin's "terror famines" and Hitler's "final solution" (Holocaust).

Both world wars were expensive in terms of human life and resources and led to enormous changes. World War I sparked colonial nationalism which, after World War II, exploded into global independence movements. Some colonies achieved independence peacefully, but others fought prolonged wars. To preserve the peace, the world turned to international organizations. The League of Nations' limited success in the political field led to differences in the structure of the United Nations which achieved better results.

QUESTIONS

1   The success of the Bolsheviks in the Russian Revolution of
November, 1917 can be explained in part by the
    1   failure of the Provisional Government to support western, liberal
ideas
    2   refusal of Tsar Nicholas II to abdicate the throne
    3   Provisional Government's continuation of Russian involvement
in World War I
    4   overwhelming acceptance of Bolshevik ideas by all elements in
the population

2   Kemal Ataturk of Turkey and Reza Khan of Persia (Iran) were similar in that both men
    1   favored traditional ways, but opposed religious control
    2   wished to avoid violence and favored civil disobedience
    3   established absolute monarchies and mercantilism
    4   opposed foreign intervention, but wanted modernization

**Base your answer to question 3 on the maps below and your
knowledge of global history and geography.**

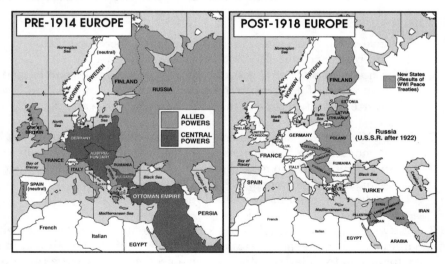

3   A significant change between the pre- and post-World War I maps of
Europe is the
    1   westward expansion of France
    2   appearance of more small nations in Eastern Europe
    3   increase in size of Russia
    4   end of largely homogenous nations in Western Europe

4   Wilson's *14 Points* and the *Treaty of Versailles* are similar in that both
   1   blamed Germany for beginning World War I
   2   called for a general arms decrease
   3   provided for reparations payments for war damage
   4   favored self determination for Eastern Europe

5   "I have nothing to offer but blood, toil, tears and sweat. We have before us an ordeal of the most grievous kind. We have before us many, many long months of struggle and of suffering. You ask, what is our policy? I will say: It is to wage war, by sea, land and air, with all our might and with all the strength that God can give us; to wage war against a monstrous tyranny..."

   In this quotation, Prime Minister Winston Churchill of Great Britain is
   1   urging the British people to prepare for a long, hard struggle against Hitler's Germany
   2   expressing the difficulties to be faced in holding the British Empire after World War II
   3   preparing the British people for the defensive nature and casualties of World War I
   4   stating his concerns about the Boer War and the Afrikaner policy of apartheid

6   The use of motorized vehicles in World War I increased global
   1   interest in the oil rich lands of the Middle East
   2   concerns about control of the Straits of the Dardanelles and Bosporus
   3   awareness of dangers to the environment
   4   desire to control inventions of new methods of warfare

7   World War I aided development of Russian communists ideas by
   1   demonstrating how governments could control the economy
   2   allowing Russia to gain control of the Dardanelles and Bosporus
   3   expanding communist influence in Eastern Europe
   4   ending the need for increased industrialization

8   "...Obliteration of the allegedly kulak elements was not only an end in itself, but a means for stampeding the rest of the population into submission to collectivization. ...the objective was to scare the poor and middling peasants themselves into merging their land, livestock, and implements."

   This quotation best describes
   1   British reaction to the Great Hunger in Ireland
   2   Mao's approach to winning Chinese peasant support
   3   Stalin's policies during the first Five Year Plan
   4   Turkish treatment of the Armenians.

9   The failure of the League of Nations members to deal effectively
     with the threats to world peace during the 1930s may be explained
     in part by its
     1   failure to hold meetings on a regular basis
     2   inability to impose sanctions on aggressors
     3   domination by the United States
     4   reluctance to oppose powerful nations

10   "...The ordinary law breaker breaks laws surreptitiously and tries to
     avoid the penalty; not so the civil resister. ...But there come occa-
     sions, generally rare, when he considers certain laws to be so unjust
     as to render obedience to them a dishonour. He then openly and
     civilly breaks them and quietly suffers the penalty for their breach."

     This quotation best expresses the ideas of
     1   Vladimir Lenin
     2   Pope John Paul XXIII
     3   Mohandas Gandhi
     4   Benito Mussolini

11   The Armenian Massacres, the Holocaust, and the killing fields of
     Cambodia have in common the
     1   attempt to wipe out a specific group of people (genocide)
     2   elimination of opposition to communist ideas
     3   killing of opposition groups during a civil war
     4   execution of the poorest groups in the population

12   The Washington Conference, the *Kellogg-Briand Pact* (Pact of Paris),
     and the *Locarno Pact* have in common the goal of
     1   expanding world wide trade during the interwar period
     2   limiting weapons of mass destruction after World War II
     3   preventing future German expansion in Europe
     4   preserving the peace between World War I and World War II

13   ***Britain Devalues the Pound***
     Viennese Banks Fail
     U.S. Unemployment Rises

     These headlines of the 1930s demonstrate the
     1   global spread of economic problems
     2   dangers of the command system
     3   need for government regulation of banks
     4   failure of the common world currency

Base your answer to question 14 on the charts below and your knowledge of global history and geography.

SOVIET v. TSARIST PRODUCTION

1913 – Tsarist Russia
1928 – New Economic Plan
1940 – After Stalin's 5-yr Plans Began

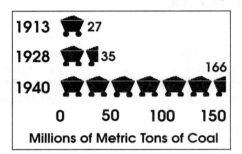

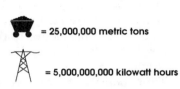

= 25,000,000 metric tons

= 5,000,000,000 kilowatt hours

Millions of Metric Tons of Coal

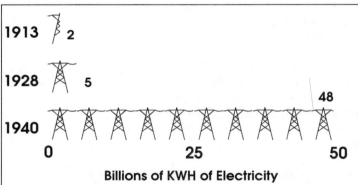

Billions of KWH of Electricity

14 Based on the charts above and your knowledge of global history, which statement is true?
  1 Soviet production during the 1930s was hampered by wartime production demands.
  2 The Five Year Plans boosted Soviet heavy industrial production during the 1930s.
  3 Widespread capitalism accounts for the rapid Soviet progress during the 1930s.
  4 Consumer industries made rapid progress in meeting people's needs in the 1930s.

15 The ability of German armies to defeat Poland quickly at the beginning of World War II can be partially explained by the
  1 pro-Nazi attitudes of a majority of the Polish people
  2 Soviet aid to the advancing German armies
  3 unwillingness of the Polish Army to offer resistance
  4 successful use of blitzkrieg tactics on the North European Plain

THEMATIC ESSAY

Directions: Write a well-organized essay that includes an introduction, several paragraphs explaining your position, and a conclusion.

Theme: change

> Throughout global history, wars have led to major changes in international affairs.

Task:

> - Select *one* war
> - Discuss this war's impact on international affairs.

Suggestions: You may use any war from your study of global history and geography. You may wish to consider the impact of the Peloponnesian War, Punic Wars, Crusades, Thirty Years War, Napoleonic Wars, Opium Wars, Russo-Japanese War, Franco-Prussian War, World War I, World War II, Arab-Israeli Wars. **You are *not* limited to these suggestions**.

PRACTICE SKILLS FOR DBQ

Directions: The following task is based on the accompanying documents. The documents may have been edited for the purposes of this exercise. The task is designed to test your ability to work with historical documents. As you analyze the documents, take into account both the source of the document and the author's point of view.

Historical Context:
In 1933, the Nazi government achieved power legally with the support of some Germans.

Part *A* – Short Answer
The documents on the next page relate to post-World War I Germany. Examine each document carefully, then answer the question that follows it.

Document 1

1   According to the information on the graph, why might the German people be looking for new leadership in 1933?

_____

_____

_____

_____

_____

Document 2

1   We demand the union of all Germans to form a Great Germany on the basis of self- determination of nations.

3   We demand land and territory [colonies] for the nourishment of our people and for settling our surplus population.

4   None but members of the nation may be citizens of the State. None but those of German blood, whatever their creed, may be members of the nation. No Jew, therefore, may be a member of the nation.

– selected 3 points fromThe 25-Point Program of the National Socialist German Workers' Party

2   What aspects of this sample of the Nazi Program would lead some Germans to support the rise of the Nazis to power?

_____

_____

_____

_____

Part *B* – Essay Response

Task: Using only the information in the documents, write a one paragraph explanation of why some Germans supported the rise of the Nazis to power.

State your thesis:

_____

_____

_____

_____

_____

_____

_____

- Use only the information in the documents to support your thesis position
- Add your analysis of the documents
- Incorporate your answers to the Part *A* scaffold questions

_____

Additional Suggested Task:

From your knowledge of global history and geography, make a list of additional factors that may have contributed to the Nazi rise to power.

_____

_____

_____

_____

_____

_____

_____

_____

_____

_____

1945 To Present

THE WORLD SINCE 1945

AD	
1945–	India and Pakistan independent (1947) *U.N. Declaration of Human Rights* (1948)
1955–	Hungarian Revolution (1956)
	Cuban Missile Crisis (1962)
1965–	European Community established (1967)
	Global oil crisis (1973)
1975–	Iranian Revolution (1979)
1985–	Tiananmen Square Massacre (1989) Destruction of the Berlin Wall (1990) U.S.S.R. collapses (1991)
1995–	India and Pakistan nuclear tests (1998)
2000–	

INTRODUCTION

In the years immediately after World War II, countries often adopted economic systems modeled on the democratic socialism of Western Europe or the command system of the Soviet Union. But, during the 1990s this trend reversed itself and countries moved toward the market system. This time period also saw the recovery of the Japanese and German economies and beginning steps toward economic

Soviets build "Iron Curtain" – The Berlin Wall

unions in Western Europe and elsewhere. As the 21st century approached, the Pacific Rim countries – along with some **LDCs** (Less Developed Countries) in other areas – became economic forces only to encounter problems from over expansion and poor government policies.

Politically, many colonies achieved independence after World War II. Some were granted independence by the colonial power; others fought wars of independence to gain it. The Cold War between the two superpowers – the Soviet Union and the United States – dominated world developments for more than a generation. The period of tension went on until the breakup of the Soviet Union in the 1990s. However, persistent hot spots around the world continued to threaten world peace.

Socially, the role of women changed and some even became leaders of their countries. However, the forces of modernization continued to struggle with traditional values especially in India and the Middle East. Attention was focused on human rights issues with varying degrees of success, with the end of apartheid in South Africa a major victory.

JAPAN AND GERMANY REBUILD

West Germany [Federal Republic of Germany] and Japan benefitted from U.S. aid while rebuilding their postwar economies. With access to the newest manufacturing, transportation and communication technology, the U.S. helped both countries to compete effectively against the older equipment and factories of Western Europe and the United States. They had labor forces with strong work ethics and a willingness to save. German chemical, iron, steel, and engineering and Japanese electronic products were of high quality.

West Germany and Japan also adopted democratic governments. The bicameral West German government was headed by a chancellor while the president represented the country internationally. In Japan, the 1946 constitution (enacted during the U.S. occupation) provided for a democratic government with the emperor as a constitutional monarch.

THE COLD WAR

Germany faced some unique problems brought about by its division into four occupation zones: U.S., British, French, and Soviet (with a similar 4-zone structure within Berlin inside the Soviet Zone). Fueled by the animosities of the Cold War, the Soviets established the **Berlin Blockade** in 1948; the allies answered with the **Berlin Airlift** to supply the city surrounded by the Soviet Zone. The Soviet refusal to allow free elections in its zone led to the establishment of the Federal Republic of Germany (West Germany) composed of the zones controlled by the allies in 1949. The Soviets answered with the formation of the German Democratic Republic (East Germany) as one of their satellites. The reunification of the two Germanies (1990) came about after the rise of Mikhail Gorbachev to power in the Soviet Union.

The Cold War between the two superpowers – Soviet Union and the United States – started as World War II ended. As the Soviet armies pressed the retreating German armies across Eastern Europe, **satellite nations** under Soviet control were established. This Soviet expansion led to the U.S. policy of **containment** and a series of rivalries and third party confrontations as each superpower tried to establish its dominance.

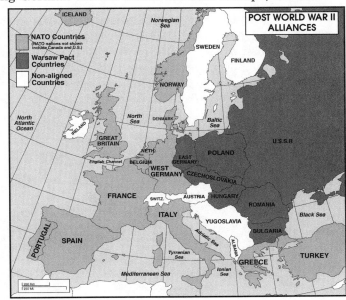

COLD WAR BEGINS

U.S.S.R. Expansion
COMECON
Warsaw Pact

COMPETITION

U.S. Containment
Truman Doctrine
Marshall Plan
NATO

OUTCOMES

Economic Markets
Space Race
Strategic Arms Race
Korean War
Vietnam War
Struggle for influence in Asia, Africa, Latin
America, Middle East

Three years after the death of Soviet dictator Josef Stalin (1953), Communist Party chief **Nikita Khrushchev** denounced many of Stalin's actions and policies as "crimes." This symbolic action unleashed a series of revolts in the U.S.S.R.'s Eastern European satellites. In Hungary (1956) and Czechoslovakia (1968) where leaders pushed for more independence from the Soviet Union, the Soviets harshly suppressed the revolts.

The Cold War rivalry was intensified by the nuclear and space races. The Soviet Union detonated its first atomic bomb in 1949, and it was quickly joined in the "nuclear club" by Britain, France, and China. The contamination of the atmosphere from nuclear tests and the proliferation of atomic weapons led to diplomatic attempts to control these threats. The *Limited Nuclear Test Ban Treaty* (1963), the *Nuclear Non-Proliferation Treaty* (1968), *SALT* (1972, 1979), and *START* (1991, 1993) were designed to limit the spread of nuclear weapons and sophisticated missile delivery systems.

THE UNITED NATIONS

The Cold War rivalry also affected the United Nations. Both superpowers had veto power and permanent seats on the **Security Council** along with Britain, France, and China. The Security Council had primary responsibility for preserving the peace. When it was blocked by a veto, the U.N. **General Assembly** (each U.N. member had one vote) could act. The **Secretary General** could be called upon to head U.N. Emergency Forces that were deployed to preserve the peace. Like its predecessor, the League of Nations, much of the U.N.'s best work was in the social and economic field. Its agencies, such as the **World Health Organization** and the **Food and Agriculture Organization**, did much to improve the global quality of life.

COMMAND V. DEMOCRATIC SOCIALISM

In the aftermath of World War II, many countries adopted democratic socialism or the command system to rebuild their economies. Both systems called for more government involvement in the economy. **Democratic Socialism** was often the choice in Western Europe. In countries such as Britain, France, and the Scandinavian countries, nationalization of key industries was combined with extensive social welfare programs. Developing nations such as India and Israel followed this example. A key feature of this approach was the prevalence of democratic governments. As problems of high taxes, labor discontent, and inflation developed, most of these nations modified their approach and moved in the direction of a market system (= mixed systems).

The **command system** was found primarily in communist countries in Eastern Europe, Cuba, China, North Korea, and some nations in Southeast Asia. The dictatorial governments of these nations were clearly in charge of the economy and central planners made the key decisions. Although extensive social welfare programs existed, there was little attempt to meet the demand for consumer products. The emphasis

CHARACTERISTICS OF MARKET AND COMMAND ECONOMIES	
Market Economy	**Command Economy**
Supply and demand determine prices	Government sets prices
Private Property	Mostly government ownership of property
Private Profit	
Market forces guide economic decisions	Mostly government ownership of profit
	Government guides economic decisions

remained on heavy industry and the military. As the Soviet Union collapsed in the early 1990s and the satellites gained freedom, most command economies struggled to move in the direction of the market system.

EUROPEAN UNITY

Another economic trend was the movement toward economic unity. This was most evident in Europe where countries learned the value of economic cooperation from the postwar Marshall Plan. Similarly, **NAFTA** provided links among the economies of Canada, United States, and Mexico in 1994. The **Latin American Integration Association**, 1960, and Mercosur, 1995, attempted to do the same for its members.

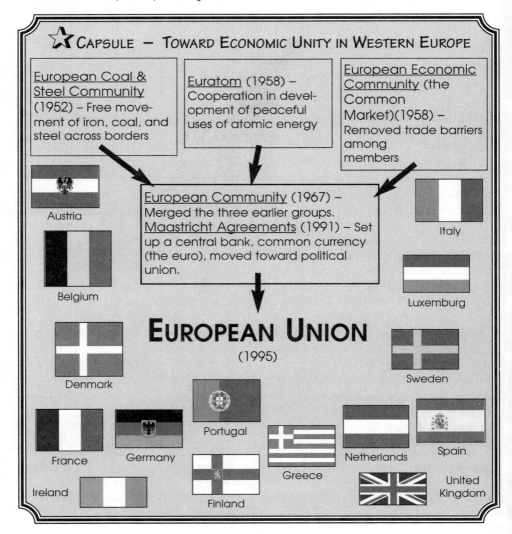

☆ CAPSULE – TOWARD ECONOMIC UNITY IN WESTERN EUROPE

European Coal & Steel Community (1952) – Free movement of iron, coal, and steel across borders

Euratom (1958) – Cooperation in development of peaceful uses of atomic energy

European Economic Community (the Common Market)(1958) – Removed trade barriers among members

Austria

Italy

European Community (1967) – Merged the three earlier groups. Maastricht Agreements (1991) – Set up a central bank, common currency (the euro), moved toward political union.

Belgium

Luxemburg

EUROPEAN UNION
(1995)

Denmark

Sweden

France   Germany   Portugal   Netherlands   Spain

Greece

Ireland   Finland   United Kingdom

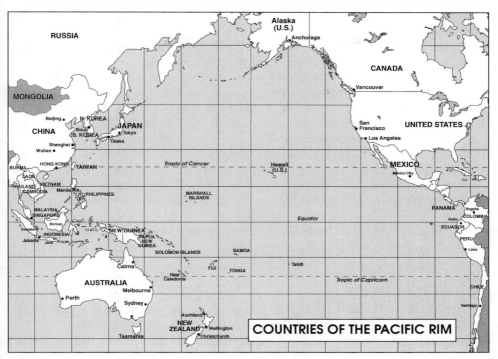

COUNTRIES OF THE PACIFIC RIM

ASIA AND THE PACIFIC RIM

The Pacific Rim countries, especially the "**Asian Tigers**" (South Korea, Hong Kong, Singapore, Taiwan) began to play an increasing role in the global economy. Originally producers of low priced products, these areas quickly attracted foreign investment and moved to produce electronics, cars, clothing, etc. In the late 1980s, Thailand, Indonesia, China, and the Philippines began to prosper. However, close ties between governments, businesses, and banks undermined confidence in their ability to reform and continue growth, and progress stalled.

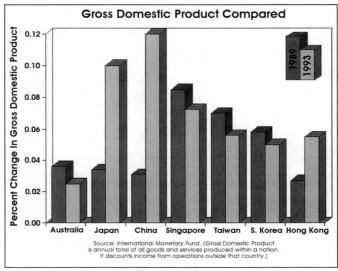

Gross Domestic Product Compared

Source: International Monetary Fund. (Gross Domestic Product is annual total of all goods and services produced within a nation. It discounts income from operations outside that country.)

THE RISE OF RED CHINA

The emergence of communism in China predates World War II. Some leaders of the 1911-1912 revolution were interested in its ideas. During the 1920s, the Chinese Communist Party allied itself with the Guomindang Party of Jiang Jieshi (Chang Kai-shek). Eventually, Jiang turned against the communists. This led to the Long March (1934-1935) of the communists under the leadership of Mao Zedong to northwestern China. In the areas they controlled, the communists implemented land reform programs and won the support of the peasants. The Guomindang and the communists uneasily joined forces to face the threat of Japanese invasion in World War II. After the War and despite aid from the United States, the Guomindang was forced to flee to Taiwan and the **People's Republic of China** was established in 1949 under the leadership of Mao. After Mao's death in 1976, subsequent leaders began to make changes in his hard-line policies.

CHINA: KEY POLICIES AND EVENTS	
Leader	**Policies**
Mao Zedong (1949-1976)	**Economic**: centralized planning and collectivized most land and property; emphasized heavy industry, but agriculture suffered in the Great Leap Forward **Social**: improved literacy, health care, and position of women; imposed censorship, propaganda, restrictions on religion, violations of human rights **Political**: Great Proletarian Cultural Revolution to eliminate opposition; terror tactics of Red Guard citing *Quotations of Chairman Mao* ("Little Red Book")
Deng Xiaoping (1976-1997)	**Economic**: proposed economic reform in the Four Modernizations Program; allowed some market reforms with the Responsibility System for agriculture, partial freedom from government control for consumer industry, and establishment of "Economic Zones" with some foreign investment **Social**: allowed increased contact with the West, sent students abroad to study, continued quality of life improvements, but class differences emerged; violations of human rights continued **Political**: harshly suppressed student protest movement at Tiananmen Square, signed 1984 agreement with Britain to regain Hong Kong
Jiang Zemin (1997-)	**Economic**: instituted reforms to increase private ownership, decrease central planning, and reform financial practices; struggled with increasing unemployment and movement from rural to urban areas **Social**: continued Deng's reforms, but concerns over human rights violations continued with accusations of forced labor in factories **Political**: imprisonment of dissidents and little toleration for opposition

GLOBAL DISINTEGRATION OF EUROPEAN COLONIALISM

After World War II, European countries were weakened and unable to maintain control of their colonies. In some instances, the Europeans honored wartime promises and granted independence. In others, colonies fought wars to gain their independence. Even after independence, the former colonial powers often remained influential. Economic and military aid and intervention to preserve peace and investments were factors in continuing European presence. Production of cash crops for export and exploitation of natural resources made it difficult for the former colonies to achieve economic independence.

☆ CAPSULE – A SAMPLER OF COLONIAL INDEPENDENCE

NIGERIA – 1957
Achieved independence from Britain after strikes, boycotts, riots, and imprisonment of independence leaders.

Problems: ethnic hostilities among Hausa, Fulani, Ibo; secession of Biafra led to civil war; continuing altercations between civilian and military governments led to instability

INDIA – 1947
Achieved independence from Britain after Gandhi's policies of non-violence, civil disobedience, boycotts and passive resistance attracted international attention and pressure; Hindu India and Muslim Pakistan established.

Problems: caste system and discrimination against untouchables; continued Hindu-Moslem hostilities especially over Kashmir, separatist pressures of Sikhs and Tamils, poverty only eased by Green Revolution

VIETNAM – 1954, 1975
Achieved independence as North Vietnam and South Vietnam at end of French phase of Vietnam War (1954); at end of American phase (1975), reunited under control of communist North.

Problems: war recovery with little foreign aid; 5-Year Plans and command system achieved little economic progress and led to adoption of some market system economic reforms in 1988

★ CAPSULE – A SAMPLER OF COLONIAL INDEPENDENCE CONTINUED

Nelson Mandela became the first president of the Republic of South Africa (r. 1994-1999).

SOUTH AFRICA – (self government under Afrikaner control - 1910; Black control in 1994).
Achieved self government after British victory in Boer War, but apartheid policies (Native Land Act, Group Areas Act) led to formation of African National Congress, eventual changes in apartheid, and election of Mandela as first Black president in 1994).

Problems: unifying Whites, Coloureds, Blacks and various tribal groups, providing equal economic opportunities and improving standard of living for all groups

KENYA – 1963
Achieved independence from Britain after Mau Mau violence.

Problems: one party state with corruption and civil rights violations, ethnic violence, economic restrictions and government control limited progress

Jomo Kenyatta nationalist leader became the first president of Kenya (r. 1964-1978).

CAMBODIA also **received independence** from France, but quickly found itself caught up in the Vietnam War. At the end of the War, the communist Khmer Rouge leader, Pol Pot seized power (r. 1975-1979). Under his leadership, a massive relocation program to the countryside occurred. Between

one and two million Cambodians died during the relocation and many more were executed for their opposition. It is estimated that about one-third of the population was killed in this genocide known as the "Killing Fields" of Cambodia. Struggles over control of the government among Soviet-backed, Vietnam-backed and Khmer Rouge troops continued for some time.

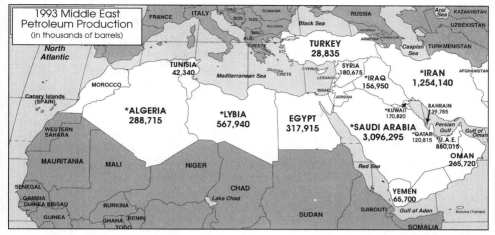

1993 Middle East Petroleum Production (in thousands of barrels)

• represents OPEC member

UNREST IN THE MIDDLE EAST

Unrest also developed in the oil-rich Middle East after World War II. In 1948, Britain withdrew from Palestine and Israel declared its independence. This led to a series of wars between the Arabs and Israelis. Both groups staked historic claims to the region. Lebanon, a country with large numbers of Muslims and Christians, got caught up in these ten-

WARS AND TERRORISM		
War / Terrorist Campaign	**Causes**	**Results**
Suez Canal Crisis 1956	President Nassar of Egypt nationalized the Suez Canal and denied Israel access.	Britain, France, and Israel attacked Egypt. U.N. arranged truce and sent peacekeepers.
Six Day War 1967	Egypt demanded withdrawal of U.N. peacekeepers; terrorist attacks on Israel; closure of Gulf of Aqaba to Israel.	Israel won control of and occupied West Bank, Golan Heights, Gaza Strip, Sinai Peninsula, and all of Jerusalem.
Yom Kippur War 1973	Desire of Arabs to regain lost territories led to attack on Israeli troops in Gaza and Golan. U.S. aided Israel; U.S.S.R. aided Syria.	U.N. arranged a cease fire.
Intifada 1987	Young Palestinians protested Israeli rule of occupied areas with attacks on troops and selected targets.	Israel retaliated by arrests, imprisonment, destruction of homes of Arabs involved, and closure of access to Israeli controlled areas to Arab employees.

sions when floods of Muslim refugees from Israel entered. The resulting refugee camps were and are used as bases to attack Israel. Involvement of Israel and Syria in Lebanese affairs complicates the problems, but there are signs of some economic recovery from the violence. The Arab **Palestine Liberation Organization** gave up terrorism in 1988, but groups such as **Hezbollah**, **Hamas**, and **Islamic Jihad** continue the use of violence.

Economic development is a fundamental issue in the Middle East. Mixed economies prevail, but population growth, water shortages, foreign investment's role, large defense budgets, and problems of traditionalism versus modernization continue to plague the area. Israel's development has been aided by Jews of every nation, especially those in the United States. High skill industries and the application of science and technology to agriculture explain much of its success. However, the Muslim countries have achieved less development.

☆ CAPSULE – ARAB / ISRAELI RELATIONS

ATTEMPTS TO PRESERVE MIDDLE EAST PEACE

1967 – *U.N. Resolution 242* – recognized sovereignty, territorial integrity, and political independence of all states in area; Israel to withdraw from territories gained in Six Day War.

1978 – *Camp David Accords* – negotiated by U.S. President Jimmy Carter, President Anwar al-Sadat of Egypt, and Prime Minister Menachem Begin of Israel - called for Israeli withdrawal from Sinai, return of U.N. peacekeepers, restoration of economic and diplomatic relations, and discussions on self-rule for Palestine.

1993 – *Declaration of Principles for Palestinian Self-Rule (The Oslo Accord)*– Prime Minister Yitzhak Rabin and Palestinian leader Yasir Arafat agreed to give Palestinians in Gaza and Jericho self-rule in 1994; extended to include West Bank in 1995.

1996 – Election of hard-liner Benjamin Netanyahu as Israeli prime minister slowed peace progress. Election of moderate Ehud Barak as prime minister in 1999 renewed hopes for progress.

☆ CAPSULE – MIDDLE EAST OVERVIEW: LEADERS, POLICIES, & PROBLEMS

EGYPT

Nasser (1952-1970) – mixed economy, nationalized Suez Canal and some businesses, land reform and irrigation projects, Aswan High Dam constructed

Sadat (1970-1981) – some foreign investment, some privatization of businesses, signed Camp David Accords.

Mubarak (1981-   ) – decreased price controls and government subsidies, liberalized trade and investment.

> **Problem**: Population growth, large foreign debts, terrorism of Islamic fundamentalists.

IRAN

Khomeini (1979-1989) – Islamic Republic, opposed westernization, reducing limited women's rights, supported seizure of U.S. embassy

Khatami (1997 -   ) – favors moderation of anti-American policies, limits on women; liberalization of conservative Islamic values

> **Problem**: High defense budget continues with Iraq tensions, high unemployment and inflation, limited foreign investment, tensions between modernizers and traditionalists and religious and secular values

LIBYA

Qaddafi (1969 -   ) – "Green Book" says Islamic socialism is a goal, but much of government revenue goes for military and terrorist support (Pan Am Flight 102, attack on West Berlin nightclub used by U.S. military personnel), nationalization of foreign businesses, limits on contacts with outside world.

> **Problem**: Failed to hand over suspects in Pan Am attack led to ban on arm sales and airline flights to Libya.

IRAQ

Saddam Hussein (1979 -   ) – expansion goals led to war against Iran and Kuwait (Persian Gulf War), harsh treatment of Kurd minority, much of government revenue used for military and development of weapons including missiles and chemical and biological agents.

> **Problem**: U.N. economic sanctions limited ability to sell oil except to make humanitarian purchases, shortages of medicines, food, and other basic necessities for much of population, Western imposed "no fly zones" to protect minorities, U.N. inspectors for forbidden weapons production denied access to facilities.

In many Muslim countries, Islamic fundamentalist groups are destabilizing influences. Algeria has an ongoing civil war which intensifies each year during the month of Ramadan when an annual average of over 600 people have been killed since 1992. In Turkey, struggles between secular forces and the fundamentalists have led to an increase in terrorism. Among the most extreme of the fundamentalist groups are the **Taliban** of Afghanistan. This group developed during the Soviet occupation of Afghanistan in the 1980s. It gained control of much of the country in the 1980s and imposed severe restrictions on women, forced men to grow a Muslim beard, and used religious police to enforce these orders.

COLLAPSE OF THE SOVIET UNION

In the last decade of the 20th century, the breakup of the Soviet Union and the collapse of communism occurred. These events led to trends toward democracy and the market system. Although neither has been successful everywhere they have been tried, significant inroads against totalitarianism and command systems took place. The gradual changes in the Soviet Union began with Nikita Khrushchev, continued with Leonid Brezhnev, and intensified under Mikhail Gorbachev.

Gorbachev's *perestroika* reforms at home frayed the social welfare safety net, cost jobs, weakened central government control, and resulted in increased class differences. As a consequence, his conservative opponents led a coup against him in 1991. Russian Federation President

EASTERN EUROPE, RUSSIA, AND CENTRAL ASIA
CONTEMPORARY NATIONS – 1990s

☆ CAPSULE – SOVIET LEADERSHIP
IN THE LAST HALF OF THE 20TH CENTURY

Nikita Khrushchev (r. 1956-1964)	**Leonid Brezhnev** (r. 1964-1982)	**Mikhail Gorbachev** (r. 1986-1991)
Foreign Affairs Suppression of Hungarian Revolution; construction of Berlin Wall; Cuban Missile Crisis; "Peaceful co-existence"	**Foreign Affairs** SALT; signed Helsinki Accords; Invasion of Czechoslovakia; Brezhnev Doctrine; Invasion of Afghanistan	**Foreign Affairs** Repealed Brezhnev Doctrine; withdrew Soviet troops from Afghanistan; increased power of republics within U.S.S.R.; allowed pro-democracy movements in satellites; Warsaw Pact ended; Soviet troops withdrawn from E. Europe
Domestic Issues Denunciation of Stalin's "crimes"; tried to increase production of consumer goods and agriculture	**Domestic Issues** Increased quality of consumer goods, quantity remained insufficient; harsh policy against dissidents	**Domestic Issues** Glasnost - increased political freedoms; Perestroika - moved toward a free market system; allowed development of pro-democracy

Boris Yeltsin led the resistance to the coup. Later, sixteen republics declared independence and Gorbachev resigned as President.

Yeltsin resigned from the Communist Party and became the first popularly elected President of Russia. However, the Communist Party remains strong in the lower house of the **Duma** (Russian parliament) and retains control of some of the independent republics. Cooperation between Russia and the republics and among the individual republics is limited. The international community worries that Russian nuclear and missile technology may reach "rogue nations" such as Libya and Iraq as

YELTSIN'S PROBLEMS

- Privatization of industry has enriched small groups called "the oligarchs"
- Crime and corruption are rampant
- GDP declined and inflation soared
- Government employees and the military often went unpaid
- People on fixed income suffered
- Violence in former republics (Georgia, Armenia, Azerbaijan, Chechnya) led to Russian involvement
- Decline in government revenue from poor tax collection led to need for international loans
- Poor personal health

the scientific and military communities experience the humiliating effects of the Russian decline as a superpower.

FALLOUT FROM THE SOVIET COLLAPSE

A positive effect of the end of the Soviet Union has been the establishment of truly independent nations in Eastern Europe. Poland, led initially by the **Solidarity** national labor union and Lech Walesa, established a democratic government and moved toward the establishment of a market system. The dismantling of the Berlin Wall led to the union of East and West Germany. The economic costs of reunification were high as the West Germans were taxed more to improve conditions in the East and to pay for the removal of Soviet troops. Ultimately, Czechoslovakia divided into the **Czech Republic** and the **Slovak Republic** in the "Velvet Revolution" because of ethnic and economic differences between the industrial west and the agricultural east.

CONTEMPORARY BALKAN STATES
Violent Ethnic Disintegration

Ethnic differences led to brutal civil war and "ethnic cleansing" in Yugoslavia. Eventually, Croatia, Slovenia, and Bosnia - Herzegovina declared independence while Serbia and Montenegro remained together as Yugoslavia. Serbia, led by **Slobodan Milosevic**, was often

Czechoslovakia divided into the **Czech Republic** and the **Slovak Republic** in the "Velvet Revolution" because of ethnic and economic differences between the industrial west and the agricultural east.

Ethnic differences led to brutal civil war and "ethnic cleansing" in Yugoslavia. Eventually, Croatia, Slovenia, and Bosnia - Herzegovina declared independence while Serbia and Montenegro remained together as Yugoslavia. Serbia, led by **Slobodan Milosevic**, was often the aggressor as he tried to establish control in the region. The attempt to "cleanse" Kosovo Province of Muslims led to the intervention of NATO and establishment of a peacekeeping force to restore order. In a fall 2000 election, Milosevic was unseated by **Vojislav Kostunica**. However, it took weeks of street demonstrations by the people before Milosevic surrendered power.

POLITICAL UNREST IN LATIN AMERICA

Some of the problems facing Latin American countries in the postwar period go back many years. The need for land reform, production of cash crops for export, gaps between rich and poor, poor living conditions in the **barrios** (urban shanty towns), increasing urbanization, population growth, and "iron triangle" alliances between the large landowners, the Roman Catholic Church, and the military are issues that most countries face.

PERON'S ECONOMIC PROGRAM
• nationalization of many industries
• improved wages and benefits for workers
• financing of public works programs
• restrictions on foreign influence in the economy

In Argentina, Colonel **Juan Peron** was elected President in 1946 with the support of the military, the poor workers (**descamisados**), and nationalists. He and his wife, Eva Duarte Peron, tried to institute reforms to benefit their supporters. However, the authoritarian government, high national debt, inflation, and opposition of the Roman Catholic Church led to a military coup. Later, the military fought the "Dirty War" against leftist guerrillas and its opponents. During this war, thousands disappeared or were arrested. This led to the formation of the Mothers of Plaza De Maya, a group which demanded information about the fate of their children. The election of **Carlos Saul Menem** (1989) after the loss of the **Falkland / Malvinas Islands War** to Britain brought pardons to those thought to be responsible for the "Dirty War."

Cuba came under the control of dictator **Fulgencio Batista** in 1953. His ties to U.S. investors won him support from the U.S. government, but his failure to help the poorest people resulted in opposition led by **Fidel**

FIDEL CASTRO

- Led communist revolution that overthrew Dictator Batista in 1959.
- Promised to improve conditions for poor.
- Established first communist state in Western Hemisphere.
- Nationalized foreign owned businesses and plantations.
- Increased literacy rate.
- Improved medical care.
- Defeated Bay of Pigs invasion.
- Faced economic crisis in mid-1990s.

Since that time, Cuba has faced economic isolation from much of the Western Hemisphere and became reliant on aid from the Soviet Union. The end to this aid during the 1980s led to an economic crisis in Cuba. More refugees tried to reach the United States. In 1998, President Clinton eased some restrictions on Cuba for humanitarian reasons. Also, Cuba began to take steps to increase tourism and institute some small market system reforms.

Instability prevailed in Central America where the "iron triangle" of the large landowners, the military, and often the conservative leaders of the Roman Catholic Church, faced the demands of leftist elements that called for land reform and more economic opportunity for the poor. In Nicaragua, dictator Anastasio Somoza was overthrown by the communist-influenced **Sandinistas** led by Daniel Ortega. A civil war resulted as the U.S. aided the **contras**, the Sandinista opponents. Eventually, a compromise was worked out between the two groups and **Violeta Chamorro** defeated Ortega in the election of 1990. Much remains to be done in terms of recovery from the civil war and help for the poor peasants.

A similar set of circumstances prevailed in Guatemala. However, after the overthrow of a left-leaning government, the military regime instituted death squads to deal with its opposition. Native Americans were a key target and thousands died. In 1994, both sides agreed to end the civil war and change the constitution to protect Indian rights. **Alvaro Arzu Irigoyent**, elected in 1996, quickly moved to control the military and improve the economy.

However, Latin America is not the only area to contain "hot spots" that threaten domestic stability and provoke international crises. Many areas around the globe have faced situations of violence and civil war. Often, international intervention by the U.N. or regional forces such as **NATO** has been necessary to restore order.

☆ CAPSULE – INTERNATIONAL HOT SPOTS

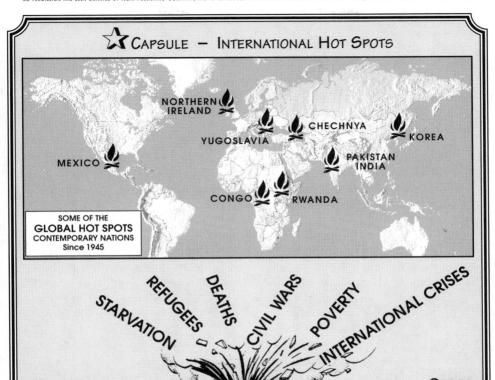

SOME OF THE
GLOBAL HOT SPOTS
CONTEMPORARY NATIONS
Since 1945

STARVATION · REFUGEES · DEATHS · CIVIL WARS · POVERTY · INTERNATIONAL CRISES

Northern Ireland
Despite a May 1998 referendum for union of the two sections of Ireland approved in both north and south, political and military problems persist.

The Koreas
North Korea's economic instability, development of nuclear capabilities, plus border and naval aggressions threaten not just South Korea, but all of East Asia.

Mexico
Native American ethnic minority (29%) continue peasant insurgency in the state of Chiapas led by Zapatista National Liberation Army, demanding better living conditions and autonomy.

Congo
Rebel forces continue to control much of an unstable Congo led by President Laurent Kabila. Troops from a half dozen countries have been caught up in the Hutu v. Tutsi conflict that has destabilized central Africa. In January 2001, Kabila was assassinated in a coup led by his own army officers and was replaced by his son, Joseph Kabila.

Yugoslavia
Long-time religious (Muslim, Eastern Orthodox, Roman Catholic) and ethnic (Serbs, Croats, Bosnians, Kosovars, Albanians) differences lead to conflicts and "ethnic cleansing" episodes involving international forces (NATO, U.N.).

LINKAGES

After World War II, the global community experienced enormous change in virtually every aspect of its existence. Economic development and power diffused significantly. Japan and Germany reemerged and the countries of the Pacific Rim became a new economic force. Many countries shifted from command and mixed economies in the direction of the market system.

Politically, this period saw the beginning and the apparent end of the Cold War between the superpowers, the Soviet Union, and the United States. However, there is rising apprehension about the power of the U.S. and its willingness to use its military might.

Socially, there were positive and negative developments after World War II. In many countries the role and position of women improved, the mass media helped to decrease global differences, and some areas saw improvements in human rights. Although the end of apartheid in South Africa was a major achievement, the world witnessed genocide in Kosovo, Central Africa, and Cambodia and varying levels of violence against minorities and dissidents elsewhere.

QUESTIONS

1   "Everyone is entitled in full equality to a fair and public hearing by an independent and impartial tribunal in the determination of his rights and obligations and of any criminal charge against him."
    – Universal Declaration of Human Rights

    Which leader would be most likely need to seek protection of the law under this provision of the *Universal Declaration of Human Rights* because of his policies and/or actions?
    1   Benjamin Netanyahu   3   Slobodan Milosevic
    2   Nelson Mandela   4   Queen Elizabeth II

2   The Vietnam War, the Korean War, the Marshall Plan, and the Truman Doctrine can be viewed as implementations of the policy of
    1   containment   3   peaceful coexistence
    2   detente   4   manifest destiny

3   Deng Xiaoping, Mikhail Gorbachev, and Fidel Castro introduced measures to
    1   end all press censorship
    2   increase use of the market system
    3   free opposition leaders from prison
    4   limit defense spending

4   The division of India into India and Pakistan after World War II, independence for Nigeria, and the breakup of Yugoslavia after the end of the Cold War all resulted in
   1   outbreaks of violence and floods of refugees
   2   religious unification, but continued economic discrimination
   3   diminished roles for women, but an end to ethnic hatreds
   4   command systems and dictatorial governments

Base your answer to question 5 on the cartoon at the right and your knowledge of global history.

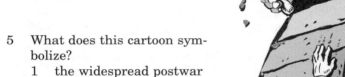

5   What does this cartoon symbolize?
   1   the widespread postwar reconstruction necessary in Berlin
   2   Soviet anger at the people of East Berlin
   3   the desire of the Soviets to isolate satellite countries from western influences
   4   Soviet seizure of German building supplies for its own reconstruction

6   Divestiture, U.N. resolutions, and boycotts were all weapons that the international community found useful in its struggle to
   1   secure the independence of Hong Kong
   2   end foreign control of the Suez Canal
   3   free South Africa of apartheid
   4   end the threat of communism in Tanzania

7   *U.N. Resolution 242*, the *Camp David Accords*, and the *Declaration of Principles for Palestinian Self-Rule* were all attempts to
   1   establish an independent Jewish state in Palestine
   2   provide for Palestinian refugees in neighboring Arab states
   3   end the threat of communist takeover in Palestine
   4   bring peace between the Jews and Arabs in the Middle East

8   Despite environmental limitations, which Middle Eastern nation is close to self-sufficiency in agriculture because of its use of science, technology, irrigation, and land reclamation?
   1   Egypt   3   Lebanon
   2   Israel   4   Jordan

Base your answer to question 9 on the timeline below and your knowledge of global history.

<pre>
        1914   1945   1985

____A____ / ____B____ / ____C____ / ____D____
</pre>

9   During which time period did the Cold War begin?
    1   A   3   C
    2   B   4   D

10 Which best describes European involvement in former African colonies in the 1990s?
    1   largely economic in nature as trading partners and with continued investment
    2   continuing with the presence of influential foreign advisors playing major roles
    3   increasing in strength as colonies try to develop more cash crops for export
    4   limited to providing military aid and training to the new armies

Base your answer to question 11 on the outline below and your knowledge of global history and geography.

11

    I._____

        A   French lose battle of Dien Bien Phu
        B   Geneva agreement results in division
        C   U.S. enters War
        D   North and South united

    Which heading is the most appropriate for the partial outline above?
    1   Korean War Ends
    2   Vietnam Wins Independence
    3   Algeria Gains Freedom
    4   Moroccans Achieve Unification

12 Which part of the world has been the site of rival power competition for control during much of the 20th century because of its possession of major waterways for world trade and petroleum?
    1   Latin America
    2   Africa south of the Sahara
    3   the Middle East
    4   the Scandinavian countries

Base your answer to question 13 on the map at the right and your knowledge of global history.

13 The best title for this map would be
   1 "World War I: Central Powers and Allies"
   2 "Imperialist Powers: Have and Have-Not Nations"
   3 "World War II Enemies"
   4 "Post World War II Alliances"

14 Mao Zedong's Great Leap Forward called for
   1 development of new consumer industries
   2 ending the agricultural communes
   3 abolishing central planning
   4 emphasizing heavy industrial production

15 Islamic Fundamentalism won support in many Islamic areas because it
   1 provides programs to meet the needs of the poor
   2 promises to promote modernization and westernization
   3 provides equal opportunities to women in the workplace
   4 promises to end censorship and provide freedom of religion

16 The election of President Mohammed Khatami of Iran in 1997 indicated that most Iranians
   1 supported the Islamic principles of Ayatollah Khomeini
   2 wished to see some moderation of Islamic limitations on daily life
   3 called for continued hostility to the United States
   4 opposed attempts of the government to promote new industries

17 Mexico and some of the Central American countries have weak human rights records when dealing with
   1 Native Americans   3 large landowners
   2 Roman Catholic priests   4 military officers

Base your answer to question 18 on the illustration at the right and your knowledge of global history and geography.

18 The left and right sides of this illustration represent the
1   benefits the poor receive from the oil wealth of the Middle East
2   search of Israelis for a new way of life
3   struggle between the forces of traditionalism and modernization
4   use of oil wealth to build a large, modern military

19 Khrushchev and Brezhnev helped to prepare the way for Gorbachev's reforms because both men
1   allowed freedom of the press
2   permitted satellite freedom of action
3   ended imprisonment of opposition
4   tried to increase production of consumer goods

20 Glasnost and perestroika were reforms associated with
1   Nikita Khrushchev   3   Boris Yeltsin
2   Leonid Brezhnev   4   Mikhail Gorbachev

THEMATIC ESSAY

Directions: Write a well-organized essay that includes an introduction, several paragraphs explaining your position, and a conclusion.

Theme: diversity

> At various times in history, people of diverse ethnic, religious, or racial backgrounds have experienced difficulties living side by side. Often problems have occurred that resulted in violence and death.

Task:

> •   Chose *two* ethnic, religious, or racial groups from your study of global history and geography which have experienced difficulty living alongside a group of different background.

> For *each* group:
> - Describe the circumstances that led to the problems between the group and its neighbors.
> - Explain how the selected group reacted, the actions it took to solve the problems, and the action, if any, of the international community.

Suggestions: You may use any example from your study of global history and geography. Some suggestions you might wish to consider include: Jews in Hitler's Germany, Roman Catholics in Northern Ireland, Sikhs in India, Blacks in apartheid South Africa, Muslims in Kosovo, Native Americans in Mexico, and Armenians in the Ottoman Empire. **You are *not* limited to these suggestions.**

PRACTICE SKILLS FOR DBQ

Directions: The following task is based on the accompanying documents. The documents may have been edited for the purposes of this exercise. The task is designed to test your ability to work with historical documents. As you analyze the documents, take into account both the source of the document and the author's point of view.

Historical Context: Sometimes the domestic and international views of a leader are different.

Part A – Short Answer
The documents below relate to the effect Gorbachev had on the Soviet Union. Examine each document carefully, then answer the question that follows it.

Document 1

"SATELLITES BECOME INDEPENDENT"
"WARSAW PACT ENDS"

1   Why did the global community support Gorbachev?

_____

_____

_____

Document 2

At home in Russia, reforms brought frustration to Gorbachev and social pain to the Russians.

2   Why was Gorbachev unpopular with many people of the Soviet Union?

_____

_____

_____

Part *B* – Essay Response

Task: Using only the information in the documents, write a one paragraph explanation of how Gorbachev could be popular in the international community, but unpopular at home.

State your thesis:

_____

_____

_____

_____

_____

_____

- Use only the information in the documents to support your thesis position
- Add your analysis of the documents
- Incorporate your answers to Part *A* scaffold questions

Additional Suggested Task:

Make *two* lists of additional information from your knowledge of global history and geography that might be applied to the task: one list of additional reasons for Gorbachev's support in the global community and one list of additional reasons for his unpopularity in the Soviet Union.

TODAY AND
INTO THE FUTURE

GLOBAL
CONNECTIONS
AND
INTERACTIONS

AD

1970–

computer processor
invented (1971)

1975–

1980–

1985–

Chernobyl nuclear
accident (1986)

Exxon *Valdez* oil spill (1989)

1990–

Earth Summit in Rio
de Janeiro (1992)

1995– 1st American on Russian
Mir Space Station (1995)

Asian Economic Crisis (1997)

2000– € comes into use (1999)

INTRODUCTION

The increasing and strengthening connections and interactions make it obvious that world problems must be addressed in a global format. Economic issues such as the tremendous differences between the **"have nations"** and **"have-not nations,"** the use of scarce resources, and choice of economic system are not likely to be solved by countries in isolation. Additionally, socioeconomic problems such as population growth, environmental questions, scientific and technological progress, and the global migration of people also require an international effort for solution.

Golden Gate Bridge
San Fransciso, CA – *PhotoDisc©*

ECONOMIC INTERACTION: THE NORTH - SOUTH IMBALANCE

The North/South imbalance is largely the result of the "have nations" being primarily in the Northern Hemisphere and the "have-not nations" primarily in the Southern Hemisphere. The "have-not nations" usually have a lower standard of living marked by lower literacy rates, lower per capita incomes, and lower life expectancies, and more children per family. Many of these "have-not nations" struggle to find an economic system

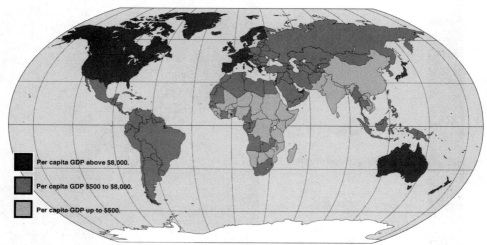

Per capita GDP above $8,000.

Per capita GDP $500 to $8,000.

Per capita GDP up to $500.

THE "HAVE" AND "HAVE NOT" COUNTRIES
Based on per capita Gross Domestic Product
This location map shows the per capita Gross Domestic Product in world nations. In general, the lower the per capita GDP, the lower the standard of living and the poorer the country is. In most cases, the low GDP countries are the "have not" or LDCs.

best suited to their needs. Although many started out with mixed systems leaning toward the command system, the 1990s saw a shift in the direction of market system. The Less Developed Countries ("have-nots," **LDCs**) must struggle with a sizable number of problems as they push for increased development.

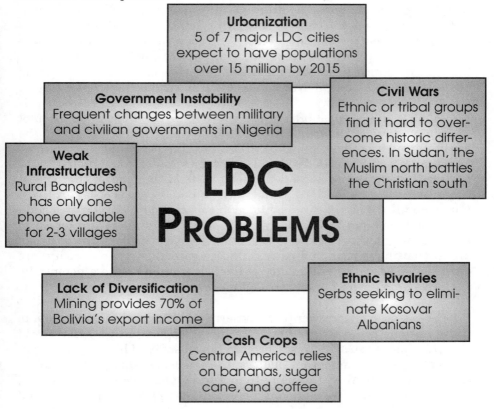

Urbanization
5 of 7 major LDC cities expect to have populations over 15 million by 2015

Government Instability
Frequent changes between military and civilian governments in Nigeria

Civil Wars
Ethnic or tribal groups find it hard to overcome historic differences. In Sudan, the Muslim north battles the Christian south

Weak Infrastructures
Rural Bangladesh has only one phone available for 2-3 villages

LDC PROBLEMS

Lack of Diversification
Mining provides 70% of Bolivia's export income

Ethnic Rivalries
Serbs seeking to eliminate Kosovar Albanians

Cash Crops
Central America relies on bananas, sugar cane, and coffee

LCD PROBLEMS

The **Arab Oil Embargo of 1973** was a serious setback for the LDCs. Most of them were oil importers, and the increased cost of oil forced them to seek loans to meet the basic needs of their people and continue development. The increased interest rates led to recessions. The international lenders then imposed financial reforms on them, and the decrease in government spending led to more economic suffering. Many nations began to shift in the direction of the market system and curb corruption in the relationship between government and business. However, by the mid-1990s, the Pacific Rim countries faced recessions brought on by over expansion, high debts, and close ties between government and business. Help from the international economic community, "belt tightening" curbs on government spending, and some reforms began to ease the crisis by the late 1990s.

Unfortunately, people in some of the LDCs use illicit drug production and sale as a means of solving economic problems. Native Americans in countries such as Bolivia, Peru, and Colombia have grown coca leaves for their own use for a long time. The international demand for cocaine and other drugs made them valuable export products. Profits often went to cartels organized to move the drugs globally, to corrupt political and military leaders, and to terrorist organizations. The U.S. government attempted to control the flow of drugs through increased border inspection and Coast Guard interceptions. Nevertheless, drug consumption in the U.S. remained high. Many believed that the correct approach would be to deal with the illegal drug demand of U.S. citizens first.

In many areas, rural inhabitants move to urban areas in an attempt to improve their standard of living. In 1950, approximately 29% of the world's population lived in urban areas, but this percentage is projected to reach 50% in 2000. In 1950, only New York had a population over 10 million, but projections indicate that by 2015, thirteen of the largest urban areas will be in LDCs. Cities such as Bombay, Lagos, Jakarta, Sao Paulo, and Karachi are expected to be in this category. This creates additional problems for LDCs. Many of the new city dwellers are forced to live in shanty towns (barrios in Latin America) on the outskirts of urban areas. Housing is poor, and basic services (water, sewers, electricity) are often non-existent. These quality of life issues often create a potentially explosive problem for already struggling governments.

For the poor, one answer to the poverty problem has been migration to "have nations" in search of better economic opportunities. After World War II, countries such as West Germany which suffered heavy war casualties welcomed the immigrant addition to their labor supply. Many "guest workers" came to West Germany from Turkey and Yugoslavia. However, reunification of the two Germanies created unemployment problems and resentment against the immigrant workers. Neo-Nazi groups led attacks on these people. Similar problems have surfaced in France where immigration from former North African colonies led to violent incidents.

Large numbers of immigrants, legal and illegal, enter the U.S. Approximately 50% of the million legal immigrants come from Hispanic and Asian areas. Illegal immigrants are estimated to total more than 500,000 yearly. Some cross borders illegally, some

LIFE EXPECTANCIES AT BIRTH (YEARS) - SELECTED COUNTRIES		
Country	1977	1993
Angola	37	47
China	59	69
Colombia	59	69
Guatemala	53	65
Haiti	48	57
Ireland	71	75
Rwanda	48	47
United States	71	76

GLOBAL MIGRATION PATTERNS

Origin:	Destination:
Turkey and Yugoslavia ———————————➤	Germany
Morocco, Tunisia, and Algeria ———————➤	France
Latin America and Asia ————————————➤	United States

overstay visas, and some pay large sums to "coyotes" to cross the Mexican border or to Chinese groups for ship passage under horrible conditions to U.S. waters. Once in the U.S., illegal aliens disappear into ethnic neighborhoods and obtain illegal work. Some enter "sweat shops" and others become migrant farm laborers. They are usually paid less than legal minimum wage, but fear deportation too much to complain.

Other social and economic problems, such as famine and hunger, plague the global community. **Famine** is caused by an insufficient amount of food for a long period of time. Famine raises national death rates. **Hunger** is the result of an inadequate supply of food which can cause weakness or illness.

Hunger exists in all countries, but famine is more likely to occur in LDCs. Among the most disturbing causes of famine and hunger are instances where food is deliberately limited by a leader or political group to increase power. For example, Josef Stalin used starvation against the kulak opposition to his regime in the 1930s. Pol Pot's policies for control led to famine in Cambodia in the 1970s. Muslim forces in northern Sudan used control of relief shipments to the Christian south to win control.

Low literacy rates and levels of education cause more social and economic problems. Much of the illiteracy is found in Latin America, Africa, and Asia. It is more common in rural than in urban areas because

CAUSES OF FAMINE AND HUNGER

- Drought, especially the failure of monsoon rains
- Pests & epidemics of plant & animal diseases
- Wars and political policies
- Poor or nonexistent infrastructure
- Soil erosion
- Reliance on cash crops at expense of **subsistence agriculture**
- Reliance on traditional farming methods

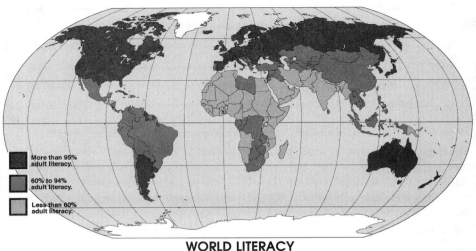

More than 95% adult literacy.

60% to 94% adult literacy.

Less than 60% adult literacy.

WORLD LITERACY

This location map shows literacy in regions of the world. In general, the highest illiteracy is found in the "have not" or LDCs. These are the poorest nations, often with the highest birthrates and lowest standards of living.

of differences in the availability of education. The twenty-five poorest nations have illiteracy rates in excess of 80%. However, countries such as Cuba, Tanzania, Nicaragua, and China have made considerable progress. Improvement in literacy is a key to economic development. Astonishingly, developed nations experience a problem of **functional literacy** (ability to meet the reading and writing demands of a complex society). Although their basic literacy rates are high, functional illiteracy may affect as much as 50% of the population.

GLOBAL ECONOMY AND EDUCATION		
COUNTRY	**(GDP) Per Capita Income (1995)**	**Adult Literacy Rate (1995)**
Bangladesh	$1,130	38%
Senegal	$1,600	33%
Laos	$1,100	57%
Haiti	$1,000	45%
Mali	$600	31%
Morocco	$3,000	44%
Afghanistan	$600	31%
Germany	$17,900	100%
United States	$27,607	96%

PROGRESS

FOR WOMEN

One area of social and economic progress is women's rights. As a result of the Industrial Revolution and the two global wars, women began to work outside the home. In most areas of the world, they gained the right to control property, to equal opportunity, and to vote. However, in some traditional areas, these gains were limited.

In developed countries, improved methods of contraception decreased child bearing and child rearing. At the same time, economic demands made two incomes a necessity for many families. Slowly, women began to move from low paying jobs such as teaching, nursing, and clerical jobs to positions of corporate leadership and the professions. In communist countries, equality of men and women was proclaimed. However, women often received less pay and were denied high positions while they continued to have full responsibility for running their households.

In LDCs, progress is slow. Until educational opportunities and attitudes change, few women will be able to advance in the work force. Islamic Fundamentalist countries often require that women assume traditional roles and sometimes refuse to allow them to work outside the home, drive cars, or vote.

U.N. LEADERSHIP

An important international presence in dealing with socioeconomic problems is the United Nations. Its Economic and Social Council tries to increase economic

EXAMPLES OF RIGHTS FOUND IN THE *UNIVERSAL DECLARATION OF HUMAN RIGHTS*
• Life, liberty, and security of person
• Freedom from slavery or servitude
• Equality before law
• Freedom from arbitrary arrest, detention, or exile

and social cooperation among nations. It also coordinates the work of specialized agencies such as **FAO** (Food and Agriculture Organization), **WHO** (World Health Organization), and **UNESCO** (United Nations Education, Scientific, and Cultural Organization). The *Universal Declaration of Human Rights* adopted by the U.N. General Assembly in 1948 reaffirms basic human rights and provides a basis for improving global conditions.

One of the main objectives of the U.N. is to work for the preservation of peace. Although it has no military forces of its own, the U.N. Security Council may request members to donate troops. During the **Korean War** (1950-1953), a U.N. army under U.S. command fought to protect South Korea from invasion from the North. The U.N. sent international peacekeeping missions to the Middle East, the Congo, Cyprus, Haiti, Angola, Somalia, Rwanda, Georgia, and the former Yugoslavia. Constant budgetary problems make it difficult to supply peacekeepers everywhere they are needed.

THE GLOBAL IMPACT OF SCIENCE AND TECHNOLOGY

The 20th century saw tremendous developments in the fields of science, technology, and medicine. The "Information Society" is one result of this progress. During World War II, an early computer was created to do calculations for the **Manhattan Project** (atomic bomb) and for artillery target estimates. By 1953, there were about 100 computers in use world-wide, today that number exceeds 100 million. The development of the microprocessor by Intel in 1971 made the personal computer possible and led to the explosion in computer use.

Home computers are used for word processing, spreadsheets, banking, bill paying, and games. Businesses use them to keep track of inventories using bar codes and scanners, to check credit cards, and to transfer funds electronically. In addition, they are used in cars, scientific research, education, and research. The Internet enables information to be sent worldwide through its global connection of computer networks.

Increased use of computers has led to concerns about privacy, viruses which destroy information and cause computer problems, and the type and availability of information on the Internet. There have been

instances where serious crimes have resulted from information obtained on the Internet or where criminals have contacted their victims via this medium. Attempts to regulate Internet information face problems involving rights of freedom of speech and press.

Computers, the key factor in the communications highway, have changed business, government, and life in general. *PhotoDisc Inc. 1994*

Space is regarded as the "new frontier." Unmanned spacecraft have sent back scientific data on the solar system and universe. Manned spacecraft do numerous scientific studies, many of which have implications for life on earth. Unfortunately, the high cost of manned vehicles limits their use, but international cooperation, especially between Russia and the U.S., helped to lessen this problem. The use of satellites circling the Earth has led to a worldwide improvement in communications. Television signals, telephone conversations, and digital data can be transmitted through orbiting satellites. These satellites have also improved weather forecasting and have proven militarily useful.

Science has also made breakthroughs in the production of food. The **Green Revolution** began in the late 1960s with new hybrid crops such as rice, wheat, potatoes, and corn. This led to an increase in food production in LDCs. Unfortunately, the high costs of petrochemical fertilizers, irrigation, pesticides, and the new seeds limit progress.

One of the reasons for the global population growth is the improvement in medical treatment. The discovery of penicillin and the development of antibiotics during World War II brought progress in the treatment of diseases such as pneumonia and tuberculosis. Unfortunately, overuse of some of these drugs has led to the development of drug resistant diseases. The development of a new generation of "wonder drugs" takes time. Vaccination programs of the WHO and governments have also done much to eliminate diseases such as polio and measles.

BIRTH RATES – SELECTED COUNTRIES			
COUNTRY	Birth rate per 1,000 (1993)	Percent Urban (1995)	Fertility Rate per woman (1995)
Afghanistan	51	20	6.9
Bangladesh	36	18	3.1
China	18	30	1.8
Chad	44	21	5.5
Kenya	44	28	4.9
Argentina	20	88	2.6
El Salvador	33	45	3.1
United States	16	76	2.0
France	13	73	1.6
Russia	11	76	1.4

Major health problems still face the global community. The human immunodeficiency virus (HIV) which causes AIDS impacts almost every area. In developed nations, expensive "cocktails" of drugs, including AZT, have extended life expectancies of victims. However, in poverty areas, these drugs are not available, and the disease continues to spread at a rapid rate. International efforts have been more successful in dealing with outbreaks of the Ebola virus in Africa and Dengue Fever in Latin America.

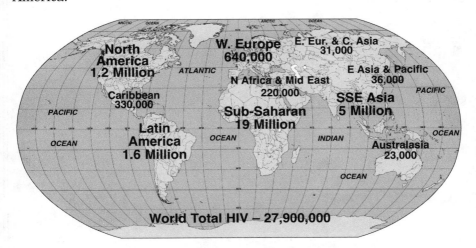

HIV – THE SPREAD ALL OVER THE WORLD
This location map shows the areas of the world where the retrovirus HIV, which causes AIDS, has had the greatest effect. Based on these 1996 statistics, the World Health Organization expresses real concern for the worldwide spread of the disease.

Medical research has found genetic markers for certain diseases that help doctors to predict who is at greatest risk. This information combined with the new drug, Tamoxifen, has been useful in treating women at greatest risk for breast cancer. Angiostatin and endostatin drugs may prove useful in blocking growth of cancerous tumor blood vessels. In addition, organ transplants, open heart surgery, and less invasive surgical procedures have helped to prolong life in developed nations.

☆ CAPSULE – ENVIRONMENTAL THREATS

Damage to the environment affects everyone

U.S.News ©

Pollution – air, water, toxic waste
High costs of clean up and proper disposal limit progress despite international agreements

Desertification – With little or no green vegetation and water, the devastating effects of desertification are evident in the appearance of emaciated Sahel cattle around Keur Mibarick, Senegal Africa

David Johnson ©

Deforestation – "Slash and Burn" – Deforestation of the Amazon Rain Forest in order to gain grazing land for cattle in Brazil, South America

PhotoDisc Inc. ©

Endangered Species – The once-numerous rhinoceros family, Rhinocerotidae, now contains only five living species. All are threatened with extinction, some imminently.

PhotoDisc Inc. ©

GLOBAL ENVIRONMENTAL CHALLENGES

Threats to the environment may be disastrous to life as we know it. Many of these threats are the result of various types of pollution. Government attempts to pass laws to regulate sources of pollution, or to force proper disposal methods for wastes, have met with some success. However, the high costs of such programs leads to violations and LDCs often find the expense prohibitive.

Deforestation is another threat to the environment. At the current rate, tropical rain forests could disappear by 2030. Hundreds of plant and animals species could disappear and the decreasing number of trees that remove carbon dioxide from the air could further the greenhouse effect. However, attempts to get "have-not nations" to limit destruction of valuable tropical rain forests encounter opposition based on the need for economic development. Attempts by the **1992 Earth Summit** in Rio de Janeiro, Brazil and the *1997 Kyoto Protocol* to decrease the emission of gases to ease the greenhouse effect have met with only limited success.

Economic problems are also partially behind the problem of **desertification**. Too many people, too much livestock, and too much cultivation of fragile desert edges leads to a spread of the desert. Natural causes such as insufficient rainfall and strong winds also contribute. A serious problem developed in the Sahel area of Africa between the late 1960s and the early 1980s. It resulted in a famine requiring international relief efforts. Some easing has occurred as rainfall amounts have returned to more normal levels.

Greed is a factor in the increasing list of endangered species. Destruction of habitats such as the tropical rain forests and coral reefs seriously decrease the numbers of certain species. The giant pandas of China are threatened because development has led to the depletion of their favorite food, bamboo. Some animals, such as the rhinoceros, are hunted for their economic value. Their horns have a medicinal value in China. The *1973 Convention of International Trade in Endangered Species* prohibited trade in plants and animals in danger of becoming extinct, but enforcement is difficult.

INTERNATIONAL TERRORISM

A political issue which continues to confront the nations of the world is terrorism. It is a frequently used weapon by those who wish to call world attention to their demands. During the latter part of the 1990s, much attention was focused on the group led by Osama bin Laden. While the leader is often out of reach in Afghanistan, his followers have been implicated in attacks on U.S. embassies in Kenya and Tanzania, the attack on tourists in Luxor, Egypt, and the bombing of the World Trade Center in New York. However, many other groups remain active around the world:

- Hamas, Hezobollah, Islamic Jihad – oppose Israel and want an independent Palestinian nation
- Zapatista National Liberation Army – wants reforms to benefit the Native American population of Mexico
- Kosovo Liberation Army – wants an independent Kosovo
- Liberation Tigers of Tamil Eelam – want an independent nation in Southeast Asia
- Islamic Salvation Front of Algeria – wants control of Algerian government

LINKAGES

Globalization is a result of the increasing connections and interactions of nations. Economically, it is impossible for a country to exist in total isolation. For example, on January 1, 1999, 11 member nations of the European Union (EU) adopted a common currency called the euro. Full adoption takes place in January 2002. The euro represents a shift in the control of EU monetary policy to the European Central Bank in Frankfurt, Germany.

Global interdependence is obvious. Necessary goods unavailable locally must be imported, and products produced in excess of needs must be sold. Unfortunately, many LDCs continue to be exporters of less expensive raw materials and importers of more expensive finished products. This imbalance of trade widens the gap between the "have" and "have-not" countries. These same LDCs often face problems of population pressure, disease, low literacy and education rates, government instability, weak infrastructures, lack of diversification, and ethnic rivalries. Attempts of international organizations to assist with these problems are not always successful. On the positive side, the connections and interactions have resulted in tremendous progress in science, medicine, technology, and to a lesser extent, women's rights and human rights in general. Unfortunately, much of this progress has made little impact on developing countries.

QUESTIONS

1   The problem of the amount of carbon dioxide in the atmosphere is a direct result of the
   1   destruction of forests and increased use of fossil fuels
   2   oil spills such as occurred in Prince William Sound
   3   improper storage of solid and nuclear wastes
   4   dumping of inorganic material into lakes and rivers

2   A major result of the Green Revolution has been a(n)
   1   decrease in the use of modern farm machinery
   2   increase in agricultural output
   3   decrease in population growth
   4   increase in the number of traditional farms

3   Josef Stalin and Pol Pot are similar in that both
   1   encouraged freedom of speech and press
   2   relocated thousands of people from the cities
   3   used starvation as a means to increase their control
   4   increasingly used market system principles

Base your answer to question 4 on the cartoon at the right and your knowledge of global history

4   What would be the best title for the cartoon shown above?
   1   Have versus Have-not
   2   Agriculture Drives Industry
   3   East Meets West
   4   Money versus Skill

5   The primary goal of the Kosovar Liberation Army and the Liberation Tigers of Tamil Eelam is to establish
   1   religious freedom
   2   collective farms
   3   independent nations
   4   a command economic system

6   During the 1990's, an important economic trend was
1   a decrease in moves to promote economic unions
2   a major increase in protective tariffs
3   an end to the power of groups such as OPEC
4   an increasing use of market system forces

Base your answer to question 7 on the chart at the right and your knowledge of global history

GLOBAL ECONOMY AND EDUCATION

COUNTRY	(GDP) Per Capita Income (1995)	Adult Literacy Rate (1995)
Bangladesh	$1,130	38%
Senegal	$1,600	33%
Laos	$1,100	57%
Haiti	$1,000	45%
Mali	$600	31%
Morocco	$3,000	44%
Afghanistan	$600	31%
Germany	$17,900	100%
United States	$27,607	96%

7   The chart indicates that
1   Germany has a higher per capita income and adult literacy rate than the United States.
2   There is a correlation between high adult literacy rates and high per capita income.
3   "Have-not" nations have high literacy rates, but low per capita income.
4   The nations with the lowest literacy rates and per capita income are in Latin America.

8   Women's rights have increased globally since the end of World War II; however, in some areas they are limited by the
1   struggle between secular and religious forces
2   increasing use of birth control methods
3   failure of international women's groups to press their goals
4   increase in media coverage

9   The oil crisis of 1973 severely impacted LDCs because
1   most of them lost expected oil revenues
2   their oil processing plants were forced to close
3   increased oil prices led to increased debt loads
4   lack of oil led to increased use of nuclear power

Base your answer to question 10 on the map below and your knowledge of global history.

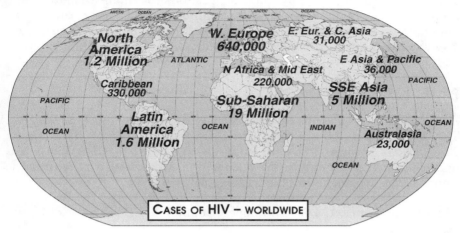

10 Which statement is most accurate?
  1 Most cases of HIV are found in the Northern Hemisphere.
  2 Sub-Saharan Africa has the highest incidences of HIV.
  3 The spread of HIV has been very limited.
  4 Few people in North America suffer from HIV.

THEMATIC ESSAY

Directions: Write a well-organized essay that includes an introduction, several paragraphs explaining your position, and a conclusion.

Theme: Technology

> The period since 1945 has been marked by tremendous progress in technology, science, and medicine. In many cases, improvements in these fields have made substantial changes to the quality of human life.

Task:

> • Describe the general impact of technology, science, and/or medicine on human development.
> • Support your opinion by discussing *two* specific ways in which technology, science, and/or medicine have improved the quality of human life since 1945. (You may select the two ways from one field or select one way from each of two fields.)

Suggestions: You may use any post-1945 examples from your study of global history and geography. Some suggestions you might wish to consider include: computers, satellite communications, Green Revolution, development of new drugs, organ transplants, and laparoscopic surgery. **You are *not* limited to these suggestions.**

PRACTICE SKILLS FOR DBQ

Directions: The following task is based on the accompanying documents. The documents may have been edited for the purposes of this exercise. The task is designed to test your ability to work with historical documents. As you analyze the documents, take into account both the source of the document and the author's point of view.

Historical Context: Less Developed Countries (LDCs) have difficulty achieving prosperity.

Part A – Short Answer
The documents below relate to the problems of LDCs. Examine each document carefully, then answer the question that follows it.

Document 1

1   What does this cartoon indicate about the relationship between LDC food production and LDC population growth?

_____

_____

_____

_____

_____

Document 2

Socioeconomic Status of Asian Countries				
Country	Per Capita GDP	Life Expectancy	Percent Literate	Birth Rate per 1000 people
Bangladesh	1,100	57	47	35
India	1,300	58	48	28
Philippines	2,500	63	89	30
Japan	20,400	79	100	11
Thailand	5,500	68	89	19

2   Why does Bangladesh qualify as an LDC?

_____

_____

_____

_____

_____

_____

_____

Part *B* – Essay Response
Task: Using only the information in the documents, write a one paragraph discussion of problems faced by LDCs.

State your thesis:

_____

_____

_____

_____

_____

_____

_____

- Use only the information in the documents to support your thesis position
- Add your analysis of the documents
- Incorporate your answers to Part *A* scaffold questions

Additional Suggested Task:

Make a list of additional information from your knowledge of global
history and geography about the problems of LDCs.

4 MILLION PLUS YEARS...
LEARNED OVER 20 MONTHS...
REVIEWED FOR A FEW WEEKS...
RECOLLECTED IN A FEW MINUTES...

STUDY HARD & GOOD LUCK!

★EXAM

1

PAGE 231

GLOBAL HISTORY
PRACTICE
EXAM

PART I : 50 QUESTIONS (55 POINTS)

1   A geographer gathering data about spatial relationships would be interested in
   1   natural, capital, and informational resources
   2   civil, criminal, and international law
   3   land forms, climate, and water bodies
   4   kinship, religion, and art forms

2   Which primary source would most likely provide an African perspective rather than a European perspective on history?
   1   a Nigerian eyewitness account of events in the 18th century
   2   a diary kept by Vasco da Gama on one of his voyages
   3   a West African history textbook written by a British author
   4   a painting of the city of Nairobi done by an early colonial settler

Base your answer to question 3 on the map below and your knowledge of global history and geography.

EASTERN MEDITERRANEAN CIVILIZATIONS
1500 BC – 500 BC

3   The topography of "Hellas" (ancient Greece) led most of the poleis to
   1   adopt monotheism
   2   unify into a powerful empire
   3   develop cash-crop economies
   4   seek their living from the seas

4   A surplus of food led to more complex societies because more individuals were
1   needed for hunting and gathering operations
2   free to trade or develop craft specialties
3   eliminated from economic competition
4   accepted into clans

5   "If the Nile smiles, the Earth is joyous,
Every stomach is full of rejoicing,
Every spine is happy,
Every jawbone crushes its food."

– ancient Egyptian hymn

The Nile's "smile" provided early civilization in Egypt with
1   shelter from violent storms
2   technology to build the pyramids
3   annual flooding for crop irrigation and soil renewal
4   protection from barbarian invasion

6   A major reason for the decline of the Roman Empire was
1   a series of military defeats in Africa
2   political corruption and the instability of the government
3   the abolition of slavery throughout the Empire
4   continued acceptance of traditional religions

7   The teachings of Confucius encouraged people to
1   set their own personal priorities
2   reject government authority
3   believe in reincarnation
4   follow a code of moral conduct

8   Which activity occurred during the Golden Age of Muslim Culture?
1   destruction of books containing Greek and Roman ideas
2   beginning of pilgrimages to Mecca
3   opposition to freedom of thought and to foreign ideas by rulers
4   major discoveries in mathematics and science

9   "The baron and all vassals of the king are bound to appear before him when he shall summon them, and to serve him at their own expense for forty days and forty nights, with as many knights as each one owes." – *Legal Rules for Military Service* (1072)
This quotation best characterizes the
1   strictness of feudal relationships
2   separation between church and state
3   power of wealth in the commercial Revolution
4   importance of codified laws in society

10 After the fall of Rome, the eastern portion of the Roman Empire
remained intact, eventually becoming known as the
1   Mongol Empire
2   Persian Empire
3   Byzantine Empire
4   Gupta Empire

11 The Protestant Reformation and the European Renaissance were
similar in that both
1   discouraged the growth of strong monarchs
2   encouraged people to question tradition
3   were led by the military
4   supported the return of the Roman Empire

**Base your answer to
question 12 on the
time line at the right
and your knowledge
of global history and
geography.**

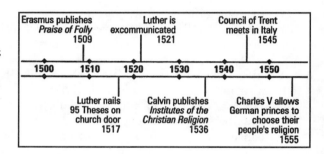

12 Which period of European history is represented by this time line?
1   Enlightenment
2   Middle Ages
3   Reformation
4   Industrial Revolution

13 A characteristic of both European and Japanese feudalism was
1   a decentralized government
2   the adoption of Christianity
3   an open democratic society
4   the many opportunities for social mobility

14 One factor that enabled the Renaissance to flourish in Northern
Italy was that the region had
1   a wealthy class that invested in the arts
2   a socialist form of government
3   limited contact with the Byzantine Empire
4   a shrinking middle class

NO PERMISSION HAS BEEN GRANTED BY N&N PUBLISHING COMPANY, INC TO REPRODUCE ANY PART OF THIS BOOK BY ANY MECHANICAL, PHOTOGRAPHIC, OR ELECTRONIC PROCESS.

Base your answer to question 15 on the map at the right and your knowledge of global history and geography.

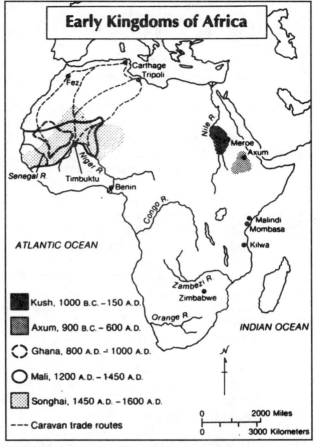

Early Kingdoms of Africa

Carthage
Tripoli
Fez
Nile R
Meroe
Axum
Senegal R.   Niger R   Timbuktu   Benin
Congo R.
ATLANTIC OCEAN
Malindi
Mombasa
Kilwa
Zambezi R.
Zimbabwe
Orange R.
INDIAN OCEAN

■ Kush, 1000 B.C. – 150 A.D.

▨ Axum, 900 B.C. – 600 A.D.

◌ Ghana, 800 A.D. – 1000 A.D.

◯ Mali, 1200 A.D. – 1450 A.D.

▨ Songhai, 1450 A.D. – 1600 A.D.

--- Caravan trade routes

N

0   2000 Miles
0   3000 Kilometers

15   Which conclusion regarding early African trade is supported by the information provided by this map?
   1   The kingdom of Zimbabwe grew rich from trade with Egypt
   2   The kingdoms of western Africa traded with the city states of eastern Africa
   3   The Congo and Zambezi Rivers played an important role in Africa's early trade.
   4   The West African kingdoms had trading contacts with the cities of the Mediterranean.

16   "God hath the power to create or destroy, make or unmake, at his pleasure; to give life or send death; to judge … and to be judged [by] none… And so do kings …"
   Which idea does the quote express?
   1   absolutism   3   socialism
   2   fundamentalism   4   nationalism

17 Spain's colonial policy of mercantilism affected the development of Latin American nations by promoting
1   the production of raw materials and cash crops
2   free and rapid trade with Asia and Africa
3   respect for the rights of indigenous people
4   isolationism as a response to international political issues

18 The *Magna Carta* and the *English Bill of Rights* are documents that
1   established England as an independent state
2   intensified the conflict between church and state
3   limited the power of the monarch
4   decreased the wealth of the nobles

19 A study of the Mayas, Aztecs, and Incas would show that these ancient American civilizations
1   produced few cultural achievements
2   lived at peace with their neighbors
3   adapted the new technology brought by European explorers
4   rivaled the accomplishments of early Middle Eastern cultures

20 Which result of the "Colombian Exchange" shows that cultural diffusion can have negative effects?
1   Europeans introduced horses and new farming techniques to Native Americans.
2   Native American crops changed the European diet.
3   Diseases native to Europe spread throughout the Americas.
4   Spanish priests spread Catholic religion and education throughout Latin America.

21 The rise of Ottoman power in the 15th century led to the
1   revitalizing of Byzantine culture
2   disrupting of trade between Central Asia and Western Europe
3   strengthening of local lords under the feudal system in Western Europe
4   decreasing of tribute from Southeast Asian kingdoms by China's Ming Emperors

22 **"Cavour Provokes War Against Austria"**
"Mazzini Establishes Young Italy Movement"
"Poles Fail in Revolt Against Russia"
These headlines best reflect the concept of
1   nationalism
2   isolationism
3   imperialism
4   totalitarianism

23 Which statement best describes an effect of geography on the development of Southeast Asia?
1 The proximity of China promotes the growth of democracy.
2 Large deposits of coal and diamonds attract Russian settlers.
3 Vast areas of desert prevent exploration.
4 The location of strategic waterways encourages trade.

Base your answer to questions 24 and 25 on the speakers' statements below and your knowledge of global history and geography.

Speaker A: I am offended by the term "Dark Continent." It implies that only ignorance and barbarism were here before European explorers and settlers invaded the continent, bringing their "enlightened" ways.

Speaker B: This hemisphere might have been a "New World" to Europeans, but it certainly was not a "New World" to the Incas, Aztecs, and other Indian Nations whose worlds were destroyed by the brutal greed of the Europeans.

Speaker C: Defeat at Dienbienphu resulted in French withdrawal from the region. I was glad to see them go. The French exploited our land, resources, and people. And now, American involvement in the region frustrates our nationalist ambitions. It will lead to more military conflict.

Speaker D: Upon arrival, we found a primitive people living in a primitive land. We built roads and bridges, sanitation systems, schools, and hospitals. We helped eliminate starvation and poverty. I feel no guilt about our past and continued presence in the region.

24 The statements of all four speakers relate to
1 socialism
2 isolationism
3 imperialism
4 feudalism

25 The statement by *Speaker A* could best be used to support the idea that
1 geographers have often disagreed on terminology
2 terminology and labeling can often lead to misconceptions and stereotyping
3 the colonial experience was welcomed by most native peoples
4 African economies are based on subsistence

26 Karl Marx and Friedrich Engels developed a theory that economic con-
    ditions would significantly improve for the working class only when
    1   governments accepted the capitalist system
    2   workers negotiated with the capitalists
    3   the bourgeoisie became the ruling class
    4   workers controlled the means of production

27 Many of the ideas of Locke, Montesquieu, and Rousseau were associ-
    ated with
    1   political reforms that ended the absolute monarchy in France
    2   the establishment of colonial empires by strong European nations
    3   the beginnings of the Spanish Inquisition
    4   British legislation that improved working conditions in factories

28 The Russian Revolution and the French Revolution both resulted in
    1   violent political change
    2   the restoration of old monarchies
    3   the establishment of direct democracies
    4   increases in the power of the Catholic Church

29 Mohandas Gandhi and Kemal Ataturk are similar because both men
    1   used violence as a weapon in the fight for independence
    2   were unwilling to accept the advances of western technology
    3   struggled to free their countries from foreign influences
    4   supported the concept of "divide and conquer"

30 Russian peasants supported the Bolsheviks in 1917 primarily
    because the Bolsheviks pledged to
    1   establish and maintain collective farms
    2   redistribute land and make peace
    3   lower key crop yields and exports
    4   limit the income of the nobility and clergy

31 One action taken by both V. I. Lenin and Josef Stalin was
    1   providing economic aid to Japan after World War I and World War II
    2   attempting to bring democracy to Russia
    3   jailing or murdering potential opponents
    4   supporting the Russian Orthodox Church

32 Which is one major reason the Holocaust is considered a unique
    event in modern European history?
    1   Jews of Europe have seldom been victims of persecution.
    2   Civilians rarely were killed during air-raids on Great Britain.
    3   Adolf Hitler concealed his anti-Jewish feelings until after he
         came to power.
    4   The genocide was planned in great detail and required the coop-
         eration of many people.

33 In the 1930s and 1940s, fascist regimes in Japan, Germany, and Italy were similar in that each emphasized
1   empathy toward African nations
2   support for free expression of ideas
3   the protection of human rights
4   imperialism as a foreign policy

34 The European Union, NAFTA, and OPEC were formed to
1   influence the course of global trade
2   increase the price of raw materials
3   remove trade barriers between nations
4   promote political union of members

Base your answer to question 35 on the cartoon at the right and your knowledge of global history and geography.

35 Which of the following offers the best title for the cartoon at the right?
1   U.N. Peacekeepers Enforce the *Declaration of Human Rights*
2   Army Assures Victory for the Solidarity Movement
3   Celebrating the Results of the Nuremburg Trials
4   Dealing With Dissent, Tiananmen Style

36 The United Nations, like its League of Nations predecessor, has been most successful in
1   solving disputes among the major powers
2   alleviating economic and social problems
3   bringing lasting peace to the Middle East
4   decreasing military preparedness

37 Major problems faced by some of the Pacific Rim countries in the late 1990s included
1   labor shortages and poor work ethics
2   command economies and collective farms
3   high debts and government corruption
4   loss of all foreign investment and World Bank loans

Base your answer to question 38 on the graph below and your knowledge of global history and geography.

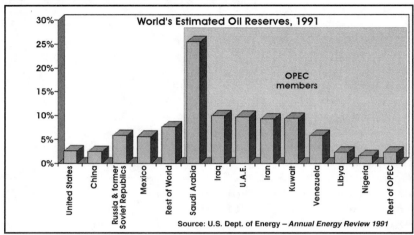

38 Based on the information on the graph above, which is an accurate conclusion?
1   Only countries in the Middle East produce oil.
2   The United States has more oil reserves than Kuwait.
3   Russian production of oil has increased since the end of communism.
4   OPEC countries have most of the world's oil reserves.

39 Which factor has most limited the development of national unity in India, Lebanon, and Bosnia-Herzegovina?
1   religious and ethnic differences
2   inability to end colonialism
3   rapid growth of industry
4   lack of natural resources

40 In the 1990s, a group of people negatively affected by the changing economic scene in Russia are those
1   employed in private industry
2   living on pensions or fixed incomes
3   between the ages of 20 and 35
4   who own factories and banks

41 Juan Peron and his wife Evita were able to rise to power in part because of the support of the
1   Roman Catholic Church
2   large landowners
3   middle class industrialists
4   poor workers or "shirtless ones"

Base your answer to question 42 on the chart at the right and your knowledge of global history and geography.

JAPAN'S BALANCE OF TRADE (IN BILLIONS OF DOLLARS)			
Year	Imports	Exports	Balance
1978	79.3	97.5	+18.2
1980	140.5	129.9	-10.6
1982	139.0	132.0	-7.0
1984	136.5	170.1	+33.6
1986	126.4	209.2	+82.8
1988	187.4	264.9	+77.5
1990	234.8	286.9	+52.1
1991	236.7	314.5	+77.8
1993	240.6	360.9	+120.3

42 Which statement best reflects the information provided by the chart?
1 Since 1984, Japan has had a favorable balance of trade.
2 Japan is the world's leading exporter.
3 In 1986, Japan had a trade imbalance that led to a recession.
4 In 1978, Japan imported more than it exported.

43 Which statement best describes an impact of topography on Eastern Europe?
1 Many different languages, religions, and customs developed.
2 A Russian tsar ruled the area as a single empire.
3 An extensive single crop agricultural system emerged.
4 Neighbors who were more powerful could not invade the region.

44 An immediate result of the Cultural Revolution in China was that it
1 helped to establish democracy in urban centers
2 led to economic cooperation with Japan and South Korea
3 disrupted China's economic and educational systems
4 strengthened political ties with the United States

45 Today, human rights violations most often occur in nations in which
1 freedom of the press exists
2 government is limited by law
3 leaders have absolute control
4 government has a multiparty system

46 As economically developing nations become more industrialized, which situation occurs most often?
1 The authority of religious leaders increases.
2 The traditional roles and values of women change.
3 The size of families increases.
4 The cost of medical care decreases.

Base your answer to question 47 on the chart at the right and your knowledge of global history and geography.

TOTAL VALUE OF WORLD EXPORTS (IN BILLIONS OF DOLLARS)	
Year	Exports
1965	186
1970	312
1980	1,393
1985	2,456

47 Which statement about the level of world exports between 1965 and 1985 is best supported by the chart?
1 Overall levels of manufacturing decreased.
2 The world inflation rate decreased.
3 Economic interdependence increased.
4 National self-sufficiency increased.

Base your answer to question 48 on the quotation below and your knowledge of global history and geography.

"In our time, in particular, there exists another form of ownership which is becoming no less important than land: the possession of know-how, technology, and skill. ...
Many people, perhaps the majority today, do not have the means which would enable them to take their place in an effective and humanly dignified way within a productive system in which work is truly central."

– Pope John Paul II, May 1991

48 What is the main idea of this passage?
1 Those who control vast stretches of territory are assured an important role in society.
2 Arable land ensures that a society will be productive.
3 As technology increases, the need for an educated labor force decreases.
4 Education and technical knowledge are needed to succeed in an industrial world.

49 José de San Martín, Jomo Kenyatta, and David Ben-Gurion all shared the common goal of
1 freeing their nations from foreign domination
2 establishing an absolute monarchy in their nations
3 establishing societies based on the ideas of Karl Marx
4 preventing the introduction of new technology in their nations

50 Which heading for the outline below would fit most appropriately in the blank space?

I. _____

    A. Stalin's Five-Year Plans
    B. Khruschev's incentive plan
    C. Gorbachev's perestroika

1 Defense Policies in Ukraine
2 Nationalism in the Soviet Union
3 Political Reform for the Baltic Republics
4 Economic Changes in the Soviet Union

PART II (45 pts.)

THEMATIC ESSAY: (15 pts.)

Directions: Write a well-organized essay that includes an introduction, several paragraphs explaining your position, and a conclusion.

Theme: Impact of Individuals

Certain individuals have had a major impact on history.

Task:

Select *three* individuals [Do *not* use an individual in United States history in your answer.] and for *each* one selected:
- Identify a nation or region associated with the individual. [Do *not* use the United States in your answer.]
- Describe *one* major event this individual influenced.
- Explain how this individual has had a significant impact on the history of this nation or region.

You may use any examples from your study of global history and geography. Some suggestions you might wish to consider include: Elizabeth I, Catherine the Great, Vladimir Lenin, Mohandas Gandhi, Fidel Castro, Nelson Mandela, Yasir Arafat.

You are *not* limited to these suggestions.

DOCUMENT BASED QUESTION: (30 PTS.)

The following task is based on the accompanying documents. The documents may have been edited for the purposes of this exercise. The task is designed to test your ability to work with historical documents. As you analyze the documents, take into account both the source of the document and the author's point of view.

Directions: Read the documents in Part A and answer the question after each document. Then read the directions for Part B and write your essay.

Historical Context: Geography and imperialism were intertwined during the 19th and 20th centuries. The documents below present information on this relationship.

Task:
> Using the information from the documents and your knowledge of global history and geography, write an essay in which you evaluate the role geography played in the development of 19th and 20th century imperialism.

Part A – Short Answer [15 pts.]

Directions: Analyze the documents and answer the questions that follow each document in the space provided.

Document 1

> "Upon the maintenance of free communication in the Mediterranean depends ... Great Britain's ... support of her influence in the Levant ... the air route to India and the Kirkuk [oil] pipelines. Great Britain has always regarded the protection of the Suez Canal as a paramount duty. ... Egypt is a focal point."
> – Royal Institute of International Affairs, *The Colonial Problem*, 1937

1   Why was Egypt important to Great Britain?

_____

_____

_____

_____

Document 2

> "During the nineteenth century, Europe at last breached [broke down] the geographical limits of its influence during the previous centuries. ...To some extent this was the result of deliberate choice, but far more of technical factors – the relative inefficiency of sailing ships for long-distance bulk carriage, the small marginal advantage provided by European armaments, problems of health in tropical climates, and so on. During the early nineteenth century, these obstacles to European expansion were removed by economic, technical and political developments within Europe."
>
> – D. K. Fieldhouse, *Economics and Empire*, 1830-1914

2   What changes were necessary for Europeans to expand into previously unclaimed areas in the 19th century?

_____

_____

_____

_____

Document 3

3   Why was Russia desirous of controlling the Straits of the Dardanelles and Bosporus?

_____

_____

_____

_____

Document 4

"The United States of America reach from ocean to ocean, and our Territory of Oregon and State of California lie directly opposite to the dominions of your imperial majesty [Emperor of Japan]. Our steamships can go from California to Japan in eighteen days, [but need to refuel before going on to China] …

"Great numbers of our people pursue the whale fishery near the shores of Japan. It sometimes happens, in stormy weather, that one of our ships is wrecked on your … shores. In all such cases we ask, and expect, that our unfortunate people should be treated with kindness, and that their property should be protected, till we can send a vessel and bring them away."

– U.S. President Millard Fillmore to the Emperor of Japan, 1853

4   Why did U.S. President Fillmore send Commodore Matthew C. Perry to open Japan in 1853?

_____

_____

_____

_____

Document 5

IMPERIALISM – CIRCA 1900			
Colonial Power	Number of Colonies	Mother Country Population	Population of Colonies
United Kingdom	50	40,559,954	345,222,239
France	33	38,517,975	56,401,860
Netherlands	3	5,074,632	35,115,711

5   What does this chart say about the possible market for the Mother Country's products in the colonies?

_____

_____

_____

_____

Document 6

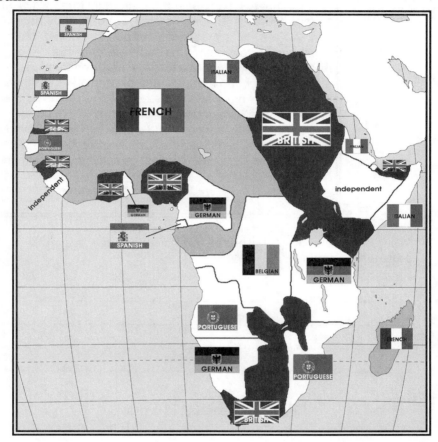

6   Why were the British and Cecil Rhodes angered by German acquisition of German East Africa?

_____

_____

_____

_____

Document 7

> "We have already said there are only three ways left to Japan to escape from the pressure of surplus population. We are like a great crowd of people packed into a small and narrow room, and there are only three doors through which we might escape, namely emigration, advance into world markets, and expansion of territory. The first door, emigration, has been barred to us by the anti-Japanese immigration policies of other countries. The second door, advance into world markets, is being pushed shut by tariff barriers. ... It is quite natural that Japan should rush upon the last remaining door [expansion of territory]."
>
> – *Sources of the Japanese Tradition*, 1931, compiled by Ryusaku Tsunoda, a Japanese government official

7   What reasons does the author of this document give to justify Japanese expansion?

_____

_____

_____

_____

Part *B* – Essay [15 pts.]

Directions:
- Write a well organized essay that includes an introduction, several paragraphs, and a conclusion.
- Use evidence from the documents to support your response.
- Do not simply repeat the contents of the documents.
- Include specific related outside information.

Historical Context:
Geography and imperialism were intertwined during the 19th and 20th centuries.

Task:
Using the information from the documents and your knowledge of global history and geography, write an essay in which you evaluate the role geography played in the development of 19th and 20th century imperialism.

Be sure to include specific historical details. You must also include additional information from your knowledge of global history and geography.

Abbasid Dynasty (8th C. Shi'ite revolt set up separate Muslim region in Persia), 88 [map], 89, 93, 105

abbot (superior of a monastery), 87, 93

abdication (giving up power or responsibility), 171

absolutism (political theory holding that all power should be vested in one ruler or other authority), 69, 70, 110, 135, 136-138, 139, 140, 150, 151

Abu Bakr (r. 632-34; father-in-law of Muhammad; 1st Caliph, religious leader of Muslims), 88, 89

Ancien Régime (see Old Regime)

acid rain (airborne pollutants precipitating far from their source), 30

Acquired Immunodeficiency Syndrome (see AIDS)

Act of Supremacy (Parliament agreed to Henry VIII's desire to make Anglicanism official religion of England, 1534), see Protestant Reformation on 119

Adriatic Sea (S.E. Europe between Italy and Balkan Peninsula), 33, 34

Aegean Sea (S.E. Europe between Greece and Turkey), 33, 34

Afghanistan (arid, mountainous, landlocked country of southwest-central Asia), 200, 201, 223-224

Africa (second-largest continent, lying south of Europe between the Atlantic and Indian Oceans), 44-46, 106-108, 129, 130, 159

African Kingdoms (Ghana, Mali, Songhai; ancient states had high cultural and economic development), 106-108

African National Congress (ANC; South African political party; sought civil rights under apartheid), 196

African slaves (imported by Spanish and Portuguese for Latin American plantations), 130, 131

Afrikaner (South African people of Dutch or French Huguenot descent, formerly also known as Boers [make up about 56 percent of South Africa's white population]; their Afrikaans language is,a derivative of Dutch), 196

Age of Augustus (golden age of ancient Rome [27 BC-14 AD), 70, 72

Age of Discovery (period of global exploration and colonization by Europeans in 15th-16th C.), 128-131

Age of Enlightenment (18th C. also called Age of Reason or Intellectual Revolution; European era of scientific and philosophical development), 148, 149, 150, 153

Age of Exploration (see Age of Discovery, 15th-17th centuries)

Age of Pericles (golden age of ancient Athens, 461-429 BC), 72

Age of Reason (see Age of Enlightenment)

agora (place of congregation, especially an ancient Greek marketplace), 64

Age of Revolutions (18th-20th centuries; centered on sweeping political, social, intellectual and economic changes especially in Western Europe); 148, 161

aggression (act of initiating hostilities or invasion), 176, 177 [chart], 205

agrarian (farm-based economy and lifestyle; see Agrarian Revolution)

Agrarian or Agricultural Revolution (18th century Britain, a revolution in land use and improving technology, dramatically increased agricultural production), 148, 155-156

AIDS (epidemic of Acquired Immunodeficiency Syndrome from retro virus HIV), 221

Akbar the Great (Mughal ruler of India [1542-1605] began golden age), 106, 136, 137

Albania (poor country of southeast Europe on the Adriatic Sea; became a republic in 1925; satellite of the U.S.S.R. in 1944; leaders broke with the Soviets and developed close economic ties with China [1961-1976]), 205

Albuquerque, Alfonso de (1453-1515; explorer; founded the Portuguese empire in the Indian Ocean; viceroy), 128

Alexander the Great (c. 324-27 BC, Hellenistic conqueror & unifier of ancient Middle East), 48, 64, 65, 71

Alemanni (group of Germanic tribes that settled in Alsace around the 4th century AD), 85

Ali (600-661; Ali ibn Abi Talib, 4th caliph of the Muslim community; regarded by Shi'ite Muslims as the only legitimate successor of the Prophet Muhammad; husband of the Prophet's daughter Fatima), 89

Alighieri, Dante (Italian Renaissance writer: *Divine Comedy*), 117 [chart]

All-India Muslim League (1906 Bengali movement sought independence for Muslims in British India), 155

Allah (Islamic name for God), 88

allegiance (loyalty or the obligation of loyalty, as to a nation, sovereign, or cause), 113

Allies (Allied Powers; in WWI, Britain, France, Russia, and later Italy and the U.S. - opponents of the Central Powers; in WWII, mainly Britain, France, Russia, and later, the U.S. and China - opponents of the Axis Powers), 169, 172 [map]

allocate (divide up), 96

alluvial or alluviums (sediment deposited by flowing water, as in a riverbed, flood plain, or delta), 48

allocate (divide up), 96

Almieda, Francisco de (1450-1510; first viceroy of Portuguese India), 128

Alps (mt. range in Central Europe), 10, 33, 34

Amazon River (massive basin in the N. center of South America), 38, 39, 40, 133, 154, 222

American Revolution (1776-1783; war between Great Britain and its mid-Atlantic American colonies; led to the formation of the independent U. S.), 148, 154

Amerindian (also Native Americans of any of the aboriginal people of the Western Hemisphere), 132, 133

Amur River (major waterway of northeast Asia; 1,800 mi. border between China and the Russia), 36, 37

Analects (Confucius' guide to correct behavior), 74

Andes Mountains (major north-south cordillera of South America), 38, 39, 133

angiostatin (drugs with the potential of blocking the growth of caner in blood vessels), 222

Anglican Church (Church of England set up as result of *Act of Supremacy* under Henry VIII), 110, 118, 119

Angola (country of S.W. Africa bordering on the Atlantic Ocean; Portuguese colony; slave trade center), 108

Anglo-Saxons (European nomadic group; conquered Britain in 5th century, AD), 69, 85

Anschluss (1938, Hitler's term for German-Austrian union), 177

antibiotic (substance, such as penicillin or streptomycin, produced by or derived from fungi, bacteria, and other organisms; can destroy or inhibit the growth of other microorganisms), 221

An'yang (walled capital of Shang Dynasty in east-central China on Huang He), 62

Apartheid (official policy of racial segregation practiced in the Republic of South Africa, involving political, legal, and economic discrimination against nonwhites), 46, 188, 196

appeasement (acquiescing to aggressors to avoid war), 176, 177

Apennines (mt. range in S.W. Europe running down the Italian Peninsula),33, 34, 67

apprentice (beginner learning a trade or occupation, especially as a member of a guild), 113

aqueduct (pipe or channel designed to transport water from a remote source, usually by gravity), 69, 128

Arab (member of a Semitic people inhabiting Arabia, whose language [Arabic] and Islamic religion spread widely throughout the Middle East and northern Africa from the seventh century), 48, 72, 88, 97, 106, 117, 174, 197, 198

Arab Oil Embargo (1973; sparked by the October Arab-Israeli War; prices tripled in a few short months and created widespread panic in world oil markets), 215

Arabian Sea (northwest part of the Indian Ocean between Arabia and western India), 47

Arafat, Yasir (Chief spokesman & negotiator of Palestine Liberation Organization), 198

Aral Sea (inland sea of Central Asia, east of the Caspian Sea; environmentally impacted by Soviet water diversion projects in Siberia), 36

Aramaic (Semitic language widely used throughout southwest Asia from the 7th century BC to the 7th century AD), 62

archbishop (bishop of the highest rank, heading an archdiocese or a province), 93

archipelago (island chain: peaks of undersea mt. ranges), 114

Archimedes (384-322 BC; Greek mathematician, engineer, and physicist; discovered formulas for the area and volume of various geometric figures, applied geometry to hydrostatics and mechanics; discovered the principle of buoyancy), 72

Arctic (northern polar region and ocean), 37, 133

Argentina (nation of southern South America), 40, 203

aristocracy (gov't. by a small, often rich, privileged class, nobility), 66

Aristotle (Greek philosopher, 384-322 BC), 72

Aristophanes (ancient Greek dramatist, d. 380), 72

Arkwright, Richard (1732-1792, British inventor - water frame), 157

armada (formidable naval force; see Spanish Armada)

Armenia (region and former kingdom of Asia Minor in present-day northeast Turkey, southeast European Russia, and northwest Iran), 37, 38, 172

artisans (craftsmen), 87

Aryans (c. 1500-500 BC, early conquerors of India), 48, 61

Ashley Report (1842, mine safety in British Industrial Revolution), 35

Asia Minor (peninsula of western Asia between the Black Sea and the Mediterranean Sea; also Anatolia, Turkey), 71, 90

Asian Tigers (also known as the "Little Dragons" - economic powers of Hong Kong [now a province of China], South Korea, Singapore, and Taiwan), 193

Asoka (r. 272-232 BC, Mauryan ruler of India), 72

assimilation (beingabsorbed into a new culture), 106

assembly (group of persons gathered together for a common reason, as for a legislative, religious, educational, or social purpose; in Rome, the house representing plebeians), 68

Assyrians (warrior people of northern Mesopotamia who spoke the same Semitic language as their Babylonian neighbors to the south; established an empire that became the dominant power in the Middle East during the 8th and 7th centuries BC), 61, 62, 63

Aswan High Dam (Egypt controversial project on Nile River under Nasser), 43, 199

Ataturk, Kemal (1881-1938; established the Republic of Turkey in 1923), 155, 175

Athens (pre-eminent poleis, center of ancient Greek democracy and culture), 33, 66, 72

Atlantic Ocean (one of the five great bodies of water on Earth; N-S between Europe/Africa and N/S America), 33, 34, 38, 39, 44, 45, 133

Atlantic Charter (14 August 1941, Allies' WWII aims became basis for U.N. Charter of 1945), 177

Atlas Mountains (North Africa), 44, 45

atomic bomb (August 1945, dropped by U.S. on Japan), 176, 190

Attica (eastern peninsula of Greece; Athens),

Attila (406-453; king of the Huns [r. 433-453] and the most successful of the barbarian invaders of the Roman Empire), 86

Attlee, Clement (British Prime Minister, 1945-1951; unseated Churchill at end of WWII), 178

Augustus (c. 27 BC, 1st Roman Emperor), 70, 72

Austro-Hungarian Empire (dual monarchy of central Europe consisting of Austria, Hungary, Bohemia, and parts of Poland, Romania, Yugoslavia, and Italy; formed in 1867 and lasted until 1918), 36, 151, 153, 153, 155, 168, 169, 170 [map]

Austro-Prussian War (1866, also Seven Weeks' War [June-August]; Prussia and Italy defeated Austria and several of the smaller German states; Prussia became the preeminent German state annexing several north German states), 155

Austro-Sardinian War (1849; unsuccessful effort to secure Italian independence; led to Sardinia merging into the new Kingdom of Italy in 1861), 155

autobahns (high speed German highways), 175

autonomy, autonomous (independence, home or self-rule), 73, 205

autocratic (government by a single person having unlimited power), 38, 83

Avars (slavic group settled in E. Europe and the Balkans after the 4th C. AD), 85, 92

Axis (*Tripartite Pact*, 1939 alliance of Italy, Germany, and Japan), 176

Axum (early Ethiopian empire - 1st-12th

centuries;also known as Aksum), 108

AZT (drug useful in combating AIDS), 221

Aztec Empire (1300-1535 AD; Central Mexico), 130

Babylonians (ancient Amorite civilization of southern Mesopotamia, dominated region c. 1900-1000 BC), 61, 62, 63

Babur (Zahir ud-Din Mohammed [1483-1530]; Mongol conqueror of India; periodic raids into India [1519-1524]; founded the Mogul dynasty), 106

Baghdad (ancient center of civilization in Iraq, capital of Abbasid Dynasty and Hulegu Khanate), 89, 93, 106

Bakewell, Robert (1725-1795, agrarian innovator, scientific breeding), 155

Baikal, Lake (southeast Siberian Russia; largest freshwater lake in Eurasia and the world's deepest lake), 36

Balboa, Vasco Núñez de (1475-1517; Spanish explorer and colonial governor who discovered [1513] the Pacific Ocean and claimed it for Spain), 128, 131

Balkans (mountainous peninsula in S.E. Europe; Yugoslavia and group of small countries often torn by nationalist /ethnic strife), 37

Baltic Sea (N.E. Europe), 33, 34, 37, 114

Bangladesh (country of southern Asia on the Bay of Bengal; formerly E. Pakistan; declared independent after 1971; civil war with W. Pakistan), 47, 218

banking houses (business establishment in which money is kept for saving or commercial purposes or is invested, supplied for loans, or exchanged), 114

Barak, Ehud (1942- , moderate, military hero, Labor Party leader, elected prime minister of Israel 1999), 198

barbarian (people considered by those of another nation or group to have a primitive civilization; fierce, brutal nomadic peoples involved in several waves of invasion of Western Europe between 350 and 1000 AD), 69, 72, 84, 85, 86, 90

barrios [los] (Latin American urban slums), 40, 203, 216

barter / barter economy (direct exchange of goods and services of equal value without use of money), 96

Basra (Persian Gulf city founded 636; important center of letters, science, poetry, finance, and commerce under the early Abbasids), 89

Bastille (fortress and prison in Paris; symbol of royal absolutism before the French Revolution; stormed by revolutionary mob on 14 July 1789), 151

Batista, Fulgencio (1901-1973, Cuban dictator deposed by Castro in 1958), 203, 204

bay (body of water partially enclosed by land but with a wide mouth, affording access to the sea), 31

Bay of Bengal (body of water off S.E. coast of India), 47

Bay of Pigs Invasion (1961, exiled Cubans with U.S. aid tried to overthrow Castro in Cuba), 204

Bayeux Tapestry (11th C., 230 foot long linen and wool embroidery depicting Norman conquest of England by William the Conqueror), 125

Begin, Menachem (Israeli Prime Minister, signed*Camp David Accords*, 1977), 198

Beijing (capital of China from Yuan Dynasty, 13th C.), 106, 138

Belgium (country of N.W. Europe on the North Sea), 46

Belisarius (505-565; Byzantine general under Emperor Justinian I; led campaigns against the barbarians in North Africa and Italy), 85

Benin (13th C. African kingdom), 108

benevolent neglect (gov't. policy of ignoring small violations of mercantilist regulations as long as reasonable revenue was realized), 131

Berlin Blockade (1948, Soviets cut off West Berlin), 189

Berlin Airlift (Allied attempt to supply German city cut off by Soviets in 1948), 189

Berlin Conference (1884-1885; also Congress of Berlin; settled the Russo-Turkish War and partially worked out African territorial claims by Europeans, triggering the imperialists' "scramble for Africa"), 159

Berlin Wall (built by Soviets in 1960s to deter escapes from communist zone of the city; dismantled in pro-democracy incident in 1990), 25, 201, 202

Bhagavad Gita (poem from Mahabharata, most widely studied sacred writings of Hinduism), 73

Biafra (breakaway province of Nigeria, civil war 1967-1970), 195

Bible (sacred scriptures of Judeo-Christian religions), 74-75, 119

bicameral (two house legislature), 110, 188

"Big Lie" (intentional distortion of the truth, especially for political or official purposes), 175

Bill of Rights (English, 1689; limited power of monarchs), 139

bin Laden, Osama (Saudi-born millionaire, sponsor of jihad against the U.S.; financier of multinational network of Islamic fundamentalist terrorist operations), 223

bishop (high-ranking Christian cleric, in modern churches usually in charge of a diocese), 74, 85, 87, 93

Bismarck, Otto von (1815-1898; "Iron Chancellor;" creator and first chancellor of the German Empire [1871-1890]; instrumental in Prussian victory over Austria [1866] and the creation of the

North German Confederation [1867]), 155, 159

Black Death (bubonic plague, wiped out nearly one-third of Europe's population in late Middle Ages), 109, 116, 119

Black Friday (stock market crash in October 1929 - harbinger of the Great Depression), 173

Black Sea (inland sea between Europe and Asia connected with the Aegean Sea by the Bosporus and the Dardanelles), 36, 37, 116

Blackshirts (1920s-1940s; Italian fascist paramilitary group), 172

blitzkrieg ("lightning war"; swift, military offensive, usually by combined air and mobile land forces; tactic used by Nazis), 176

Boer War (1899-1902, British v. Boers of Transvaal and Orange Free State), 46, 196

Boers (18th and 19th century Dutch settlers of South Africa), 196

Bolívar, Simón (1783-1830; Creole leader of So. American independence movement; founder of Gran Colombia), 39, 154

Bolshevik Revolution (November 1917 phase of Russian revolution led by Lenin), 171

Bolsheviks (left-wing majority group of the Russian Social Democratic Workers' Party that adopted Lenin's theses and seized power in November 1917), 171

Bonaparte, Napoleon (see Napoleon)

Bosnia and Hercegovina (west central Balkan nation broke from Yugoslavia 1991), 37, 169, 202, 205

Bosporus (w/ Dardanelles, straits between the Aegean and Black Seas near Constantinople [Istanbul]; crossing point for invasions between Europe and Asia) 34, 41, 42, 155

Bourbon Dynasty (French royal family descended from Louis I, Duke of Bourbon, 1270-1342; ruled in France [1589-1793 and 1814-1830], Spain, and Naples and Sicily), 110

bourgeoisie (member of the French mercantile class of a medieval European city, see also burgher [German] and burgesses [England]), 21, 129, 135, 150

Boxer Rebellion/Uprising (1899-1900; organized, armed attacks on Chinese Christians and foreigners), 160

boycott (economic sanction: customers refuse to purchase goods or services), 174, 195

Brahman Nerugna (Hindu Deity, the creator), 30, 55, 73 [chart]

Bramaputra (river of southern Asian river flows 1,800 mi. s.w. from the Himalaya Mountains through northeast India; joins Ganges River to form a vast delta in central Bangladesh), 47

Brahmins (Hindu priests), 73, 94

Brazil (largest nation in South America; Portuguese colony and culture), 40-41, 129, 154, 170

Brezhnev Doctrine (Soviet pledge to intervene in any nation whose actions endangered communism), 201

Brezhnev, Leonid (1906-1982; Soviet leader [1965-1983]), 200, 201

Britain (see, Great Britain or England)

British East India Co. (trading company financed through stock sales; became base for British imperialism in India), 114

bubonic plague (contagious, often fatal epidemic disease caused by bacterium [Yersinia pestis] transmitted from person to person or by the bite of fleas from an infected host), 109, 116

Buddhism (major religion of eastern & central Asia, 6th C. BC), 18, 48, 51, 72, 73, 83, 91, 97, 104, 105, 106, 114, 115

Buddha (6th C. BC, India, Siddhartha [Siddarta] Gautama, founder of Buddhism), 72

bureaucracy (a core of administrators, clerks, and officials that carry out the laws, policies, programs of a gov't.), 69, 83, 93, 104, 109, 137, 138

burgesses (members of the English medieval mercantile class see also bourgeoisie [French] and burgher [German]), 129, 135

burgher (member of the German mercantile class of medieval city, see also bourgeoisie [French] and burgess [England]), 129, 135

Burma (country of southeast Asia on the Bay of Bengal and the Andaman Sea; ancient kingdom; also a province of British India from 1886 until 1948; contemporary nation is called Myanmar), 106

bushido (traditional code of the Japanese samurai, stressing honor, self-discipline, bravery, and simple living), 115

Byzantine Empire (East. Roman Empire 4th-15th C. AD; also style of architecture developed from the 5th century AD characterized by a central dome resting on a cube formed by four round arches), 82, 83, 84, 85, 86, 88, 90, 91, 92, 96, 97, 107, 117

Cabot, John (1451-1498; explorer, English claims to Canada) , 128

Cabral, Pedro, (1467-1520; explorer who discovered Brazil [1500] and claimed it for Portugal), 129

Caesar Augustus (Octavian; c. 27 BC, first Roman Emperor), 72

Caesar, Julius (100-44 BC; Roman general, statesman, and historian who subdued Gaul, invaded Britain and Egypt; given a mandate to rule as dictator for life [45BC]), 70

Cairo (capital and largest city of Egypt, in the northeast on the Nile River; built c.

642 as a military camp [Fustat] by the Fatimid dynasty), 111

caliph (also calif or khalifa; title for successor to Muhammad as leader of Islam), 18, 88, 89

calligraphy (artful writing), 62

Calvin, John (1509-1531, Swiss theologian, Eur. Protestant Reformation, *Institutes of the Christian Religion*), 118, 119

Cambodia (also Kampuchea; country of S.E. Asia once ruled the entire Mekong River valley; fell after the 15th century; became part of French Indochina in the 19th century; proclaimed independence in 1953), 48, 196, 217

Camp David Accords (1979 Middle East peace agreements), 198, 199

Canaan (ancient region of Palestine or the part of it between the Jordan River and the Mediterranean Sea; referred to as "the Promised Land" in *Old Testament*), 62

Canton (now Guangzhou; city of southern China on a delta near the South China Sea), 111

capital (wealth in the form of money or property, used or accumulated in a business by a person, partnership, or corporation.), 114, 156

capitalism (economic system in which the means of production and distribution are privately or corporately owned and reinvestment of profits recurs habitually), 114, 120, 128, 130, 157

Caribbean Sea (arm of the western Atlantic Ocean bounded by the coasts of Central and South America and the West Indies), 38

Carpathians (1,400 mi. long mountain system of cent. Europe; link the Alps with the Balkan Mts.), 36

carte blanche (unqualified support), 169

cartel (combination of economic units to limit competition), 216

Carter, James Earl, Jr. (Known as "Jimmy."; 39th U. S. President [1977-1981]; negotiated the *Camp David Accords* between Egypt and Israel, 1979), 198

Carthage (powerful Phoenician trading city in western N. Africa; 4th and 3rd C. BC rival of Rome in Mediterranean), 62, 63, 65, 68, 70, 106,

Cartier, Jacques (1491-1557; French explorer who navigated the St. Lawrence River [1535] and laid claim to the region for France), 128

cartoon (drawing representing current public figures or issues symbolically and often satirically), 13

Cartwright, Edmund, (1743-1823; invented the power loom), 157

cash crop (agricultural crop, such as tobacco, grown for direct sale), 215

Caspian Sea (salt lake between S.E. Europe and W. Asia; water decreasing because of former Soviet dam construction on the Volga River), 36

caste system (rigid social structure, esp. Hindu India, often dictating one's rank and occupation), 48, 62, 63, 83, 93, 94, 195

Castro, Fidel (1927- ; Cuban president [1959-]; overthrew Batista dictatorship in 1959 and established a socialist state; aided communist liberation struggles in Latin America and Africa), 203, 204

Catherine the Great (Empress of Russia [r.1762-1796]; vastly increased the territory of the Empire through conquest and three partitions of Poland), 37, 138, 150

Caucasus (750 mi. long mountain range between Russia and Georgia and Azerbaijan; part of natural boundary between Europe and Asia), 36

caudillos (strong men; warlords; local chieftain usually with military connections), 153

Cavour, Conte Camillo Benso di. (1810-1861; Italian political leader; premier of Sardinia [1852-1859 and 1860-1861] and assisted in the unification of Italy), 154

Celt (Indo-European people originally of central Europe and spreading to W. Europe, the British Isles, and S.E. to Galatia during pre-Roman times, especially a Briton or Gaul), 67, 85

censorship (official removal or suppression of books, films, or other material considered morally, politically, or otherwise objectionable), 170, 175, 194

Central America (region of southern North America extending from the southern border of Mexico to the northern border of Colombia; separates the Caribbean Sea from the Pacific Ocean; linked to South America by the Isthmus of Panama), 11

Central Powers (Germany-Austria-Ottoman-Bulgarian alliance of World War I), 170 [map]

Cervantes, Miguel de (Spanish Renaissance writer: *Don Quixote*), 115 [chart]

Chad River (river of north-central Africa), 44, 45

Chaldeans (ancient people of the Persian Gulf whose leaders briefly dominated Babylonian Empire [626-539 BC]), 62

Chamorro, Violeta (1929- president of Nicaragua [1990-1996] brought an end to the 8-year civil war between the Sandinista government and the U.S.-backed contra rebels), 204

Champlain, Samuel de (1567-1635; French explorer who established first French settlements on the site of present-day Quebec), 128

Chandragupta Maurya (r. 321-297 BC, king of Magadha), 64

Chang Jiang River (see Yangtze)

Chao Phyra (major river system of S.E. Asian Peninsula), 47

Charlemagne (see Charles the Great)

Charles I (British king, dethroned & beheaded in Puritan Revolution, 1625-1649), 138, 139, 140

Charles II (British king, restored to monarchy after Cromwell's death in 1658), 139, 140

Charles V (absolutist, r. 1516-1556, grandson of Ferdinand of Aragon, elected Holy Roman Emperor), 136, 137

Charles the Great (r. 771-814, also Charlemagne; king of the Franks [r. 768-814]; founder of the first empire in western Europe after the fall of Rome; oversaw a cultural rebirth in Europe), 86

charter (written grant from the sovereign power conferring certain rights and privileges on a person or group), 129

charts and tables (an orderly, columnar display of data), 12

Chaucer, Geoffery (English Renaissance writer: *Canterbury Tales*), 117 [chart]

chauvinism (militant devotion to and glorification of one's country; fanatical patriotism; also prejudiced belief in the superiority of one's own gender, group, or kind), 153, 173

Chechnya (S.W. Russia; former Soviet Republic, largely Muslim, rebelled for independence in 1991; truce signed 11996), 38, 205

Cheng Ho (see Zheng He)

Chiang Kai-shek (see Jiang Jieshi)

Chiapas (state in southern Mexico, mainly Native Americans, revolted against gov't., 1994), 205 [map]

Ch'in Dynasty (see Q'in Dynasty)

China (E. Asian nation/ancient empire) 37, 47, 48, 49, 50, 51, 82, 91, 92, 96, 104, 106, 111, 114, 120, 128, 136, 138, 140, 155, 159-161, 190, 191, 193, 194

China, People's Republic of (also Red China; renamed after communists won the civil war in 1949), 194

China's Sorrow (see Yellow or Huang He River), 49

chivalry (principles and customs idealized by knighthood or bushido in Japan; bravery, courtesy, honor, and gallantry toward women), 116

Chou (see Zhou) Dynasty

Christendom (Christians considered as a group; the Christian world), 91

Christian Church (monotheistic religion based on teachings of Jesus Christ; includes Roman, Eastern and Russian Orthodox, and Protestant denominations), 18, 43, 69, 74, 86, 88, 90-91, 92, 93-94, 109, 117

Christianity (monotheistic religion with roots in Judaism, based on life and teachings of Jesus Christ), 18, 43, 69, 74, 86, 88, 90-91, 92, 93-94, 97, 118-120, 197

Church of England (see Anglican Church)

Churchill, Winston (1874-1965, British Prime Minister during WWII), 177, 178

circumnavigate (to proceed completely around), 128

city-states (small, independent countries built around an urban area; the poleis of ancient Greece; Monaco, Singapore, or Vatican today), 65, 66

civil disobedience (disobeying a law on grounds of moral or political principle; often adopts tactics of nonviolence and passive resistance; can take active forms such as illegal street demonstrations or peaceful occupation of premises; differs from rebellion because the civil disobeyer invites arrest and accepts punishment), 174, 195

civilization (level of human society - complex social, political development), 60

classical period (most artistically developed stage of a civilization), 64, 65, 71

Clemenceau, George (1841-1929, French Premier at the Paris Peace Conference of 1919), 170

clergy (church officials)

climate (Classifications throughout this book are according to Wladimir Peter Koppen's *Handbook of Climatology*; rainfall amounts and frequency patterns as key determinants along with winter temperatures [chart]), 33

Clinton, William J. (1946- ; 42d president of the U.S. [1993-2001]), 204

Clovis (466-511 AD; 1st generally recognized king of the Franks; united most of present-day France), 86

coalition government (gov't. by alliance; a temporary union of individuals, factions, parties, or nations, especially in parliamentary governments), 173

Code of Hammurabi (ordered arrangement of rules dealing with labor, personal property, and business, Babylonian c. 1792 to 1750 BC), 62

codified laws (organized and written social rules), 62, 69, 150

Colbert, Jean Baptiste (1619-1683, mercantilist finance minister and advisor to France's absolutist King Louis XIV), 129

Cold War (post-WWII global power clash between democratic and communist superpowers), 38, 153, 168, 178, 188, 191

collectivization (system of ownership and control of the means of production and distribution by the people acting as a group), 172

Colombia (nation of N.W. South America), 40, 219

colonialism / colonization (subjugation of a territory by an outside power; see imperialism), 140, 168, 174, 178, 188, 195

colony (region politically controlled by a distant country), 129, 130, 131, 132, 135, 174

Coloureds (racially mixed South Africans; largely the descendants of European settlers, Khoikhoi, and slaves from Madagascar and Asia; most speak Afrikaans, are Christian, and conform to a way of life typical of the Afrikaner, who are white, but were restricted under now defunct Apartheid system), 196

Columbus, Christopher (1451-1506; Italian explorer in the service of Spain who determined that the Earth was round and attempted to reach Asia by sailing west from Europe, thereby discovering America), 128, 131

COMECON (Post-WWII Soviet-sponsored common market for Eastern European nations; a Cold War answer to the Marshall Plan), 190

command economy (economic system in which decisions about productive resources are made by a central authority), 172, 188, 191, 200

Commercial Revival or Revolution (economic movement which opened Europe to worldwide trade enterprises [11th-18th C.]), 113, 114, 120, 128

Common Market (Western European trade assoc.; see European Union, formerly European Community), 192

Commonwealth Government (see Puritan Revolution)

communism (idealistic system of gov't. and economics in which the state plans and controls the economy; in practice, a single, often authoritarian party holds power, claiming to make progress toward a higher social order in which all goods are equally shared by the people; Marxist-Leninist version of communist doctrine advocates the overthrow of capitalism by the revolution of the proletariat), 50, 157, 171, 172, 175, 191, 194, 195, 201, 203, 204, 219

Communist Manifesto (1848, Marx and Engels' work; socialist doctrine), 21, 157

computers (development as key to modern technological and economic advancement), 220

concept (general idea derived from specific occurrences), 26

conclusion (in essay writing, the summary of facts plus the final judgment or decision reached after deliberation of the facts), 18, 19, 22, 23, 24

Concordat of 1801 (ended more than 10 years of hostility and violence between the Church and the French Revolution; reestablished Roman Catholicism as a state-supported religion; served as a model for agreements with various emerging national states throughout the 19th century), 151

Confucius (c. 551-479 BC, also Kongzi, ancient Chinese teacher/political advisor), 62, 72, 74, 83, 105, 115

Congo, Democratic Republic of (central African country; former Belgian colony; called Zaire [1971-1997], called Republic of Congo in 1997; sometimes called Congo-Kinshasa [cap.] to distinguish it from the Congo Republic to its south with capital at Brazaville), 46, 205, 219

Congo River (also Zaire River; cent. Africa; flowing about 2,900 mi north, west, and southwest through Congo to the Atlantic Ocean), 44, 45, 46

Congress Party (India's Hindu-dominated nationalist movement & most powerful political faction), 174

Congress of Vienna (1814-15; organized restoration of political power in Europe after Napoleon's defeat), 46, 152

conquistadores (Spanish conquerors of Latin American Indian empires, set up colonial rule), 134

conservative (groups favoring traditional views and values; tending to oppose change, usually for minimal governmental interference), 173

Constantine the Great (r. 306-337 AD, Roman emperor; issued the *Edict of Milan* in 313 AD), 18, 69, 84, 85

Constantinople (Turkey's capital; earlier called Byzantium, central city of Eastern Roman Empire; center of Ottoman Empire), 84, 111

constitution (system of fundamental laws and principles that prescribes the nature, functions, and limits of a gov't. or another institution), 68

constitutional monarchy (monarch limited in power by parliamentary body), 139, 189

consul (chief magistrates of the Roman Republic, elected for a term of one year), 68

Consulate (France, 1799-1804; oligarchy of three rulers dominated by Napoleon Bonaparte), 151

containment (U.S. policy attempted to limit the spread of communism during the Cold War), 189, 190

continents (principal land masses of the Earth, usually regarded as including Africa, Antarctica, Asia, Australia, Europe, North America, and South America), 31

contras (rebel group sought to overthrow communist rule in Nicaragua, 1980s), 204

Convention of International Trade in Endangered Species (1973, prohibited trade in plants or animals in danger of becoming extinct), 223

Copernicus, Nicolaus (1473-1543; Polish astronomer; advanced the theory that the earth and other planets revolve around the sun), 149

cordillera (extensive chain of mountains or mountain ranges; e.g., Andes of South America), 31, 39, 133

Cordoba, Francisco Hernandez de (Spanish explorer, active in Mexico, 1517), 131

Corn Laws (series of British laws in force before 1846 regulating the grain trade and restricting imports of grain; triggered Great Hunger in Ireland), 158

Corpus Juris Civilis ("Body of Civil Law;" a collection of Roman law prepared during the reign of the Byzantine emperor Justinian I [r. 527-565]), 69, 83

corruption (venal, dishonest, immoral violations of public trust), 196, 202, 215

Corsica (island in the Mediterranean Sea north of Sardinia), 68

Cortés, Hernando (1485-1547; Spanish explorer and conquistador who conquered Aztec Mexico), 131

council of ministers (also cabinet; executive arm of parliamentary gov't.; can also mean a junta or oligarchy in non-democratic forms)

Council of Mutual Economic Assistance (see COMECON)

Council of Trent (16th C. reorganization of the Catholic Church in response to the Protestant Reformation), 119

count (nobleman in some European countries), 86

Counter Reformation (offensive drive by Roman Catholic Church in the 16th-17th C. against the Protestant Reformation), 119

coup or coup d'état (sudden overthrow of a gov't. by a usually small group of persons in or previously in positions of authority), 200, 203

craftsman (an artisan; person who practices a craft with great skill), 113, 116

Creoles (also criollos, Spanish subjects born in the American colonies), 131, 132

Crete (island of southeast Greece in the eastern Mediterranean Sea; ancient Minoan civilization was one of the earliest c. 1600 BC; subsequently fell to the Greeks, Romans, Byzantines), 65

criollos (see creoles)

Croatia (N.W. Balkan nation broke from Yugoslavia 1991), 37, 202

Croats (people of N.W. Balkan area), 37, 205

Crompton, Samuel (1753-1827, invented the spinning mule), 157

Cromwell, Oliver (1599-1658; British Puritan dictator; declared Lord Protector of the Commonwealth in 1653), 138, 139

Crusades (military expeditions undertaken by European Christians in the 11th, 12th, and 13th centuries to recover the Holy Land from the Muslims), 89, 90-91, 96, 97, 104, 111, 112

Cuba (island country in the Caribbean Sea south of Florida), 203-204

Cuban Missile Crisis (1962 Cold War crisis), 201, 203

culture (a people's whole way of life: language, traditions, customs, institutions, religions, folkways), 60

cultural diffusion (cultural patterns spreading from one people to another), 43, 48, 51, 63, 71, 91, 96, 130, 132

cuneiform (ancient Sumerian system of writing using wedge-style ideographs on wet clay tablets), 62

Curie, Marie (1867-1934) and Pierre (1859-1906) (French physicists - proved that atoms could be split), 168

Cyprus (island country in the eastern Mediterranean south of Turkey; site of an ancient culture, settled by Phoenicians c. 800 BC; later conquered by the Assyrians, Egyptians, Persians, Macedonian Greeks, Romans [58 BC] and Byzantines [395 - 1191]), 65, 219

Cyrus the Great (c. 539 BC, Persian king conquered Lydia near Ionian coast), 64, 65

cyrillic (old Slavic alphabet ascribed to Saint Cyril, at present used in modified form for Russian, Bulgarian, certain other Slavic languages), 92

Czar (see "tsar")

Czechoslovakia (state uniting the Czech and Slovak peoples, existed in Central Europe from 1918 to 1939, and again from 1945 to 1993; late 1960s,reformers tried to change the Communist system ["Prague Spring"], decentralizing the economy, ending censorship, and allowing more political activity; U.S.S.R. invaded with Warsaw Pact troops on in Aug. 1968), 177, 190, 201, 202

Czech Republic (western half of former Czechoslovakia, independent in 1992; see Velvet Revolution), 202

Da Gama, Vasco (15th C. Portuguese explorer; reached India via Cape Horn in Africa in 1498), 128

da Vinci, Leonardo (1452-1519; Italian painter, engineer, musician, and scientist), 117 [chart]

daimyo also daimio ("Great Lords" of Japan's feudal era, 1300-1600; warrior land holders), 104, 105, 115, 138

Damascus (capital and largest city of Syria, in the southwest part of the country; inhabited since prehistoric times, the city became a thriving commercial center under the Romans), 89, 93

Danish Wars (1848-1850, 1864; wars between Germany and Denmark; Denmark ceded its claims to the territory by the Peace of Vienna; entire region was annexed by Prussia in 1866, following the Seven Weeks' War), 155

Dante (see Alighieri)

Danton,Georges Jacques (1759-1794; French Revolutionary leader; guillotined for opposition to the Reign of Terror), 151

Danube River (major trade route of south-central Europe rising in Germany and flowing 1,770 miles southeast through Austria, Hungary, Yugoslavia, and Romania to the Black Sea), 36, 37

Daode Jing (The Way and Its Power by Laozi, the most important text in Chinese Daoism; believed to date from the 4th century BC), 74

Daoism (ancient Chinese philosophy; also Taoism), 62, 74

Dardanelles (w/ Bosporus, straits between the Aegean and Black Seas near Constantinople [Istanbul]; crossing point for invasions between Europe and Asia) 34, 41, 42, 155

Darius I (reformer king of Persia, 522-480 BC), 64

Das Kapital (1867, Marx's elaboration of communist philosophy), 157

data-based questions (overview of varieties on Global History and geography examinations), 8-15

da Vinci, Leonardo (central figure of Italian Renaissance art, Mona Lisa, Last Supper), 117

Dawes Plan (1923; Charles G. Dawes of the U.S. negotiated a system for lowering WWI reparation payments and provided loans to Germany), 173

DBQ (document-based question; a two-part thematic response combining a series of "scaffolded" short-answer questions that become the prewriting building blocks for an expository essay), 6, 16, 17, 24, 25, 27

de León, Ponce (see Ponce de Leon)

Deccan Plateau (occupies most of the peninsula area of India and holds much mineral wealth), 47

Declaration of Principles for Palestinian Self-Rule (see Oslo Accord)

Declaration of Rights of Man and of the Citizen (1789; French Revolution document justified overthrow of monarchy with Enlightenment ideas), 151

deficit spending (see Keynes; spending of public funds obtained by borrowing rather than by taxation), 174

deforestation (over-cutting of timber resources), 222, 223

Delhi Sultanate (Delhi Sultanate was a Muslim kingdom in northern and northwestern India ruled by a succession of Afghans from the late 12th century to the 16th centuries), 107 [map]

Delian League (naval alliance with Athens as central polis), 66, 72

demand (amount of a resource or service people are ready and willing to consume), 114 demesne (manorial land retained for the private use of a feudal lord; also domain), 95

democracy (governing power in the hands of many; gov't. by the people, exercised either directly or through elected representatives [indirect democracy]), 65, 66, 176, 191, 200

democratic socialism (mixed economic systems in European nations with extensive welfare systems; basically aimed at society in which full democratic control would be exercised over wealth, and production would be controlled by a group of responsible experts working in the interests of the whole community), 188, 191

Democritus (460-370 BC, Greek philosopher who expounded elementary ideas about the basic composition of matter, the atom), 72

Deng Xiaoping, (1904-1997, reformist communist Chinese leader after Mao), 50, 194

Dengue fever (sporadically infectious disease of warmer climates, although painful, dengue fever usually ends in complete recovery within a few week, fever has caused numerous deaths in children in recent years), 221

depression (economic contraction; period of drastic decline in a national or international economy, characterized by decreasing business activity, falling prices, and unemployment), 168, 173-174

desert (barren or desolate area; dry, often sandy region of little rainfall, extreme temperatures, and sparse vegetation; also Koppen-type Bw climate), 41, 42, 44, 106, 222, 223

descamisados (Argentina; poor industrial working classes), 203

desertification (transformation of arable or habitable land to desert, as by a change in climate or destructive land use), 222, 223

developing nations (see LDCs)

dharma (Hindu concept of sacred duty one owes to family, caste, social custom, civil law; in Buddhism, the principle or law that orders the universe; the essential function or nature of a thing [soul]), 18, 94

Dias, Bartolomeu (1450-1500; Portuguese navigator who was the first to round the Cape of Good Hope), 128

Diaz, Porfirio (Mexican dictator, 1876-1911), 153

dictator/dictatorship (an absolute ruler, a tyrant, a despot), 70, 172, 191

Diocletian (r. 284-305 AD, Roman emperor who divided Roman Empire into eastern & western regions), 69, 84

Directory (French Revolution; group of five men constituting the governmental executive [1795 to 1799]; chosen by the legislature; one director was replaced each year.), 151

"Dirty War" (Argentina 1979, military resorted to kidnapping, torture, and murder of dissenters), 203

dissenters (see dissidents)

dissidents (those who disagree with institutional authority), 194, 201

divine right (absolute power coming from God with ruler having no responsibility to those ruled), 62, 83, 109, 135, 138, 140

Dneiper River (river system in western Russia and Ukraine), 36 [map]

document-based writing questions (see DBQ)

dogma (doctrine relating to matters such as morality and faith, set forth in an authoritative manner by a church), 89

domestic system (commercial production done in homes and coordinated by an entrepreneur), 20, 156

Don River (1,198-mi. commercial trade route in central Russian uplands flowing southward to the Sea of Azov), 36, 37

Dorians (1100 BC, northern warlike people, precursors of ancient Greeks), 65

dowry (money or property brought by a bride to her husband at marriage), 87

Drakensberg Mountains (southern Africa), 44, 45

drought (long period of abnormally low rainfall, especially one that adversely affects growing or living conditions), 217

due process rights (established course for judicial proceedings or other governmental activities designed to safeguard the legal rights of the individual), 140

Du Fu (c. 750, T'ang poet) 83

Duma (national legislative body under tsars in 19th and 20th C.), 201

Dutch (of or relating to the Netherlands or its people or culture; see Netherlands)

Dutch East India Company (trading company financed through stock sales; became base for Netherlands imperialism in India, Indonesia, China), 114

dynasties (family of hereditary rulers)

Earth Summit (1992 U.N.-sponsored global meeting on environmental issues), 223

East Asia (China, Mongolia, Korea, Japan), 49-51, 205

East China Sea (arm of the Pacific Ocean between the Chinese mainland and Formosa; connects with the Yellow Sea to the north and South China Sea to the south), 49

East Germany (see German Democratic Republic)

Eastern and Russian Orthodox (Catholic) Church, 74, 83, 92, 96, 118

Eastern Europe: 7, 36-37, 83, 104, 191

Eastern Hemisphere (continents of Africa, Europe, Asia, and Australia)

Ebola (Ebola virus causes Ebola fever, highly virulent, 90% death rate, discovered in 1976 in the Ebola River area in northern Zaire), 221

economic nationalism (stimulation of internal development using gov't. policies to eliminate outside competition [i.e., protective tariffs]), 174

economic system (social institution that deals with the production, distribution, and consumption of goods and services and their management), 172 [chart], 191 [chart]

Edict of Milan (granted freedom of worship to all Christians in Roman Empire, 313 AD), 18, 86

Edo (center of Japan's Tokugawa gov't., later called Tokyo), 136

Edward VI (short-lived English monarch; son of Henry VIII; his regents continued Anglican Church reforms), 110

Egypt (eastern North African nation; one of the earliest known civilizations, 3100-1000 BC; later fell to the Assyrians, Persians, Alexander, and the Romans), 41, 61, 71, 88, 106, 197, 198, 199

Eightfold Path (Buddhism's basic concepts), 73

Einstein, Albert (1879-1955, German, expressed Curies' concept - formula, $E=MC^2$ - Theory of Relativity), 168

Elders, Council of (formed the judiciary and counseled the Assembly in Sparta), 65

Elizabeth I (r. 1558-1603; absolutist monarch of England, established the nation as a power in Europe; restored power of Anglican Church; began colonization of New World), 110, 139

embargo (an official declaration of refusal to sell or trade)

Enclosure Acts (16th-19th C. British government allowed farm lands to be fenced for pasture purposes), 155

encomiendas (feudal-type land grants in Brazil, Portuguese colonial plantations), 131

endangered species (plant or animal threatened with extinction), 222, 223

endostatin (drugs with the potential of blocking the growth of cancer in blood vessels), 222

Engels, Frederick (collaborator with Karl Marx on Communist Manifesto, 1848), 157

England (country that evolved in southern Britannia; originally settled by Celtic peoples, subsequently conquered by Romans, Angles, Saxons, Jutes, Danes, and Normans; see Great Britain or United Kingdom)

English Channel (narrow strait N.W. Europe between France, Netherlands, and England), 33, 34

English Civil Wars (see Puritan Revolution)

enlightened despot (tyrant who uses autocratic power for the benefit of the people), 138, 148, 150

Enlightenment (see Age of Reason)

environment (the habitat or setting in which people live), 222-223

Ephors, Council of the 5 (ancient Spartan oligarchy of magistrates with veto power over actions of the Kings, Elders, and the Assembly), 65

epidemic (rapidly and extensively spreading infection affecting many individuals in an area or a population at same time), 116

Erasmus, Desiderius (Netherlands Renaissance writer, In Praise of Folly), 117 [chart], 119

Eritrea (region of N. Ethiopia bordering on the Red Sea; proclaimed an Italian colony in 1890; focal point of Italy's conquest of Ethiopia [1935-1936]; part of Ethiopia in 1952; independent in 1993 after 30 years of civil war), 177

Estates General (French parliament or national assembly under Bourbon monarchs), 150, 151

Ethiopia (ancient East African kingdom, invaded by Italy 1880, finally take by taken by Mussolini in 1936, freed by Allies in WWII), 159

ethics, ethical behavior (rules or standards governing human conduct), 26, 74

ethnic group (people sharing a common and distinctive racial, national, religious, linguistic, or cultural heritage), 7, 196, 202, 205

ethnic cleansing (genocidal policy in war-torn Balkan nations between Christians and Muslims; attempt to eliminate racial, religious, tribal or cultural group), 202

ethnocentrism (tendency to regard the beliefs, standards, and code of behavior of one's own culture or subculture as superior to those found in other societies), 50, 72, 138

Etruscans (ancient civilization of west-central Italy in present-day Tuscany and parts of Umbria before founding of Rome [c. 700 BC]), 67, 68

Euphrates River (see Tigris-Euphrates)

Euratom (European Atomic Energy Community; post-WWII consortium of Western European nations to deal with nuclear power management), 192

Euripides (5th C. BC Greek dramatist), 72

euro (common currency of the European Union), 192, 224

European Coal and Steel Community (1951 co-op plan of Robert Schuman [French] for 5 W. European nations; forerunner of "Common Market"/European Union), 192

European Community / European Economic Community (EC; see renamed European Union [1994]; originally "Common Market"), 192

European Union (originally the "Common Market," then the European Community; ongoing attempt to unify European nations' trade and commerce; integration broadened and formalized in the 1991 Maastricht Treaty), 33, 192, 224

exam blueprint (format for global history and geography examinations), 6

excommunication (depriving of the right of church membership by ecclesiastical authority), 119

export (to send or transport abroad merchandise, especially for sale or trade), 129

Fairs (gatherings held at specified times and places for the buying and selling of goods; a market), 113

Falklands-Malvinas Islands War (1982; Argentina v. Britain, Britain won with U.S. spy satellite help), 203

famine (drastic, wide-reaching food shortage resulting in severe hunger and starvation), 116, 172, 217

FAO (Food and Agricultural Organization, U.N. agency research and coordinating organization to develop programs in the field of world food supply.), 191, 219

Far East (western euphemism for East Asia; also "the Orient"), 159

Fashoda Crisis (1898; confrontation between Great Britain and France over territory in Africa), 159

fascism (system of gov't. marked by centralization of authority under a dictator, stringent socioeconomic controls, suppression of the opposition through terror and censorship, and typically a policy of belligerent nationalism and racism), 172, 173, 175-176, 177

Fatamid Dynasty (Islamic dynasty that reigned in North Africa and later in Egypt [909 - 1171]), 111

fealty (allegiance, loyalty, faithfulness to obligations, duties), 87

Ferdinand, Archduke Franz (d. 28 June 1914, with wife, Sophie, assassinated in Sarajevo by the Serbian rebel group, "the Black Hand" - blamed for immediate "cause" of WWI), 169

Ferdinand VII of Aragon (1784-1833, ruled unified Spain with Isabella of Castile), 109

Fertile Crescent (Middle East region between the Tigris and Euphrates Rivers considered to be the Cradle of Civilization), 32, 61

feudal / feudalism (land holding-based lord / vassal economic-political-social system; Medieval Europe, Japan), 62, 85, 87, 90, 96, 97, 104, 115, 116

Fichte, Johann Gottlieb (1762-1814, *Addresses to the German Nation* [1808] strongly influenced the development of German nationalism.), 155

fief (fiefdom; also called feud; self-sufficient feudal manor granted by a lord to a vassal on condition of homage & service), 85, 87

filial piety (in Confucian society, the special bond between parents and children, lends stability and ordered), 74

First Estate (French Roman Catholic Church officials in the Estates-General - the rarely called national assembly under the French monarchs), high gov't. officials), 150

Five Pillars (basic beliefs and duties of Muslim faith),74

Five Power Naval Armaments Treaty (Washington Naval Arms Conference agreement [1922]; Britain, France, U.S. Japan, Italy agreement to control production of war ships), 176

Five-Year Plans (gov't. command in communist and socialist economies), 172, 195

fixed income (non-growing amount of money on which to live [pensions; inheritances]; difficult to manage expenses when prices rise and income does not [inflation]), 202

Food and Agricultural Organization (see FAO)

"Four Modernizations" (revision of China's economic priorities under Deng Xiaoping), 194

Four Noble Truths (basic beliefs of Buddhism), 73

Four Power Treaty (Washington Naval Arms Conference agreement [1921]; Britain, France, U.S., Japan agreement to respect possession in E. Asia), 176

Fourier, Charles (1772-1837; utopian socialist; favored ideal communities where all shared in the work and received the benefits of joint labor according to need), 157

Fourteen Points, The (WWI peace plan for Europe drawn up by U.S. President Wilson, 1918; became partial basis for the Treaty of Versailles, 1919), 172

France (country of western Europe on the Atlantic Ocean and the English Channel), 33, 34, 109, 110, 120, 128, 129, 136, 150-152, 158, 169, 174, 189, 190, 191, 192, 196, 197

Francis I (autocratic king ruled France from 1515 to 1547; personified the splendor of the Renaissance), 110

Franco, Francisco (directed the Nationalist rebel armed forces that defeated the Republicans in the Spanish Civil War [1936-1939]; ruled as fascist dictator [1939-1975]), 177

Franco-Prussian War (1871; to complete the unification of Germany begun in 1866, Bismarck provoked France into an act of war to frighten the south German states into alliance with Prussia, then persuaded all the German rulers to join together in forming the new German Empire with the king of Prussia as emperor), 155

Franks (5th C. AD, people of the central and western sections of Gaul [France]), 84, 85, 88

Frederick the Great of Prussia (1740-1786, enlightened despot), 138, 150

French Empire (1804-1814, ruled by Napoleon Bonaparte as emperor by plebiscite), 151, 152 [map]

French Revolution (rebellion against Bourbon monarchy c. 1789; transformed the country into a republic), 150, 151, 152, 154

Freud, Sigmund (1856-1939, founded the field of psychoanalysis), 168

Fulani (Muslim people in north of Nigeria), 195

functional literacy (just meeting the minimum reading and writing demands and standards needed in a complex society - a sub-cause of poverty in industrialized nations), 218

fundamentalism (see Islamic fundamentalism)

Fustat (N. Egyptian city was a center of learning and administration in Muslim Era under the Abbasids), 89, 93

Galileo Galilei (1632, used telescope to prove planets revolved around Sun), 149

Gandhi, Mohandas K. (1869-1948, non-violent Indian independence movement leader, assassinated 1948), 174, 195

Ganges River (river of N. India and Bangladesh flows 1,560 mi. east from the Himalaya Mountains a through a vast plain to the Bay of Bengal), 47

Garibaldi, Guiseppe (1807-1882; Italian general and nationalist who led volunteers in the capture of Sicily and Naples [1860] which conquest led to the formation of the kingdom of Italy [1861]), 155

Gaul (ancient region of Western Europe south and west of the Rhine River, west of the Alps, and north of the Pyrenees, corresponding roughly to modern-day France and Belgium), 67, 70

Gaza Strip (narrow band of desert-like land along the western Mediterranean coast; part of the British mandate of Palestine; controlled by Egypt after the Arab-Israeli War of 1948 until the Six-Day War of 1967; PLO and Israel signed accords on Palestinian self-rule in Gaza and the West Bank in 1993, 1994, and 1995), 197, 198

GDP (Gross Domestic Product; total value of goods and services produced annually [even by foreign owned firms] within a particular nation; excludes income from foreign business operations by firms not owned by that nation), 202

General Assembly (see U.N. General Assembly)

genocide (deliberate elimination of a racial or cultural group), 168, 175, 196

geographic influences (core ideas essential to mastering global history and geography exams), 25, 29-58

German Democratic Republic (also East Germany; official name for country created by Soviets from their N.E. zone of occupation after WWII before reunification in 1989), 191

Germany (country of north-central Europe; occupied since c. 500 BC by Germanic tribes;part of the kingdom of the Franks by the time of Charlemagne; later a loose federation of principalities and nucleus of the Holy Roman Empire), 37, 85, 120, 129, 153, 154, 155, 158, 168, 169, 172, 171, 175, 176, 188, 191, 202, 219, 217

Germany, Federal Republic of (official name for West Germany before reunification in 1989; official name after *Treaty of Final Settlement* 12 Sept. 1990 reunified E. & W. Germany), 188, 191, 202

Gestapo (German internal security police as organized under the Nazi regime, known for its terrorist methods), 175

Ghana (West African empire 7th-11th C. AD), 108

Ghats (two mountain ranges of southern India; extend 1,000 miles along each coast; separated by the Deccan Plateau), 47

ghettoes (ethnic or cultural area or neighborhood; section or quarter imposed or evolving because of social, economic, or legal pressure; also see *barrios*)

Gibraltar, Strait of (narrow sea passage connecting the Mediterranean Sea and the Atlantic Ocean between Spain and northern Africa), 33, 34

Gilgamesh (ancient Sumerian epic tale of heroic king), 62

glasnost ("openness"- Gorbachev's political reform policies), 201

Glorious Revolution (Catholic James II deposed; placed Protestant William III [of Orange] & Mary II on English throne in 1688), 139

GNP (Gross National Product; total value of goods and services produced annually by a nation at home and abroad; replaced in international financial statistics in 1980s by Gross Domestic Product; see GDP)

Gobi Desert (desert of S.E. Mongolia and N. China), 49

Golan Heights (hilly plateau in southwestern Syria disputed among Israelis, Palestinians, and Syrians since 1967 War), 197

golden age (period of intellectual and creative achievement), 71-72

Golden Age of Islamic culture (Abbasid Dynasty, 750-1258 AD), 89

Golden Age of Greek culture (also Age of Pericles,461-421BC), 9, 72

Golden Horde, Khanate of (1223, name given to the Mongol state established in S. Russia), 106, 107

goldsmith (artisan who fashions objects of gold; also trader or dealer in gold articles), 113-114

Gorbachev, Mikhail (1931- , Soviet reform president 1985-1991), 189, 200, 201

Goths (barbarian tribes occupied Italy and Spain 5th C.), 84, 85

government (agency that exercises control and administration of a political unit), 65

Gran Colombia (short-lived union of Venezuela, Colombia, Peru, and Ecuador [c. 1820]), 39, 154

Gran Chaco (arid, uninhabited lowland plain of central South America divided among Paraguay, Bolivia, and Argentina), 38, 39

graphs (pictorial device, such as a pie chart or bar graph, used to illustrate quantitative relationships), 8, 10-11

Great Britain (island nation off the N.W. coast of Europe; nation formed by 1707 union of England, Wales, and Scotland; built world empire from 16th to 20th C.; also England and United Kingdom), 35, 46, 51, 152, 155, 156, 158, 159, 160, 169, 170, 174, 177, 189, 190, 191, 192, 196, 197, 203

Great Depression (1930s worldwide economic collapse; cause of social and political upheaval), 169, 173-174, 176

Great Hunger, The (1845; also called the Potato Famine, in Ireland; a potato blight damaged crop to the extent that 3/4 million died from starvation and famine), 158

Great Leap Forward (Mao's major economic reorganization of the late 1950s in China), 194

Great Proletarian Cultural Revolution (Mao's major political and social reorganization of the late 1960s in China; damaged the credibility and morale of the Communist party), 194

Great Rift Valley (geologic depression of S.W. Asia and E. Africa from the Jordan River valley to Mozambique; marked by volcanic faults), 44, 45

Great Wall of China (c. 219 BC; built as an invasion defense on northern borders of China in Q'in period), 72

Greco- (prefix for Greek; eg. Greco-Roman classical culture), 32, 117

Greece (country of S.E. Europe on the S. Balkan Peninsula; includes numerous islands in the Mediterranean, Aegean, and Ionian seas; one of the most important centers of early civilization), 48, 63, 168, 192

Green Revolution (1960s' scientific breakthroughs in agriculture), 18, 49, 195, 220

Greenhouse effect (Earth's atmosphere traps solar radiation, absorbing heat radiated back from the Earth's surface), 223

Gross Domestic Product (see GDP)

Gross National Product (see GNP)

Group Areas Act (1950; divided 13% of So. Africa among 10 Bantu homelands), 196

Guatemala (country of northern Central America), 204

guerrillas (small mobile, irregular armed force that takes limited surprise actions as part of a larger political and military strategy), 203

guild (also gild; association of persons of the same trade or pursuits, formed to protect mutual interests and maintain standards, as of merchants or artisans), 113, 116

gulag (forced labor camp or prison, especially for political dissidents), 172

gulf (large area of a sea or ocean partially enclosed by land, especially a long land-locked portion of sea opening through a strait), 31

Gulf of Tonkin (see Tonkin, Gulf of)

Guomindang (also Kuomintang or Nationalist Party, formed by Sun Yixian and associates during Chinese Revolution [1911]), 175, 194

Gupta (320-550 AD, ancient dynasty of India), 9, 82, 83, 94, 96

Gutenberg, Johann (German Renaissance inventor of the movable type, printing ink, letter press process, published Mazarin Bible, c. 1455), 118 [chart], 119

Habeas Corpus Act (17th C., guaranteed arrested English subjects a statement of charges, bail, and a fair and speedy trial), 139

habitats (native environment of a plant or animal), 223

Habsburg (also Hapsburg; German royal family that supplied rulers to a number of European states from the late Middle Ages until the 20th century; reached the height of their power under Charles V of Spain in the 16th C.), 110, 135, 136, 137

haiku (traditional Japanese poem of only 3 lines), 115

Hamas (Palestinian group commits acts of terrorism against Israel and any supporters of the Jewish State), 198, 224

Hammurabi (c. 1792-1750 BC, 6th king of Babylonia, giver of laws [code]), 62

Han Dynasty (210 BC-219 AD, expanded China's control over Central Asia), 72, 75, 83, 84, 91, 92

Handbook of Climatology (climate classification system developed by Wladimir Peter Koppen, 1846-1940), 33

Hannibal (247-183 BC, Carthaginian general; terrified Rome during the Second Punic War (214-199 BC), 68

Hanover Dynasty (English ruling family 1714-1901; the ruling dynasty of the kingdom of Hanover in Germany; supplied five British monarchs between 1714 and 1837), 139

Hanseatic League (protective alliance and confederation of free towns in northern Europe [Lübeck, Hamburg] 1241-1669), 10, 114

Harappa (locality in the Indus River valley of the Punjab [Pakistan]; archaeological finds dating back to the 3rd millennium BC include well-laid-out city and links between Indian and Sumerian cultures), 62

hard-line (firm and uncompromising, as in policy, position, or stance, strict, orthodox), 194, 198

hard-surfaced roads (Thomas Telford and John MacAdam; invented during the 19th C. industrial revolution), 157

Hargreaves, James (1730-1778, invented spinning jenny), 157

Hausa (predominantly Moslem people inhabiting northern Nigeria and southern Niger; also West African Islamic city-state of the 14th C.), 195

"Have and Have Not Nations" ("Have" refers to higher levels of per capita incomes, life expectancies, literacy, etc., "Have not" the opposite - lower levels), 214, 215, 216, 218

Hebrews (also Jews; descendants of a northern Semitic people, claiming descent from Abraham, Isaac, and Jacob; ancient monotheistic civilization of Middle East), 61, 62

Hegira (flight of Mohammed from Mecca to Medina in 622, marking the beginning of the Muslim era), 88

Heian (medieval capital of Japan founded in 794; also major cultural period of early Japan), 105, 115

Hellas (ancient Greeks' name for their region), 66, 71

Hellenes (name used by ancient Greeks to identify themselves), 66

Hellenic / Hellenistic culture (c. 324-27 BC, extension of ancient Greek influence by Philip of Macedon and Alexander the Great), 69, 71, 72, 83

helots (Ancient Greece; conquered peoples, neither free or slave who served as farm servants or serfs), 65

Helsinki Accords (1973-1975; Conference on Security and Cooperation in Europe; U.S., Canada, the U.S.S.R., and 32 European agreed to legitimize the U.S.S.R.'s World War II territorial gains, provide scientific, technological, and cultural exchanges, respect human rights), 201

hemisphere (either the northern or southern half of the earth as divided by the equator or the eastern or western half as divided by N-S meridians), 31

Henry II (r. 1154-1189, England, set up impressive administrative framework, justice system became basis of legal systems of most English-speaking people), 110, 110, 139

Henry IV (r. 1598-1610, France, 1st king of Bourbon Dynasty), 110

Henry VII (1457-1509; founder of the Tudor dynasty of English monarchs), 110, 139

Henry VIII (1491-1547; Tudor king, created Anglican Church), 110, 119, 139

Henry the Navigator (also Prince Henry, 1394-1460; Portuguese noble founded a center at Cape St. Vincent for navigational studies and expedition planning), 114

heretic (person who dissents from officially accepted dogma of a religion), 119

Hezbollah (Palestinian group commits acts of terrorism against Israel and supporters of the Jewish State), 198, 224

Hidalgo, Miguel (1753-1811; Catholic priest began Mexican independence movement), 152

hierarchy (body of persons having authority), 95, 119

hieroglyphics (ancient system of picture writing, such as that of ancient Egypt), 61

hill (well-defined natural elevation smaller than a mountain), 31

Himalaya Mountains (central Asia, world's highest mountains), 39, 47, 48, 49, 63

Hindenburgh, Paul Ludwig Hans Anton von Beneckendorff und von (1847-1934; served as a German field marshal in WWI and president of Weimar Republic), 176

Hindu / Hinduism (major religion of India), 18, 48, 62, 73, 91, 94, 106, 155, 174, 195

Hindi (widely spoken native language of India)

Hippocrates (Greek father of medicine), 72

Hitler, Adolf (German;, Nazi Party leader, chancellor, dictator [r., 1933-1945]), 36, 153, 172, 174, 175-176, 177, 178

Hittite Empire (confederation of Indo-European-speaking peoples who established a kingdom in central Anatolia after c. 1750 BC; powerful E. Mediterranean - Middle Eastern empire that flourished in the 14th and 13th centuries BC), 61, 62

HIV virus (known cause of AIDS disease), 221

Hobbes, Thomas (1588-1679, English political theorist, defended absolutism as part of natural law), 135

Holocaust, Jewish (Nazi genocide against Jews, estimated 6 million killed), 175, 178

Holy Land (Middle East; Israel-Palestine area where major Christian, Islamic, and Judaic religious shrines are located), 90

Holy Roman Empire (central European state, never truly strong, begun when Charlemagne was crowned by Pope Leo

III [800 AD] and lasted into early modern times), 86, 107, 110, 111, 120, 135, 136, 137

homage (ceremonial recognition by a vassal of allegiance to his lord under feudal law; also fealty), 87

Hong Wu (1328-98; formerly Zhu Yuanzhang; overthrew Mongol authority; launched the Ming Dynasty), 138

Horace (65-8 BC; Roman lyric poet), 72

Houses of Lords and Commons (the two chambers of the British Parliament; Lords for the nobles; Commons for the burgesses, and later ordinary citizes), 110, 139

Huang He River Valley (see Yellow River Valley), 62

Hudson, Henry (d. 1611; English navigator and explorer who discovered the Hudson River on a 1609 expedition for the Dutch East India Company), 128

Hulegu Khanate (also called Ilkhan; Persia - one of four kingdoms resulting from division of Genghis Kahn's Mongol Empire; 1258-1353), 106, 107

humanism (cultural and intellectual movement of the Renaissance that centers on human beings and their values, capacities, and worth [secular rather than spiritual of existence]), 117

humanitarian (devoted to the promotion of human welfare and the advancement of social reforms), 204

human rights (basic rights and freedoms to which all human beings are entitled, often held to include the right to life and liberty, freedom of thought and expression, and equality), 188, 194

Hundred Years' War (1337-1453, France v. England battled over dynastic claims in France), 109

Hungarian Revolution (1956; after Stalin's death Hungarian leaders sought to overthrow the communist system; Soviet forces invaded and put down the insurrection), 190, 201

hunger (lack of sufficient nutrition for quality of life functions - good health, life expectancy), 217

Huns (nomadic invaders of Europe in the 4th and 5th centuries AD; defeated in 455), 37, 85, 105

hunter-gatherer (early humans; lived off the land, both meat and farming), 60

Hussein, Saddam (1937- ; President of Military Council of Iraq [r. 1979-]; waged territorial war against Iran [1980-1988]; invaded and occupied Kuwait [1990], forced out by international forces), 199

Hutu and Tutsis (central African ethnic violence; 1994 flight of 2 million Hutus to Zaire [Congo]; forced from Zaire in 1996; thousands died in reprisals), 205

Iberian Peninsula (S.W. Europe; Spain and Portugal)

Ibn Buttuta (14th C. visitor to Yuan Dynasty of Kublai Khan), 112

Ibn Sina (Islamic chemist known in the West as Avicenna, wrote *Canon of Medicine*, c. 900 AD), 89

Ibo (African people inhabiting south central Niger-Congo area), 195

icon (representation or picture of a sacred or sanctified Christian personage, traditional to the Eastern Church), 83

Ieyasu, Tokugawa (see Tokugawa Ieyasu)

Ilkhan Khanate (see Hulegu Khanate)

IMF (see International Monetary Fund)

Immigration (enter and settle in a country or region to which one is not native; see "guest workers in Germany), 216-217

Imperator Caesar Augustus (r. 27 BC-14 AD, "exalted" title of 1st Roman emperor), 70, 72

imperialism (policy of extending a nation's authority by territorial acquisition or by the establishment of economic and political dominance over other people), 158-161, 169

import (to bring or carry in from an outside source, especially to bring in [goods or materials] from a foreign country for trade or sale), 129

import taxes (see tariffs)

Inca Empire (1200-1535 AD; Andes Mountains - Peru, Ecuador, parts of Chile, Bolivia, & Argentina), 130

India (country of S. Asia; site of one of the oldest civilizations in the world, centered in the Indus River valley c. 2500-1500 BC),37, 48-50, 82, 94, 97, 104, 106, 130, 136, 137, 155, 174, 188, 191, 195

Indian National Congress (founded in1885; leading organization in India's independence movement; dominant political party in independence;), 115

Indian Ocean (body of water extending from southern Asia to Antarctica and from eastern Africa to southeast Australia) 42, 44, 45, 47, 128

indigenous (originating and growing or living in an area or environment), 130

Indochina (peninsula of Southeast Asia; also French colony that was divided into modern Vietnam, Laos, Cambodia [1950s]), 106

Indo-Gangetic Plain (flatlands, valleys of N. India), 47

Indonesia (country of S.E. Asia in the Malay Archipelago comprising Sumatra, Java, Sulawesi, the Moluccas, parts of Borneo, New Guinea, and Timor, and many smaller islands), 47

Indus River (river of south-central Asia flows 1,900 mi. N.W. from Tibet through northern India and southwest through Pakistan to the Arabian Sea; valley was the site of an ancient civilization lasting from 2500 to 1500 BC), 47, 62, 71, 88

Industrial Revolution (economic, social, political change when production of basic necessities becomes organized mechanically), 20-24, 148, 155-157, 159, 218

industrialization (to develop industry in a country or society; organize the production of something as an industry), 20-24, 155-157, 172

inflation (persistent increase in the level of consumer prices or a persistent decline in the purchasing power of money), 203

infrastructure (basic systems needed for the running of society such as transportation and communications systems), 69, 72, 215

Institutional Revolutionary Party (PRI, dominant political party in Mexico, formed in 1929), 153

Intellectual Revolution, The (see Age of Enlightenment, also Age of Reason)

interdependence (mutual dependence of people on each other), 224

Internet (global connection of computer networks), 220

Intifada (1987-1988 revolt by Palestinians against Israeli military occupation in Israeli occupied territories), 197

Iran (S.W. Asian nation; also Persia), 37, 42, 174, 199

Iran-Iraq War (1980-1988), 42, 199

Iraq (S.W. Asian nation; see also Persia), 199, 201

Ireland (island in the N. Atlantic Ocean west of Britain; invaded by Celts c. 500 BC; joined Great Britain in 1801; Easter Rebellion [1916] and a civil war [1919-1921] split island into the independent Irish Free State [now Republic of Ireland] and Northern Ireland - still allied with Great Britain), 158, 205

Irigoyen, Alvaro Arzu (1996 leader in Guatemala, protect Indian rights, reduced military, privatization plans), 204

"Iron Chancellor" (see Bismarck)

"Iron Curtain" (After WWII, Churchill coined phrase describing the prevention the free flow of ideas between democratic W. Europe and communist E. Europe), 188

"iron triangles" (in Central America, cooperation & conspiracy among large land holding elite, military, and leaders of Roman Catholic Church), 152, 203, 204

Irrawaddy (chief river of Burma [Myanmar] flows 1,000 miles southward to the Bay of Bengal), 47

irrigation (to supply dry land with water by means of ditches, pipes, or streams), 61, 62, 199

Islam (major world religion founded in Middle East by prophet Muhammad [7th C. AD]), 18, 32, 43, 74, 93, 97, 106, 107, 118

Islamic Empire (622-1216 AD; military conquest of region stretching from the Indus across S.W. Asia and N. Africa into Spain; ruled by caliphs [successors to the Prophet Muhammad]), 82, 88, 89, 92, 107

Islamic fundamentalist movement (concerned with the reconstruction of a genuine *ummah* [community of the faithful submissive to God's will as expressed in the *Sharia*]; demands creation of a new Islamic authority through an Islamic state; views modern Muslim societies as un-Islamic), 43, 199, 200, 219

Islamic Jihad (Middle East terrorist movement; claimed responsibility for a series of bombings, murders, and kidnappings against U.S., French, Israeli, and other installations and personnel since 1983), 198, 224

Islamic Salvation Front of Algeria (FIS; popular resistance group), 224

Islamic World (combined global regions where Islam is predominant religion and cultural influence), 32, 91

Israel (ancient Mid-East kingdom of Hebrews; also independent nation since 1948), 42, 43, 191, 197-198

Italy, 129, 153-155, 172, 176-178

Ivan IV (the Terrible; Russian Tsar, 1533-1584), 137

Jagatai Khanate (central Asia; Turkestan, one of four kingdoms resulting from division of Genghis Kahn's Mongol Empire), 106, 107

Jahangir (also Jahngir; 4th Indian Mogul ruler, 1605-1627, continued golden age of father Akbar), 106

James I (1566-1625, English king of the Stuart Dynasty of Scotland), 139

James II (1633-1701, English king deposed in Glorious Revolution, 1688), 139

Japan (archipelago country off the N.E. coast of Asianmainland; traditionally settled c. 660 BC), 50, 71, 91, 92, 104-106, 114, 120, 135, 136, 138, 140, 158 [illus.], 159, 176-179, 188, 189

jati (India: social subclasses or castes), 94

Java (island of Indonesia; converted to Islam before the arrival of the Europeans in the late 16th century), 106

Jefferson, Thomas (1743-1826; 3rd President of the United States [1801-1809]; member of the 2nd Continental Congress; drafted the *Declaration of Independence* [1776]), 154

Jerusalem (capital of Israel; occupied as far back as the fourth millennium BC; became the capital of King David c. 1000 BC; later ruled by Greeks, Romans, Persians, Arabs, Crusaders, and Turks and by Great Britain), 43, 90, 197

Jesus of Nazareth (founder Christianity; major world religion), 74

Jews (member of the widely dispersed people originally descended from the ancient Hebrews and sharing an ethnic heritage based on Judaism), 37, 88, 90, 120, 174-176 [chart], 198

Jiang Jieshi (1887-1975; also Chiang Kai-shek; military leader of Chinese Nationalist [Guomindang or Kuomintang] gov't. after Sun Yixian; self-exiled to Taiwan after defeat by communists [1949]), 175, 194

Jiang Zemin (1926- , paramount leader of China since death of Deng Xaioping in 1997), 194

jihad (Muslim crusades and struggles to spread the faith, often through armed conquest), 18, 88, 198, 224

joint stock company (private enterprises used by English to finance exploration and colonization projects, 16th-19th C.), 97, 129

Jordan River (river of S.W. Asia flowing about 198 mi. from Syria to the N. end of the Dead Sea), 41

Joseph II (1741-1790; reformer; enlightened Habsburg king & Holy Roman Emperor; son of Maria Theresa of Austria), 150

journeyman (one who has fully served an apprenticeship in a trade or craft and is a qualified worker in another's employ), 113

Juarez, Benito Pablo (1806-1872; Mexican reformer, 1st Native American to be elected president), 153

Judaism (monotheistic religion of the Jews having its spiritual and ethical principles embodied chiefly in the *Bible* and the *Talmud*; cultural, religious, social practices, and beliefs of the Jews), 43, 62, 69, 73

junta (group of military officers ruling a country after seizing power; council or small legislative body in a government), 65

Justinian (r. 527-565, Byzantine emperor), 83, 85

Justinian Code (*Corpus Juris Civilis*; 6th C. AD collection of Roman civil law), 83

Kabila, Joseph (1970- ; replaced father in Jan. 2001 army coup in Democratic Republic of Congo), 205

Kabila, Laurent (1941 -2001; leader of 7-month rebellion in 1997 that ousted President Mobutu in Zaire [now Democratic Republic of Congo]), 205

kabuki (traditional Japanese dramatic form originated in the 16th C.), 115

Kalahari (desert basin in Southern Africa), 44, 45

Kalidasa (c. 400 AD, ancient sanskrit author), 83

Kampuchea (Cambodia was renamed [also Khmer Republic] briefly in 1970s; see Cambodia), 196

Kanem-Bornu (Islamic state northeast of Lake Chad destroyed by French in 19th C.), 108

karma (Hindu concept - person's actions carry unavoidable consequences and determine the nature of subsequent reincarnation [fate]; the total effect of a person's actions and conduct), 94

Kasatriya (Hindu varna: warriors and political leaders), 94

Kashmir (territory in N.W. India claimed by both India and Pakistan), 195

Katanga (now Shaba; rebellious province of S.E. Congo [Zaire]), 46

Kay, John (1704-1764, invented flying shuttle), 157

Kellogg-Briand Pact (1928 Pact of Paris; proposed a worldwide non-aggression structure), 173

Kennedy, John F. (U.S. President 1961-1963; Cuban Missile Crisis), 203

Kenya, Republic of (E. Africa; independence from Britain, 1963), 196, 224

Kenyatta, Jomo (1891-1978, nationalist leader; 1st President of Kenya), 196

Keynes, John Maynard (1883-1946; English economist called for deficit spending and tariff reductions as a way for governments to stimulate national economies in the Great Depression), 174

khan (Mongol ruler), 106, 111

Khan, Batu (d. 1255; grandson of Genghis Kahn, leader of Mongol Golden Horde), 106

Khan, Genghis (1162-1227; also Jenghiz; 13th C. Asian conqueror established Mongol Yuan Dynasty in China, proclaimed "universal ruler"), 105, 106

Khan, Kublai (1215-1294; grandson of Genghis Khan; Mongol emperor of China; moved capital to Beijing; opened China to world trade), 105-106

Khan, Reza (r. 1925-1941, Iranian reformer; overthrew the Persian Shah, expelled Soviet troops, established Pahlavi Dynasty [1925-1978]), 174

khanates (realm of khans [Mongol chieftains] or kingdoms), 105, 106, 107, 111, 112

Khanate of the Golden Horde (12th-14th C. Mongol realm in West-Central Asia & Russia; established by Batu Khan), 106

Khatami, Mohammed (president of Iran, 1997, improved relations with West), 199

Khmer Rouge (communist insurgent group in Cambodian civil war, 1960-1980), 196

Khomeini, Ruhollah (1900-1989; leader of Iranian Shi'ite Muslims; overthrew Shah in 1978), 199

Khrushchev, Nikita S. (1894-1971; Stalin's successor; 1st Secretary, U.S.S.R. [1956-1964]), 190, 200, 201, 203

kibbutz (collective farm or settlement in modern Israel), 42

Kiev ([Kyiv] Ukraine; important trading center for the Slavs after 900 AD; also called Kievan Rus), 92, 105, 106

knighthood (behavior or qualities befitting a knight; chivalry), 87

Knox, John (1514-1572, Scots; applied Calvin's ideas to founded Presbyterian Church), 119

Kongo (African trading kingdom, 1200-1800 AD), 108

Kongzi (see Confucius)

Koppen, Wladimir (1846-1940 Austrian geographer, created a system of classification of climates), 33

Koppen Climate Types (system of classification of climates), 33 [chart]

Koran (see *Qur'an*)

Korea (peninsula and former country of E. Asia between the Yellow Sea and the Sea of Japan; after W W II, the Soviet(N.)- and U.S.(S.)- occupied territories formed separate republics), 50, 51, 91, 92, 104, 107, 114, 191, 205

Korean War (1950-1953; under U.S. command; first use of U.N. army "peacekeepers"), 190, 219

Kosovo (Yugoslavia 1998, southern province with Muslim Albanian majority revolted against Orthodox Serb-dominated Yugoslav gov't.), 37, 203, 205, 224

Kostunica, Vojislav (1944- ; replaced Milosevec as president of Yugoslavia in 2000 election), 203

Kufa (inland city on Tigris; major trade and cultural capital in early Muslim Era), 88, 89, 93

Kulak (prosperous landed peasant in Russia; resisted Stalin's collectivization in 1930s0, 217

Kulikovo (battle site; Russian princes wrested Russia from Mongols of the Golden Horde, 1390 AD), 106

Kunlun Mountains (mountain system of western China extending from the Karakoram Range eastward along the northern edge of the Xizang [Tibet] plateau; isolate China), 49

Kuomintang (see Guomindang)

Kurds (pastoral and agricultural people inhabiting the transnational region of Kurdistan in Northern Iraq; persecuted by Saddam Hussein), 199

Kush (ancient kingdom of North Africa [northern Sudan]; flourished from the 11th century BC to the 4th century AD, when its capital fell to the Ethiopians), 63, 108

Kuwait (oil-rich country of the northeast Arabian Peninsula at the head of the Persian Gulf), 42, 199

Kyto Protocol (December 1997 Earth Summit on Global Warming, agreement [not ratified by U.S.] to reduce carbon dioxide and other greenhouse gases down from the 1990 levels), 223

Laissez-faire (economic doctrine opposes governmental regulation or interference in commerce beyond the minimum needed), 157

lake (large inland body of fresh water or salt water), 31

Laos (country of S.E. Asia; united as a kingdom by 1353; became part of French Indochina in 1893; gained its independence in 1953), 48

Lao -tsu (see Laozi)

Laozi (6th century BC;Chinese philosopher who is traditionally regarded as the founder of Taoism.), 74

Latin (Indo-European language of the ancient Latins and Romans), 69, 72, 96

Latin America (countries of the Western Hemisphere south of the United States, especially those speaking Spanish, Portuguese, or French), 8, 32, 38, 131, 132, 148, 152-153, 154, 203-204, 217, 221

Latin American Integration Association (Lat. Am. Free Trade Association formed in 1960 to lower trade barriers transformed in 1980), 192

Latium (ancient country of west-central Italy bordering on the Tyrrhenian Sea), 67

latitude (angular distance north or south of the earth's equator, measured in degrees along a meridian), 32

Laws of the Twelve Tablets (c. 450 BC, basis for the Roman legal system), 68

LDCs (Less Developed Countries of the world, the "have nots," generally with poor economies, poor health and education, and little industrialization), 11, 188, 214-219, 220, 223

League of Nations (1920-1945; world peace organization established after WWI), 41, 170, 174, 176, 177, 178, 191

Lebanon (country of Southwest Asia on the Mediterranean Sea; occupied by Canaanites in ancient times; torn by civil and religious strife), 197, 198

leftist (people and groups who advocate liberal, often radical measures to effect change in the established order, especially in politics, usually to achieve the equality, freedom, and well-being of the common citizens of a state), 204

Legalism (strict, literal adherence to the law or to a particular code, as of religion or morality; 3rd C. BC, Chinese philosophy - punishment should be very severe for even minor offenses), 62

Legion of Honor (in 1802 Emperor Napoleon I instituted the Légion d'Honneur; the Legion of Honor is awarded in five classes; the most common modern French decoration), 151

Lena River (river of eastern Siberia [Russia] rising near Lake Baikal and flowing about2,670 mi northeast and north to the Laptev Sea), 36

Lenin (Vladimir Ilyich Ulyanov, 1870-1924; a.k.a. "Nikoli" Lenin; Marxist leader of Bosheviks in 1917 Russian Revolutions), 171

Leopold II (King of Belgium; established Belgian Congo colony; began the imperialist "Scramble for Africa," c. 1880s), 46

Less Developed Countries (see LDCs)

Leviathan (1651; English philosopher Thomas Hobbes compares the state to the largest of natural organisms--the whale, or leviathan; that the modern state requires a single controlling intelligence to direct its motion), 135

levee en masse (French Revolution protest against drafting civilians into the military), 151

Li Bo (c. 750 AD, T'ang Dynasty poet), 83

Liu Qi (see Wudi)

Liberation Tigers of Tamil Eelam (1990, Indian-Sir Lanka, separatist responsible for thousands of deaths), 224

Liberia (West African nation created with abolitionists' help by former slaves from America; independent from 1822), 159

Libya (country of northern Africa on the Mediterranean Sea; achieved independence in 1951; became an important oil producer during the 1960's; ruled by Muammar al-Qaddafi since 1969), 199

life expectancy (number of years that an individual is expected to live as determined by statistics), 216 [chart]

Limited Nuclear Test Ban Treaty (1963; outlawed tests in the atmosphere), 190

literacy (condition or quality of being literate, especially the ability to read and write; literacy rate [% literate] = number of literate persons / tot. population), 204, 217, 218

Liu Qi (see Wudi)

Livy (59 BC - 17 AD hid history of Rome originally consisted of 142 volumes), 72

llanos (large, grassy, almost treeless plain, especially one in Latin America), 38, 39

Lloyd-George, David (1863-1945, British Prime Minister at Paris Peace Conference, 1919), 170

L'Overture, Francois Dominique Toussaint (1743-1803; revolutionary liberator of Haiti, ruler 1798-1802), 154

Locarno Pacts (1926, diplomatic agreements helped establish European boundaries after WWI), 173

Locke, John (1632-1704, English Enlightenment philosopher, *Two Treatises of gov't.*, 1690), 149, 150, 154

Lombards (nomadic invaders, replaced Goths in Italy 6th C.), 84, 85, 86

London (capital and largest city of the United Kingdom, on the Thames River in southeast England), 35

Long March (1934-1935, general retreat of Mao's communist forces in which 45,000 died), 175, 194

longitude (imaginary N-S dividing the Earth into 24 segments, each representing 1-hour of time), 32

lord (person of high rank in a feudal society or in one that retains feudal forms and institutions [king, noble, or proprietor of a manor), 95

Louis XIV (of France 17th C.; divine right ruler), 33-34, 136

Louis XVI (of France (18th C.; executed by the French Revolutionaries), 150, 151

Luther, Martin (1483-1546, German cleric began Protestant Reformation; also Lutheran Churches), 118, 119

Luzon Strait (key shipping passage of northwest Philippines),47

Lydians (ancient civilization of Western Turkey, seafaring traders, precursors of ancient Greeks), 63, 65

MacAdam, John (1756-1836, with Thomas Telford, invented hard-surfaced, crowned roads), 157

Macedon/Macedonia (ancient: 3rd C. BC Balkan kingdom of Philip & Alexander the Great; modern: independent south Balkan nation broke from Yugoslavia in 1991), 66, 71

Machiavelli, Nicoló (1469-1527; wrote *The Prince, Discourses* - advice on how to increase and hold power), 118 [chart]

machiavellian (characterized by expediency, deceit, and cunning), 136

Madurai (city of southern India south-southwest of Madras; Hindu pilgrimage site with ancient carvings on temples), 83

magistrate (government official, such as a justice of the peace, having administrative and judicial authority), 68

Magna Carta, (guarantee of rights for nobles signed in 1215 by English King John), 110, 139, 140

Magellan, Ferdinand (1519-1522, Spanish explorer; expedition circumnavigated globe, claimed many Pacific Islands), 128, 131

Magyars (principal ethnic group of Hungary), 37, 85

Mahabharata (100,000 verse epic from Sanskrit contains teaching of the Hindu god Krishna), 73

Malaya (peninsula of Southeast Asia), 106

Mali (West African Islamic kingdom, c. 1000-1400 AD), 106, 107, 108

Manchukuo (N.E. Chinese "puppet" industrial state set up by Japanese in Manchuria, 1932-1945), 177

Manchuria (region of northeast China; homeland of the Manchu people who conquered China in the 17th century),51, 177

mandate (right or command; also League of Nations, authorized Allies rule of former territories of Central Powers to prepare for independence in post-WWI Era), 41, 174

mandate of heaven (China's modified divine right system), 62, 83, 105

Mandela, Nelson (1918- , So. African anti-apartheid leader; elected President, r. 1994-1999), 196

Manhattan Project (1942-1945; U.S. scientific project to build the atomic bomb), 220

manor (district over which a lord had domain and could exercise certain rights and privileges in medieval western Europe), 95, 96, 113

manorialism (relationship between lords and serfs), 95, 97, 120

Mansa Musa (legendary 14th century Mali emperor in Central Africa), 106

Mao Zedong (1893-1976, "the Great Helmsman," Chinese leader, established communist regime in 1948), 50, 175, 194

maps (representation, usually on a plane surface, of a region of the earth or heavens), 10

Marat, Jean Paul (1743-1793; radical French revolutionary leader of the National Convention), 151

Marco Polo (Italian visitor to the court of Kublai Khan, 13th C.), 112

Maria Theresa of Austria (1740-1780, Habsburg Empress, reform-minded enlightened despot), 138, 150

Marius, Gaius (r. 104-100 BC, Roman reform consul), 70

market system (economic decisions based on free interaction of consumers and producers, minimal gov't. regulation; also capitalism), 172, 188, 191, 192, 195, 200, 201, 202, 215

Marshall Plan (1947; formally the U.S. *European Recovery Act* gave assistance in rebuilding Europe after WWII), 190, 192

Mary I (English Tudor monarch; daughter of Henry VIII succeeded her brother, Edward VI; tried to overturn Anglican Church), 110

Mary of Orange (with William III, took over throne of England after the Glorious Revolution 1688), 139, 140

Marx, Karl (1818-1883, see Marxism, author *Communist Manifesto, Das Kapital*), 21, 156, 157

Marxism (socialist interpretation of history as class struggle [workers v. capitalists]; Marx's works [*Communist Manifesto, Das Kapital*] form the basis of all communist theory), see Industrial Era

Mass (Public celebration of the Eucharist in the Roman Catholic Church and some Protestant churches), 94

Mau Mau (1950s; anti-European guerrilla movement by the Kikuyu people of British-ruled Kenya), 196

Maurya, Chandragupta (r. 321-297 BC, king of Magadha, see Maurya Empire), 64

Maurya Empire (north-central India; ancient empire of Indo-Gangetic Plain, 321-185 BC, centered in Magadha), 61, 72

Mayan Empire (50 BC - 1400 AD, Southern Mexico, Yucatan, Guatemala, Central America), 134

Mazarin, Cardinal (chief minister who dominated the gov't. during reign of Louis XIV), 136

Mazzini, Giuseppe (1805-1872, organizer of 19th C. nationalists in Italy), 155

Mecca (Islamic holy city, S.W. Saudi Arabia), 88

Medieval Christian Church (see Christian Church)

Medieval Era (500-1500 AD, Europe, also considered the Feudal Era, or Middle Ages), 87, 96, 135, 161

Medina (city of western Saudi Arabia north of Mecca; Muhammad lived here after fleeing from Mecca in 622), 88

Mediterranean Sea (between S. Europe and N. Africa), 10, 32, 33, 34, 41, 42, 67, 68, 69, 70, 82, 85, 90, 106, 111, 112, 116, 117

Mediterranean World (basin area surrounding the Mediterranean that was a cradle to early civilizations), 32

Meghaduta (c. 400 AD, ancient Sanskrit work by Sanskrit poet Kalidasa), 83

Meiji Restoration (imperial name for emperor Mutsuhito [r. 1867-1912] who presided over the overthrow of the Shogun and the transformation of feudal Japan into a modern constitutional and industrial nation), 159

Mekong River (river of southeast Asia flowing 2,600 mi. from S.E. China to the South China Sea through a vast delta in southern Vietnam.), 47, 48

Menem, Carlos Saul (1930- , elected Argentine president in 1989 after loss in Falkland Islands War with Britain; economic reformer), 203

mercantilism (theory and system of political economy based on national policies of accumulating bullion, establishing colonies and a merchant marine, and developing industry and mining to attain a favorable balance of trade), 129-131, 135

Mercosur (1995 international economic association [Argentina, Brazil, Paraguay, and Uruguay] eliminates tariffs and sets common tariffs on imports from outside), 192

meridian (of longitude; imaginary great circle on the earth's surface passing through the North and South geographic poles), 31

Mesoamerica (cultural region occupied by the native people extending south and east from central Mexico to include parts of Guatemala, Belize, Honduras, and Nicaragua), 130, 134

Mesopotamia (ancient region of S.W. Asia between the Tigris and Euphrates rivers in modern-day Iraq), 62

Metternich, Prince Klemens von (1773-

1859; Austrian statesman; worked to restore the pre-French Revolution European status quo and limit Prussian power), 152

mestizos (racial mixture: European colonizers of Latin America intermarried with Indians), 132, 153

Mexican Revolution (civil war 1910-1930; also the 1810 struggle for independence against Spain), 152-153, 154 [map]

Mexico (country of south-central North America), 205, 217

Michelangelo Buonarotti (Italian Renaissance artist: *Sistine Chapel, Pieta, Moses,* and *David*), 117 [chart]

microprocessor (computer component, integrated circuit that contains the entire central processing unit of a computer on a single chip invented by Intel in 1971), 220

Middle Ages (see Medieval)

middle class (members of society occupying a socioeconomic position intermediate between those of the lower working classes and the wealthy), 113

Middle East (traditional name used by Western scholars for region where Southwest Asia and North Africa meet), 41-43, 48, 188, 197-200, 219

Middle Kingdom (traditional Chinese ethnocentric concept that China was the center of civilization located between the dark world of barbarism and celestial paradise), 50, 138

militarism (a policy in which military preparedness is of primary importance to a state), 169

millennium (thousand year period of time)

Milosevic, Slobodan (1941- ; Yugoslav president 1989- ; backed Serbian insurgents after secession of Croatia [1991] and Bosnia-Hercegovina [1992]; continued Serb aggressions sanctioned by the U.N.; accused before World Court of ethnic cleansing campaigns; launched repression against Albanian Muslims in breakaway province of Kosovo, fomenting NATO intervention in 1999), 202

Mimana (area on southern tip of Korean Peninsula; colonized by Japan c. 400 AD), 92

Ming Dynasty (China, 1368-1644; restorers of traditional Chinese society), 111, 112, 136, 138, 140

Minoans (seafaring traders of E. Mediterranean, percursors of ancient Greeks), 65

Missouri-Mississippi River System (drains central North America), 133

mixed economic system (combines elements of market and command; see socialism), 191, 198, 199

Model Parliament (English legislative prototype, established the concept of the power of the purse in 1295), 139

Mogul (also Mughal; Mongol rulers of India, 16th-19th C. AD), 106

Mohenjo-daro (c. 3000 BC, India's earliest civilization), 62

moksa [moksha] (liberation from the world and union with Brahman Nerugna), 73

monarchy (government power in the hands of a single person, ruler, king, etc.), 65, 66, 109, 113, 135-140

monastery (religious communities bound by vows and often living in partial or complete seclusion), 94

money (exchangeable equivalent of all other commodities used as a measure of their comparative values), 113, 224

Mongols (Central Asian nomads, extensive conquests & empires, 12th-14th centuries), 38, 89, 92, 104, 105, 106, 111, 112, 116, 120

monk (man who is a member of a brotherhood living in a monastery and devoted to a discipline prescribed by his order), 94

monopoly (company or group having exclusive control over a commercial activity), 129, 137

monotheism (religion-one god belief), 73, 74

monsoons (prevailing winds in East, South, and Southeast Asia; reverses direction in summer and winter), 30, 47, 62, 217

Montesquieu, Baron de la Brede de (1689-1755, French Enlightenment writer; separation of power in gov't.), 149

Montenegro (S.W. Balkan nation joined with Serbia in new Yugoslavian state in 1991), 202

Moors (Christian name for Muslims, mainly in Spain), 109

More, Thomas (statesman and author Renaissance England; *Utopia*), 117 [chart], 119

mosaic (picture or decorative design made by setting small colored pieces, as of stone or tile, into a surface), 83

moshav (Israeli cooperative settlement consisting of small separate farms), 42

mosque (Islamic house of worship), 74, 89

mountain (natural elevation of the earth's surface having considerable mass, generally steep sides, and a height greater than that of a hill), 31

Mubarak, Mohammed Hosni (1928- , replaced al-Sadat as president of Egypt), 199

Mughals (Mongol/Islamic rulers of India, 16th-19th C. AD), 48, 106, 136, 138, 140

Muhammad (570-632 AD; originator and major prophet of Islamic faith; also referred to as "the Prophet;" also spelled Mohammed or Mohammet), 88

mulattos (African-Caucasian intermarriage in Latin America), 132

multinational empire (super state ruling over many ethnic groups and nationalities), 168 multiple-choice questions (overview of varieties on global history and geography examinations), 6-15

Munich Conference (1938 summit meeting at which Britain and France appeased Hitler, yielding Czech territory), 177

Murasaki Shikibu (see Shikibu)

Muslim (variant of "Moslem," preferred in scholarly circles; in Arabic, "one who surrenders;" a follower of Islam), 37, 48, 85, 86, 88, 89, 90, 91, 96, 106, 114, 120, 195, 197, 198, 200, 203, 205, 217

Mussolini, Benito (1883-1945, Italian Fascist leader, 1922-1940s), 172, 175, 177

Mexico, 152-153, 192

Mexico City (most populous city in the world [1999]), 40

Myron (5th C. BC; classical greek sculptor; *The Discus Thrower*), 72

Mycenaeans (Aegean civilization that spread its influence to many parts of the Mediterranean region; first Greek-speaking people), 66

NAFTA (North American Free Trade Association; Canada, Mexico, U.S. trade treaty and zone), 192

Nanking, Treaty of (now Nanjing, city of east central China; 1842 Treaty forcefully opened China to limited trade with the West), 159

Napoleon Bonaparte (1769-1821, ruler of France), 36, 151-152, 154

Napoleonic Code of Laws ([Code Civil] legal system for 19th C. French Empire), 151

Napoleonic Wars (periodic warfare in Europe c. 1802-1815 Britain, Austria, Russia v. France), 37, 46

Nara (city of south-central Honshu, Japan; ancient cultural and religious center; first permanent capital of Japan, 710-784), 105, 115

Nasser, Gamal Abdel (1918-1970, nationalist leader of Egypt in 1950s), 43, 197, 199

nation (relatively large group of people who share common customs, origins, history, and frequently language, organized under a single, usually independent gov't.), 109

nation-states (political unit consisting of an autonomous state inhabited especially by a predominantly homogeneous people), 109

National Assembly (declared by the Third Estate at the beginning of the French Revolution), 151

National Convention (also National Assembly; legislature in midst of French Revolution), 151

nationalism (belief that nations will benefit from acting independently rather than collectively, emphasizing national rather than international goals), 152, 153, 159, 168, 169 [illus.], 177, 178, 191

nationalization (governmental takeover of private enterprises), 199, 203, 204

Native American (aboriginal peoples of the Western Hemisphere, also Amerindian), 39, 132, 133, 153, 205, 224

Native Land Act (1913 apartheid rule forbade black South Africans to own land off reservations), 196

NATO (North Atlantic Treaty Organization; post-WWII multilateral security alliance, Western Europe, Canada & U.S.), 190, 203, 204

natural law (a body of moral principles common to all humankind; Enlightenment philosophical theories), 135, 149

Nazi Party (1921-1945; National Socialist German Workers party [Nationalsozialistische Deutsche Arbeiterpartei]; political organization built by Adolf Hitler and followers; took power in 1933 and created totalitarian regime that fomented World War II), 175-176

Nazi-Soviet Pact (1939; non-aggression and trade agreement between Stalin and Hitler pledging peace and upsetting the European balance of power; also contained a secret protocol that provided for a German-Soviet partition of Poland and cleared the way for the Soviet occupation of the Baltic states), 13, 172, 176

Nazi Youth Movement (1930s; German youth cult that emphasized sports and paramilitary outdoor activities under Hitler), 175

Neolithic Age / Revolution (c. 5000-9000 BC, life began centering on agriculture), 60, 75, 133

Netherlands (European country located on the south shore of the North Sea; achieved its independence as the United Provinces in 1648 after the Thirty Years' War; active in commerce and colonization), 33, 46, 120, 128, 129, 135, 136

Netanyahu, Benjamin (1946- , conservative Prime Minister of Israel in 1996-1999), 198

neutrality (policy of being neutral, especially non-participation in war), 176

New Deal (U.S. President Franklin Roosevelt's program [1933-39] of relief, recovery, and reform that aimed at solving the economic problems created by the Depression of the 1930s), 174

New Economic Policy (NEP, 1921-1927; Lenin's socialist economic structure for the U.S.S.R.), 171

New Spain (northern sector of Spain's American/ Caribbean empire 15th to 19th C.), 131

New World (Western Hemisphere; term first used by Italian historian Peter Martyr [1457-1526], whose *De Rebus Oceanicis et Novo Orbe* chronicled the discovery of America), 44

New Testament (Christian scripture - primarily the Gospels of Matthew, Mark, Luke, and John), 74

Newton, Sir Isaac (1643-1727, universal law of gravitation; Principa), 149

Nicaragua (country of Central America on the Caribbean Sea and the Pacific Ocean), 204

Nicholas II (r. 1894-1917; last Romanov Tsar during Revolutions & WWI, abdicated, killed w/family by Bolsheviks), 171

Niger River (river of western Africa flowing about 2,000 mi through Mali, Niger, and Nigeria to the Gulf of Guinea) 44, 45

Nigeria (country of West Africa on the Gulf of Guinea; exploited by Portuguese, British, French, and Dutch slave traders, 15th-19th centuries), 108, 195

Nightingale, Florence (1820-1910, British nurse - founder of modern nursing), 168

Nile River (longest river in the world, flows 4,150 miles through eastern Africa from Burundi to a delta on the Mediterranean Sea in northeast Egypt; used for irrigation in Egypt since at least 4000 BC, now regulated by the Aswan High Dam), 32, 40, 41, 42, 43, 44, 45, 61, 62

Nine Power Treaty (Washington Naval Arms Conference [1922]; nations pledged respect for the independence and territory of China), 176

Nirvana (in Buddhism, the ultimate condition of rest, harmony, stability, or joy in which one has attained disinterested wisdom and compassion), 73

noble (having hereditary rank in a political system or social class sometimes derived from a feudalistic stage of a country's development), 66, 90, 93, 95, 109, 110, 113, 129, 135, 136

nomad / nomadic (life-style of constant migration, seeking food), 30, 60, 105, 133, 134

Noh (theatrical plays of 14th C. Japan - myths and history), 115

North Atlantic Treaty Organization (see NATO)

North(ern) European Plain (open region running from Russia to France), 33, 34, 36

North German Confederation (1866, union of German states established by Prussia after the Austro-Prussian War), 153 [map]

North Sea (N.W. Europe off Norway and Scotland), 10, 33, 34

North/South imbalance (division between the "have and have-not" nations), 214

Northern Ireland (northeastern part of Ireland, majority of Protestants), 205

Nubia (desert region and ancient kingdom in the Nile River valley of southern Egypt and northern Sudan), 61, 106, 108

Nuclear Nonproliferation Treaty (1968; attempted to stop spread of nuclear weapons to countries not already having them), 190

Nuclear Test Ban Treaty (see Limited Nuclear Test Ban Treaty 1963)

Nuremberg Trials (1945-1946; 22 Nazi leaders tried for war crimes [12 sentenced to death, four, including Karl Doenitz and Albert Speer, were sentenced to up to 20 years]), 178

nun (woman who belongs to a religious order or congregation devoted to active service or meditation), 94

Ob River (2,300 mi. long river in western Siberia; flows northward to the Arctic Ocean), 36

ocean (body of salt water that covers more than 70 percent of the Earth's surface; any of the principal divisions of the ocean, including the Atlantic, Pacific, and Indian oceans), 31

Octavian (63-14 BC; 1st Roman emperor [Augustus]), 70, 72

O'Higgins, Bernardo (1778-1842; Chilean general and politician who ruled Chile [1817-1823] after its revolt against the Spanish), 154

Old Regime (ancien régime; allowed the king to wield absolute power over a tight-knit social hierarchy), 150, 151

Old Testament (of the Bible; Judeo-Christian teachings and law on moral behavior), 73

oligarchy (government power in the hands of a small group), 65, 67

OPEC (Organization of Petroleum Exporting Countries; cartel of oil producing states), 41, 197

Opium Wars (1839-1841, Anglo-Chinese power struggle), 159

Orinoco River (river of Venezuela flowing more than 1,500 mi., partly along the Colombia-Venezuela border, to the Atlantic Ocean), 38, 39

Ortega, Daniel (1945- ; leftist Sandinista National Liberation Front [FSLN] leader; president of Nicaragua from 1985 to 1990), 204

Orthodox Christian Church (adhering to the Christian faith as expressed in the early Christian ecumenical creeds; also Eastern, Greek Orthodox or Orthodox Catholic Church, not accepting supremacy of Roman Pope), 37, 74, 92, 96, 137, 205

Oslo Accord (1993 agreement between PLO and Israel setting up a Palestinian National Authority to administer a school system, a police force, banks, a television station, courts, taxation, a postal service and other services; PNA is charged with keeping the peace in the parts of the formerly Israeli-occupied territories now under Palestinian self-rule), 198

Ottoman Empire (Muslim Turkish state; encompassed Anatolia, southeastern Europe, and the Arab Middle East and North Africa from the 14th to the early 20th century; succeeded both the Byzantine Empire the Arab caliphates), 130, 136, 137, 140, 170

overlord (one in a position of supremacy or domination over others), 87, 115

Ovid (43 BC - 17 AD; Roman poet: the *Art of Love* [c. 1 BC] and *Metamorphoses*), 72

Owen, Robert (1771-1858, English utopian socialist, founded New Lanark, Scotland, and New Harmony, Indiana, U.S.), 156, 157

Pacific Rim (broad term for countries sur-rounding the Pacific Ocean), 128, 140, 188, 193, 215

Pacific Ocean (largest of the five great bod-ies of water on Earth; N-S between Asia/Australia and N. & S. America), 36, 38, 39, 47, 49, 50, 111, 133

pagan (professing no religion; heathen; unbeliever), 18

pagoda (structure, such as a garden pavil-ion, built in imitation of a many-storied Buddhist tower), 83

Paine, Thomas (1737-1809; British-born American writer and revolutionary leader; wrote the pamphlet *Common Sense* [1776] arguing for American inde-pendence from Britain; also published *The Rights of Man* [1791-1792], a defense of the French Revolution), 154

Pakistan (south Asian Muslim nation bor-dering India on the west carved out of India by British as a country for Muslims; originally had an Eastern section which is now Bangladesh), 195

Palestine (historical region of southwest Asia between the eastern Mediterranean shore and the Jordan River roughly coex-tensive with modern Israel and the West Bank), 61, 90, 174, 197, 198

Palestine Liberation Organization (PLO; seeks separate Palestinian Arab state in areas occupied by Israel; involved in ter-rorist activities), 198

Pamirs (region of high mountains and val-leys in central Asia sometimes called "the roof of the world;" extends from Tajikistan, into northeastern Afghanistan and Xinjiang, China), 63

Pampas (vast plain of south-central South America extending 1,000 mi. from the lower Paraná River to south-central Argentina), 38, 39

Panama Canal (51 mi. long ship canal built by the U.S. opened in 1914; crossing the Isthmus of Panama and connecting the Caribbean Sea with the Pacific Ocean), 38, 39, 40

parallels (of latitude; imaginary lines repre-senting degrees of latitude that encircle the earth parallel to the plane of the equator), 31

Paraná River (river of central South America flowing 1,800 mi. southwest to the Paraguay River then south to the Uruguay River and forming the Río de la Plata estuary in Argentina), 38

Paris Peace Conference of 1919 (see *Treaty of Versailles*)

parliament (national representative body having supreme legislative powers within a state), 110, 136, 138, 139, 140

Parthenon (ancient Athenian temple), 72, 110, 138-139

Pasteur, Louis (1822-1895, French chemist who founded modern microbiology, invent-ed the process of pasteurization, and developed vaccines for anthrax, rabies, and chicken cholera), 168

patricians (member of one of the noble fam-ilies of the ancient Roman Republic [before the 3rd century BC had exclusive rights to the Senate and the magistra-cies]; aristocrats), 68

Pax Mongolia (brief era of peaceful Mongol rule), 112

Pax Romana (31BC-476 AD; 400 year domi-nation of ancient Mediterranean World by Roman civilization), 70, 112

"Peace, Land, and Bread!" (popular demands of Russian Revolutionaries in 1917 [end Russia's part in WWI, reform the near-feudal land system, provide food for near-famine conditions], 171

Peaceful Coexistence (Khrushchev's U.S.S.R. foreign policy of minimizing con-frontations with Western powers), 201.

peasant (member of the class constituted by small farmers and tenants, sharecrop-pers, and laborers on the land where they form the main labor force in agriculture), 94, 95, 115, 116, 132, 175

Peasants' War (religious conflict 1524-1526; German peasants, small-town artisans, and laborers sacked castles and monas-teries), 120

Pedro I / Pedro II (Portuguese rulers exiled to Brazil during the Napoleonic occupa-tion; Pedro II set up an independent empire in 1822), 154

Peking (older spelling of Beijing; China's capital)

Peloponnesian League (c. 4th C. BC mili-tary alliance of ancient Greek poleis formed by Sparta), 65, 66

Peloponnesian Wars (rival alliances of poleis led by Sparta and Athens respec-tively battled from 431-404 BC), 66

penicillin (group of broad-spectrum antibi-otic drugs from molds or produced syn-thetically; used in the treatment of vari-ous infections and diseases), 221

peninsula (land that projects into a body of

water and is connected with the mainland by an isthmus), 31, 49, 65, 67

peninsulares (Iberian-born nobles who acted as crown-appointed rulers in colonial Latin America), 31, 47, 131, 132

Pepin III (c. 714-768; first Carolingian king of the Franks, father of Charlemagne; aligned Frankish Kingdom with Papacy), 86

People's Republic of China (Communist regime came to power in 1949), 194

per capita income (total national income ÷ population = share per person), 214

perestroika (Gorbachev's proposals for restructuring U.S.S.R.'s economy and bureaucracy), 200, 201

Pericles (ancient Greek statesman, 461-429 BC), 72

Peron, Juan (1895-1974 Argentine ruler), 203

Peron, Eva (1919-1952; wife of Juan Peron; reformer; "Evita"), 203

Perry, Commodore Matthew (c. 1853, U.S. naval commander negotiated reopening of Japan to international trade), 51, 158 [illustration], 159

Persia (present day Iran; vast empire of southwest Asia founded by Cyrus II after 546 BC and brought to the height of its power and glory by Darius I and his son Xerxes), 61, 62, 64, 66, 71, 83, 89, 106, 111, 136, 137, 174

Persian Gulf (arm of the Arabian Sea between the Arabian Peninsula and southwest Iran; important trade route since ancient times; strategic significance after the 1930s discovery of oil), 41

Persian Gulf War (1990-1991, Iraq invaded Kuwait, U.S. led coalition forces drove Iraq out), 42, 199

Persian Wars (series of conflicts between the ancient Greek poleis and Persian Empire c. 546-480 BC), 66

Peru (nation of N.E. South America), 39

Peter I, the Great (Tsar, 1682-1725, Westernized Russian culture and economy), 37, 136, 137

Petition of Right (1628 act strengthened British Parliament), 139, 140

petrochemical (chemical products derived from oil, plastics, fertilizers, pesticides), 220

pharaohs (rulers in ancient Egypt), 62

pharmacology (science of drugs, including their composition, uses, and effects), 62

Phidias (c. 490-430 BC, greatest of the ancient Greek sculptors), 72

Philip II of Macedon (359-336 BC; ruler of Hellenes; father of Alexander the Great),65, 66, 71

Philip II of Spain (defeated by Elizabeth I of England in famous English Channel battle 1588), 129, 136

Philippines (West. Pacific island nation), 8

philosophes (French Enlightenment scholars who analyze processes of reason), 128, 150, 153

Phoenicians (ancient Mediterranean traders of coastal strip of Palestine-Syria; under Egyptian imperial control (to c.1200 BC), then independent falling to the Assyrians (860BC); developed an alphabet code in which each letter stood for only one distinct sound), 61, 63, 65, 68, 85

pictograph (picture representing a word or idea; a hieroglyph), 62

Pindar (c. 518-438 BC, lyric poet of ancient Greece), 72

Pizarro, Francisco (1475-1541; Spanish conquistador, conquered Incas), 131

plague (widespread affliction or calamity), 66, 116

plain (extensive, level, usually treeless area of land), 32

Plantagenet (family name of a line of English kings from Henry II to Richard III [1154-1485]), 139

plantation (large estate or farm on which crops are raised, often by resident workers), 129, 130

plateau (elevated, comparatively level expanse of land), 31

Plato (philosopher of Ancient Greece, c. 428-347 BC; presented his ideas in the form of dramatic dialogues, as in *The Republic*), 72

plebeians (common people- farmers, merchants, artisans - of ancient Rome), 68, 72

plebiscites (election in which voters express their will on an issue directly at the polls), 154, 155

PLO (see Palestine Liberation Organization)

Pol Pot (1928-1998; Khmr Rouge Cambodian premier [1975-1979], violent purges of 1970s caused over 3 million to die), 196, 217

Poland (central European republic bordering on the Baltic Sea; major power in the 15th and 16th centuries; carved up among other states until reformed as a republic in 1918; Soviet satellite 1945-1989), 37, 176, 189 [map], 190 [cartoon], 202

poleis (plural of polis)

polis (city-states of ancient Greece), 65, 66, 68, 72

political spectrum (broad range of related governmental qualities, ideas, or activities; on the right is usually reactionary authoritarian rule for an individual or small elite [conservative]; on the left usually are advocates of radical measures to effect change in the established order [liberal]), 172

pollution (contamination of soil, water, or the atmosphere by the discharge of harmful substances), 21, 222-223

Polo, Marco (Italian visitor to the court of Kublai Khan, 13th C.), 112

polytheism (belief in multiplicity of gods), 73, 88

Pompey, Gnaeus (c. 70 BC, Roman consul, one of a reform triumvirate with Crassius and Caesar), 70

Ponce de Leon, Juan (1460-1521; credited with the discovery of Florida), 131

Pope (bishop of Rome and head of the Roman Catholic Church), 74, 86, 90, 119

Pope Leo III (crowned Charlemagne as Holy Roman Emperor 800 AD), 86

Pope Urban II (called for a crusade to regain control of the Holy Land from the Muslim Turks in 1095), 90

Portugal, 33, 46, 90, 108, 114, 129, 135, 154

Portuguese (relating to Portugal or its people, language), 46, 111, 120, 128, 129, 159

Potato Famine (see the Great Hunger)

Potsdam Conference (1945, disagreements among WWII Allies), 178 [chart]

praetor (an annually elected magistrate of the ancient Roman Republic), 68

Praxiteles (370-330 BC, Greek sculptor), 72

"prime the pump" (economist Keynes plan of deficit spending to overcome economic depression), 174

Prince Henry (see Henry the Navigator)

Princip, Gavrilo (Bosnian assassin of Austrian Archduke Franz Ferdinand; fomented WWI), 169

privatization (turn gov't.-operated facilities into private businesses; opposite of nationalization), 199, 202

pro-democracy movements (organized activities to pressure governments for more openness to the people; seeking voting rights), 194, 201

proletariat (poorest class composed of industrial wage earners who, with neither capital nor production means, must earn their living by selling their labor)

propaganda (use of media to promote or oppose a cause), 194

Protestant Reformation (16th-18th C. Europe religious reform movement), 109, 110, 119-120

Protestantism (faith and practices founded on the principles of the Protestant Reformation, especially in the acceptance of The Bible as the sole source of revelation, in justification by faith alone, and in the universal priesthood of all the believers), 18, 109, 110, 119-120

Prussia (kingdom of north-central Europe including present-day northern Germany and Poland [1701]; expanded by Emperor Frederick II; instrumental in the unification of Germany), 36, 151, 155

Provisional Government (Russia; set up when Russian Tsar Nicholas II abdicated, 1919), 171

Punic Wars (264-146 BC series of three protracted conflicts for Mediterranean dominance between Carthageand Rome), 68

purge (to get rid of people considered undesirable; elimination of any opposition; ex. Stalin brutally purged Soviet Communist Party in 1930s - 20 million est. dead), 171, 172

Puritan Revolution (1642; overthrow of English monarchy; creation of a commonwealth form of government, 1649-1659), 139

Puritans (Calvinist reformers of the Anglican Church, C. 16th-17th C.), 139

Pyrenees (mt. range in S.W. Europe between France and Spain), 33, 34

pyramids (massive monument of ancient times having a rectangular base and four triangular faces culminating in a single apex; often built over or around a crypt or tomb), 43, 62

Pythagoras of Samos (ancient Greek mathematician; principles of geometry, d. 500 BC), 72

Q'in (Ch'in) Dynasty (unified China, 217-210 BC), 64

Q'ing Dynasty (1644-1912; China's last dynasty; increasing Western influence and trade led to the Opium Wars with Britain and the Boxer Rebellion [1898-1900]), 161

Qaddafi, Muammar al- (1942- ; Libyan leader, overthrew monarchy, 1969; imposed socialist policies and Islamic orthodoxy; involved in international terrorism against western powers), 199

Qur'an (Koran - Islam's sacred text), 74, 93

Rabbi (scholar trained in Jewish law, ritual, and tradition and ordained for leadership of a Jewish congregation; chief religious official of a synagogue), 73

Rabin, Yitzhak (1922-1995; Israel's prime minister from 1974 to 1977 and 1992-1995; set up Palestinian self-rule with Yasir Arafat [1993] and a peace agreement with King Hussein I of Jordan [1994]; given Nobel Peace Prize [1994]), 198

radar (WWII invention, method of detecting distant objects and determining their position, and velocity by analysis of very high frequency radio waves reflected from their surfaces), 176

Ramadan (ninth month of the year in the Moslem calendar often associated with violence against Jews and Westerners), 200

Ramayana (3rd C. BC, 24,000 verse epic from Sanskrit), 73

Raphael (1483-1520; Italian painter whose works, including religious subjects, portraits, and frescoes, exemplify the ideals of the Renaissance), 117 [chart]

Rasputin, Grigory (1865-1916, dissolute monk, consultant to Tsarina Alexandra), 171

recession (extended decline in general business activity, typically three consecutive quarters of falling real gross national product), 215

Reconquista (13th - 14th C., Spanish European kingdoms driving out Islamic Moors), 109

Reds (epithet/nickname for communist groups; see also Bolsheviks), 171

Red River (also Song Hong; river of S.E. Asia flows 730 mi. from S. China through N. Vietnam to a fertile delta on the Gulf of Tonkin), 47

Red Sea (narrow sea between N.E. Africa and the Arabian Peninsula; linked to Mediterranean by the Suez Canal), 41

refugee (person who flees in search of refuge, as in times of war, political oppression, or religious persecution), 12, 198, 204

region (large areas with common physical, political, economic, and / or cultural traits), 31, 32

Reign of Terror (1790s: French Revolution, the execution of between 15-45,000 opponents), 151

Reichstag (lower house of the German parliament c. 1930s), 176

religion (personal or institutionalized system of belief in and reverence for a supernatural power or powers regarded as creator and governor of the universe), 17-18

Renaissance (humanistic revival of classical art, architecture, literature, and learning that originated in Italy in the 14th century and later spread throughout Europe), 9, 38, 109, 117, 118, 119, 120, 128, 148, 149

reparations (compensation or remuneration required from a defeated nation as indemnity for damage or injury during WWI), 173

republic (representative democracy form of gov't.; people elect representatives to make decisions), 67

Responsibility System (instituted by Deng Xiaoping, each family was to be responsible for itself), 194

revenue (income, especially gov't. income from taxes, tariffs, and fees), 46, 110, 174, 202

Rhine River (major waterway in Germany), 33-34

Richelieu, Cardinal Armand (1585-1642, chief minister to and given full authority by, Louis XIII), 110

Río de la Plata (wide estuary of S.E. South America between Argentina and Uruguay formed by the Paraná and Uruguay rivers and opening on the Atlantic Ocean), 38, 39

river (large natural stream of water emptying into an ocean, a lake, or another body of water and usually fed along its course by converging tributaries),

Robespierre, Maximilien Francois Marie Isidore de (1758-1794; radical, incorruptible French revolutionary leader; architect of the Reign of Terror), 151

Rock Edicts (pillars inscribed with laws placed throughout India's empire under Asoka, 272-232 BC), 72

Rocky-Sierra Madre Cordillera (north-south mountain chain along the western half of North American continent), 32, 39, 133

rogue nations (unprincipled, deceitful, and unreliable countries, often engaging in terrorism, and guerrilla warfare against others), 201

Roman Catholic Church (relating to the ancient undivided Christian Church [followers of Jesus] under the Pope [Bishop of Rome] that became the predominant social institution of Europe in the Middle Ages), 37, 69, 93, 118-120, 129, 153, 203, 204, 205

Romans / Roman Civilization (dominant political and cultural civilization in ancient Mediterranean and Western Europe from 700 BC-400 AD), 7, 18, 32, 67, 83, 85

Roman Empire (27 BC-476 AD; empire succeeded the Roman Republic during the time of Augustus; at its greatest extent it encompassed territories stretching from Britain and Germany to North Africa and the Persian Gulf; after 395 it was split into the Byzantine Empire and the Western Roman Empire), 69, 70, 72, 75, 83, 84, 95, 96, 112

Roman Republic (500-27 BC; dominant civilization in ancient Mediterranean after 250 BC), 67

Rome-Berlin-Tokyo Axis (1939; pre-WWII alliance of Italy, Germany, and Japan; also called the Tripartite Pact), 176

Roosevelt, Franklin D. (1882-1945; U.S. President, 1933-45), 174, 177, 178

Rousseau, Jean-Jacques (1712-1778; French Enlightenment writer), 149, 150, 154

Rub al Khali (Arabian Peninsula; desert region of S.W. Asia sometimes called "the Empty Quarter"), 41, 42

Ruhr Crisis (1923; Germany suspended reparations payments in 1922, provoking French to occupy the Ruhr area; miners and factory workers resisted by striking which brought on economic collapse), 173

Russia (early civilization of easternmost Europe; spread into Central Asia under Tsars; overthrown by Bolshevik Revolution, 1917; also see U.S.S.R. and Russian Federation), 30, 36-38,83, 92, 106, 136, 137, 151, 168, 169, 171, 201, 201-202, 220

Russian Civil War (1917-1921, Bolshevik Reds v. anti-communist Whites), 171

Russian Revolution of 1905 (defeat in Russo-Japanese War led to strikes, protests and riots in Russia; Tsar Nicholas II allowed establishment of Duma [legislature] but reneged on most reforms he'd promised), 171

Russian Revolutions of 1917 (tensions arose from rapid industrialization, strains placed on traditional institutions by Westernization, and defeats in World War I; social upheaval involved angry peasants expropriating gentry land, rigidness of absolutist monarchy, and a struggle for a new, more equal society; moderate socialists [Cadets] forced the Tsar's abdication in March and formed a weak Provisional Government, more radical Bolsheviks overthrew the moderates' government in November), 171

Russification (conquered or subjected people forced to adopt Russian language, culture and religion to increase unity), 172 [chart]

Russo-Japanese War (1904-1905; Japan became the first modern Asian nation to defeat a major European state; led to political upheaval in Russia), 159

Sadat, Muhammad Anwar al- (1918-1981; Egyptian President [r. 1970-1981], *Camp David Accords*; shared the 1978 Nobel Peace Prize with Israeli Prime Minister Menachem Begin; assassinated 1981), 198, 199

Sadler Report (1832 British Parliamentary investigation on factory conditions), 21

Safavids (Islamic mystics became a ruling dynasty that dominated Iran in the 16th and 17th centuries), 136, 137

Sahara (vast desert of northern Africa extending east from the Atlantic coast to the Nile Valley and south from the Atlas Mountains to the region of the Sudan), 41, 42, 44, 45, 106-108

Sahel ("edge of the desert;" drought-stricken area of West Central Africa), 44, 222, 223

Saint Augustine (early Christian church father and philosopher who served [396-430] as the bishop of Hippo [in present-day Algeria], 94

Saint Patrick (Christian missionary and patron saint of Ireland), 94

Saint Simon, Count de (1760-1825, Claude Henri de Rouvroy - utopian; favored planned societies with public ownership of the means of production), 157

Saladin (also Yusuf ibn Ayyub Salah ad-din [1138-1193]; Muslim warrior, Fatimid vizier, founder of the Ayyubid Dynasty, Sultan of Egypt and Syria; effectively repulsed the Crusaders), 111

SALT agreements (U.S.-U.S.S.R. arms limitation treaties, 1970s), 190

Salt March (1930; M.K. Gandhi imprisoned for 198-mile non-violent protest of British monopoly in India), 174

Samnites (ancient civilization of west-central Italy before founding of Rome c. 700 BC), 67

Samarkand (important central Asian commercial center along Silk Route), 63, 105

samurai (Japanese feudal military - professional warrior belonging to the aristocracy), 105, 115

San Martín, José de (1778-1850; Argentine revolutionary leader who played a major part in expelling the Spanish from Chile [1818] and Peru [1821]), 154

Sandinistas (Nicaraguan communist guerrilla movement, ruled 1979-1990), 204

sangha (community of the followers of Buddha; sometimes a monastic order), 73

Sanskrit (ancient language of India), 48, 62

Sappho (c. 630 BC, most famous woman poet of classical Greece), 72

Sardinia (island of Italy in the Mediterranean Sea south of Corsica; settled by Phoenicians, Greeks, and Carthaginians before the sixth century BC), 68

Sassanid Empire (Persian dynasty [AD 220-651] last line of Persian kings before the Arab conquest), 63, 83, 88

satellite (nation and gov't. dominated by an outside power; Eastern Europe under Soviets 1945-1990), 192, 201

savanna (tropical or subtropical grassland [Bs climatic type]), 31

Saudi Arabia (kingdom occupying most of the Arabian Peninsula in S.W. Asia; independent in 1932), 41, 42

Scandinavia (region of northern Europe consisting of Norway, Sweden, and Denmark. Finland, Iceland, and the Faeroe Islands are often included in the region), 191

scapegoat (One that is made to bear the blame of others), 175

Scientific Revolution (composite work of 17th century pioneers--Francis Bacon, Galileo, Descartes, Leibniz, Isaac Newton, and John Locke--who had developed fruitful methods of rational, empirical inquiry, and the application of knowledge for human benefit), 148, 149

Scramble for Africa (European imperialist race to develop colonies in Africa in the late 19th C.), 159

sea (a tract of water within an ocean; relatively large body of salt water completely or partially enclosed by land; relatively large landlocked body of fresh water), 31

Sea of Japan (enclosed arm of the western Pacific Ocean between Japan and the Asian mainland), 49 seclusion policy (isolating a country from the outside world as in Japan under the Tokugawa Shoguns), 104, 138

Second Estate (nobility in French Estates-General - the rarely-called national assembly under the French monarchs), 150

sect (a religious body, especially one that has separated from a larger denomination; a small faction united by common interests or beliefs) , 73, 74

Security Council (see U.N. Security Council)

Sei Shonagon (c. 966-1013, poet produced *The Pillow-Book*, a diary describing court life in Japan), 115

Seine River (major waterway in central; France), 33-34

self-determination (desire for local independence or sovereignty), 7

Seljuk Turks (11th C. conquerors of Asia Minor [Turkey]), 89, 90, 105

Senate, (Roman advisory body to the Etruscan kings; main legislative body in the Republic; returned to advisory status by emperors), 68

Senegal (country of western Africa on the Atlantic Ocean; center for slave trade, 15th-19th centuries), 108

Serbia (central Balkan nation forms main part of Yugoslavia), 168, 169, 172 [map], 202

Serbs (dominant ethnic group in central Balkans), 37, 169, 205

serfs (peasants; feudal class of people in Europe, legally bound to the land and owned by a lord), 95, 116

Seubi (Germanic invaders during early Medieval era), 84

shah (traditional title for the hereditary monarch of Iran), 18, 174

Shah Jahan (1627-1658; Mughal Indian ruler, continued golden age begun by Akbar), 106

Shaka (1787-1828; Zulu conqueror of S.E. Africa, area included present-day Mozambique, Zimbabwe, Malawi), 159

Shakuntala (ancient Sanskrit work by Kalidasa c. 400 AD), 83

Shang Dynasty (first documented Chinese civilization, 1700 BC), 61, 62

Shari'a ("the way" - Islamic moral rules incorporated into a code of law), 74, 89, 93

Shi Huangdi (see Zheng)

Shi'ites (member of the branch of Islam that regards Ali and his descendants as the legitimate successors to Mohammed; Muslim fundamentalist sect), 18, 89

Shikibu, Murasaki (c. 978-1026, wrote *Tale of Genji*, an early novel of life among the court nobles in Japan), 115

Shinto, Shintoism (religion native to Japan, characterized by veneration of nature spirits and ancestors and by a lack of formal dogma), 92, 104, 114

shogun / shogunate (Japan, 11th to mid-19th C.; hereditary military commander / chieftain who exercised absolute rule), 104, 105, 115

Shotoku Taishi (573-621, Japanese noble created a central authority based on laws related to China's Confucian social order), 104, 105

Siberia (mineral rich, vast plain region composing northern part of Asiatic Russia), 36, 37, 172

Sicily (island of southern Italy in the Mediterranean Sea west of the southern end of the Italian Peninsula; colonized from the 8th century BC by Greeks, who displaced the earlier Phoenician settlers), 65, 68

Sierra Madres (cordillera in Mexico and Central America), 38

Sikhs (Hindu sect founded in 15th C.), 195

Silk Route or Road (merchant routes through deserts and mountains of Central Asia between Middle East and East Asia), 63, 96

Silla (Korean dynasty expelled the Japanese from Mimana and set up a strong state in the 6th and 7th century AD), 92

Sinai Peninsula (peninsula linking southwest Asia with northeast Africa at the northern end of the Red Sea between the Gulf of Suez and the Gulf of Aqaba; Israel occupied the Peninsula in 1956 and from 1967 to 1982, when it was returned to Egyptian control under the terms of the *Camp David Accords* (1978) and an Egyptian-Israeli treaty (1979), 197, 198

Sino-Japanese War (First, 1894-1895; Japan defeated China to signaling its emergence as a modern military power), 51, 159

Six-Day War (1967 Arab-Israeli War), 43, 197, 198

slash and burn (systematic, mechanical method of felling and clearing large tracts of forested land), 222

Slavs, Slavic (eastern European settlers and linguistic group; ancestors of Poles, Slovaks, Czechs, Slovenes, Croats, Serbs), 37, 92

slavery (a social system in which one individual is owned and exploited by another), 40-41, 44-45, 108, 129, 130, 132

Slovak Republic (Slovakia eastern region of former Czechoslovakia; independent 1992), 202

Slovenia (N.W. Balkan country; broke away from Yugoslavia, 1991), 37, 202

Smith, Adam (1723-1790; social philosopher and economist; founder of modern economics; promoted doctrine of laissez-faire in masterwork, *The Wealth of Nations* [1776]), 157

socialism (Marxist influenced systems seeking abolition of the private-enterprise economy and its replacement by "public ownership," or state control over production and distribution), 156, 157, 191

socialists (backers of political systems in which the means of producing and distributing goods are owned collectively; methods of transformation advocated by socialists range from constitutional change to violent revolution), 191

society (organized groups of individuals which have a set of behavioral rules that are transmitted from one generation to another)

Socrates (c. 469-399 BC, Greek philosopher), 72

Solidarity (Polish labor union, headed by Lech Walesa, won 1989 elections), 202

Somoza, Anastasio (1925-1980, Nicaraguan dictator overthrown by communists, 1979), 204

sonar (WWII; system using transmitted and reflected underwater sound waves to detect and locate submerged objects), 176

Song (also Sung) Dynasty (960-1279 AD), 82, 105

Songhai (powerful 13th C. West African trading kingdom), 108

Sophists (5th C BC; pre-Socratic philosophers who inquired about and speculated on theology, metaphysics, mathematics, and the natural and biological sciences), 72

Sophocles (497-406 BC, Greek dramatist), 72

South Africa (Republic of; country of Southern Africa on the Atlantic and Indian oceans first settled by the Dutch in then passed to Great Britain in 1814), 46, 188, 196

South China Sea (arm of the western Pacific Ocean bounded by southeast China, Taiwan, the Philippines, Borneo, and Vietnam), 47, 107

South & Southeast Asia, 47, 130, 191,

sovereignty (supreme independent authority), 110, 155

soviets (popularly elected councils of workers, peasants, and soldiers in the U.S.S.R.; also later epithet given to inhabitants of the U.S.S.R.)

Soviet-Afghanistan invasion (1978; Soviets aided communist gov't. against Mujahadin rebels), 201

Soviet Union (Russian Empire renamed by communists, 1917-1991), 7, 13, 38, 153, 171-172, 175, 176, 178, 188, 191, 190, 192, 196, 197, 198-203, 204

Space Exploration, 190, 220

Spain (country of Southwest Europe comprising most of the Iberian Peninsula), 33, 70, 97, 108, 109, 110, 128, 129, 130, 131, 132, 134, 135, 136, 137, 154, 177

Spanish Armada (fleet of warships; [1588] Philip II sent his armada to conquer England and was defeated in one of the great battles of European history), 35, 129, 136

Sparta (ancient Greek city-state, ruled as military oligarchy, became dominant after Peloponnesian Wars c. 400 BC), 65, 66, 71

Sphinx (figure in Egyptian myth having the body of a lion and the head of a man, ram, or hawk), 60

Spirit of the Laws, The (French philosophe and jurist Montesquieu's 1748 treatise outlining separation as a means of limiting power in government), 149

SPQR (Senatus Populusque Romanus ["the Senate and the People of Rome"]; popular motto in ancient Rome carried on standards of Roman battle legions), 68

Stalin, Josef (Soviet dictator, 1925-1953), 172, 176, 177, 178, 190, 217

standard of living (level of quality of life, including per capita income, housing, education, medical care, etc.), 214

START (Strategic Arms Reduction Talks, 1991, 1993; continued work of SALT), 190

Stephenson, George (1781-1848, invented the steam locomotive), 157

steppes (semi arid, open grassy plains; Koppen-type Bs climate), 36, 82, 105

stock exchange (association of stockbrokers who meet to buy and sell stocks and bonds according to fixed regulations), 173

strait (narrow channel joining two larger bodies of water), 31

Strait of Gibraltar (Western [Atlantic] entrance to the Mediterranean), 33, 34 [map]

Strategic Arms Limitation Treaty (SALT I placed limits on certain types of missiles; SALT II placed limits on delivery vehicles, warheads), 190

Strategic Arms Race (competition among superpowers in nuclear armaments), 190

Stuart Dynasty (absolutist Scottish monarchs succeeded Tudors in England, deposed in the Puritan Revolution, restored, deposed again finally in Glorious Revolution), 136, 138-139

stupa (dome-shaped Buddhist shrines in India), 83

subcontinent (large land mass, such as India, that is part of a continent but is considered either geographically or politically as an independent entity), 30

sub-Saharan (relating to the region of Africa south of the Sahara Desert), 44, 111

subsistence (barely maintaining life), 96, 217

Sudetenland (historical region of northwest Czech Republic along the Polish border; seized by the Germans in September 1938; restored to Czechoslovakia in 1945), 177

Sudan (north central Africa / Saharan nation, area of starvation due to ethnic, religious barriers), 217

sudras (fourth of the four Hindu classes, comprising artisans, laborers, and menials), 94

Suez Canal (strategic link between Red Sea and Mediterranean; oil shipping), 43, 197, 199

Suez Canal Crisis (1956, Egypt nationalized canal and denied Israel access), 41, 43, 197, 199

suffrage (right to vote), 170

Suleiman I ("The Magnificent;" ruled over golden age of Ottoman Empire, 1520-1566), 136, 137

Sulla, Lucius (c. 88 BC, Roman civil war general), 70

Sumer/Akkad (3000-2000 BC; first of major Mesopotamian civilizations), 62

Sumerians (ancient civilization of southern Mesopotamia, c. 3000 BC-2000 BC; creators of many basic and lasting features of Mesopotamian civilization), 62

Sun Yixian (also Sun Yat-sen; 1866-1925, early 20th C. Chinese nationalist leader; established the Republic of China, 1911), 161, 175

Sung Dynasty (see Song Dynasty)

Sunna (also Sunnah; way of life prescribed as normative in Islam), 74

Sunn'i (majority Islamic sect), 88

superpowers (enormously powerful political states; e.g., U.S. and former U.S.S.R. in the Cold War Era), 168, 188, 191, 202

supply (amount of resource or service available for meeting a demand), 114

surpluses (key economic concept - quantities in excess of what is needed; usually leads to trade for items needed, or freeing up productive resources [land, labor, capital] for other uses), 60, 113

"sweat shops" (shop or factory in which employees work long hours at low wages under poor conditions), 217

synagogue (house of worship or congregation of Jews for the purpose of worship or religious study), 73

synod (council or an assembly of church officials or churches; an ecclesiastical council), 86

Syria (see also ancient Assyria; modern country of southwest Asia on the eastern Mediterranean coast; a province of the Ottoman Empire [1516-1918]; became a French territory in 1920; independent in 1944), 88, 197, 198

Taiga (subarctic, evergreen coniferous forest of northern Eurasia located just south of the tundra and dominated by firs and spruces), 37

Taiping Rebellion (1850-1864, Chinese nationalist reformers failed to overthrow the Q'ing Dynasty), 160

Taishi, Shotoku (see Shotoku Taishi)

Taiwan (Republic of China; E. China Sea island [Formosa] stronghold of Jiang Jieshi's Chinese nationalists after their exile in 1949), 193

Taj Mahal (Agra, India; mausoleum for the emperor Shah Jahan's wife; acknowledged to be the greatest masterpiece of Indian Mogul architecture; one of the world's most beautiful buildings), 48, 106

Taliban (militant 1980s-1990s fundamentalist movement arose during Soviet occupation of Afghanistan in the 1980s), 200

Talmud (holy book of Judaic faith, knowledge, and ethics), 73

Taklamaken (desert of western China between the Tien Shan and the Kunlun Mountains), 63

Tamils (member of a Dravidian people of southern India and northern Sir Lanka), 195, 224

Tamoxifen (drug maybe useful in prevention or treatment of breast cancer), 222

T'ang Dynasty (China; revived Confucianism, 618-907 AD), 82, 83, 84, 92, 96, 105

Taoism (also Daoism, ancient Chinese philosophy of Lao-tzu C. 6th century BC), 62

tariffs (import taxes one country charges a duty or tax to another country to sell goods inside the first; high "protective tariffs" are used to discourage foreign competition as a form of economic nationalism rather than a mere way to raise government revenues), see trade barriers

Tashkent (important central Asian commercial center along Silk Route), 63, 105

Tatar (member of any of the Turkic and Mongolian peoples of central Asia who invaded western Asia and eastern Europe in the Middle Ages), 106

technology (application of science, especially to industrial or commercial objectives), 20

Teheran Conference (1943; WWII Allied leaders meeting), 178

Telford, Thomas (1757-1783; with John MacAdam, invented hard surfaced roads), 157

Ten Commandments (Judaism, basic laws), 74

terracing (raised bank of earth having vertical or sloping sides and a flat top), 39, 48, 73

terrorism (unlawful use or threatened use of force or violence by a person or an organized group with the intention of intimidating or coercing societies or governments, often for ideological or political reasons), 197, 198, 199, 200, 223-224

Teutonic invaders (Germanic tribes; Vandals, Goths, Saxons, Alemanni, Franks), 97

Teutonic Knights (independent military

order founded in 1190 to aid during the 3rd Crusade; set up a military state in Prussia and the Baltic area), 90

Thailand (country of southeast Asia on the Gulf of Thailand;an arm of the South China Sea; formerly Siam), 47, 48, 193

Thames River (major waterway in S. England), 33-34

thematic writing questions (overview of varieties on global history and geography examinations), 6, 16-18

theocracy (government ruled by or subject to religious authority), 65, 134

Theodosius (347-395 AD; last ruler over both eastern and western Roman Empire), 86

Theory of Relativity (Albert Einstein - time, space, and motion relative), 168

thesis (in the introduction to an essay, a proposition to be maintained by argument of the facts put forth in the body of the essay), 16, 17, 18, 19, 22, 23

Third Estate (the common people - bourgeoisie, proletariat, and peasantry), 150

Third World (older term for economically underdeveloped nations, also LDCs)

Thirty Years' War (1618-1648, last major religious struggle in Europe), 120

Three Principles of the People, The (political beliefs of Sun Yixian), 161

T'iananmen Square Massacre (1989; 6 weeks of prodemocracy demonstrations by Chinese students and workers; erected a plaster statue of the "Goddess of Democracy" that became a symbol of the movement; by order of Deng Xiaoping, Army units cleared Tiananmen Square and killed between 800 and 1,000 civilians), 194

Tiber River (river of central Italy flowing 252 mi. south and southwest through Rome), 67

Tibet (region of central Asia between the Himalya and Kunlun mountains; center of Lamaist Buddhism), 48, 49, 63, 107

Tien Shan Mountains (mountain range of central Asia; isolates China),49

Tientsin (also Tianjin; 1858 treaties imposed on China by Britain, France, Russia, and the United States after its defeat in the second Opium War; among the many unequal treaties that opened that country to Western penetration and deprived it of territory), 159

Tigris-Euphrates Rivers (S.W. Asia cradle of civilization; Fertile Crescent), 32, 41, 42, 62

time line (linear representation of dates for an era with text to pinpoint key events), 5, 13, 29, 59, 81, 103, 127, 147, 167, 187, 213

Timbuktu (ancient West Africa Islamic trading city), 106

tithe (tenth part of one's annual income

contributed voluntarily or due as a tax, especially for the support of the clergy or church), 86, 94

Tokugawa Shogunate (1603-1867, began the official isolation of Japan), 51, 104, 115, 128, 138

Tokugawa Ieyasu (first daimyo from whom the Tokugawa shoguns were descended, began Japan's isolation from the outside world, c. 1603-1867), 104, 136, 138

Tonkin, Gulf of (arm of the South China Sea, forming most of northern Vietnam's coast), 47

Torah (Hebrew holy scripture), 73

totalitarian government (government which exercises absolute and centralized control over all aspects of life, and the individual is subordinated to the state), 172, 174, 175-176, 200

Townshend, Viscount Charles "Turnip" (1674-1738, prominent agricultural innovator), 155

toxic materials and waste (dangerous poisons, chemicals, and materials), 222-223

Treaty of Brest-Litovsk (removed Russia from WWI), 171

Treaty of Kanagawa (1854, Japan-U.S. agreement, opened trade, see Perry)

Treaty of Nanking (see Nanking)

Treaty of Versailles (1919, ended WWI), 170, 173, 176

tribune (officer of ancient Rome elected by the plebeians to protect their rights from arbitrary acts of the patrician magistrates), 68

tribute, tributary (payment in money or other valuables made by a feudal vassal to an overlord to show submission or as the price of protection or security), 50, 87, 106

Tripartite Pact (see Rome-Berlin-Tokyo Axis)

Tripitaka (3 part Buddhist sacred text: the *vinaya* [on monastic discipline], the *sutra* [on Buddha's discourses], and the *abhidharma* [elaborations on the elements of reality]), 73

Triple Alliance (pre-WWI alliance of Germany, Austria-Hungary [1879], and Italy [1882])

Triple Entente (1907, pre-WWI alliance of France, Russia, and Britain)

Trotsky, Leon (major figure of Bolshevik Revolution in Russia), 172

Truman, Harry S (1884-1972; U.S. President, 1945-1953; dropped atomic bombs; set up Marshall Plan, containment policies in Cold War), 176, 178

Truman Doctrine (1947; designed by U.S. to help Greece and Turkey resist the threats of communism), 190

tsar (title of Russian Emperor, also commonly spelled as czar and tzar), 137, 171

Tudor Dynasty (English ruling dynasty

[1485-1603] including Henry VII and his descendants: Henry VIII, Edward VI, Mary I, and Elizabeth I), 35, 110, 139

Tull, Jethro (1674-1741, agrarian innovator, seed drill), 155

tundra (treeless area between the icecap and the tree line of Arctic regions, having a permanently frozen subsoil and supporting low-growing vegetation; cf.: Alaska, Canada, Greenland Norway, Finland, Russia), 37

Turkey (S.W. Asia / E. Mediterranean nation; see also Ottoman Empire), 37, 155, 175, 200, 216, 217

Turks (dominant Mid East group 1450-1915 AD, also see Ottoman Empire), 89, 90, 111, 120, 155, 170

Two Treatises on Government (John Locke's 1690 work outlining government as servant of the people), 149

tyrant (modern: ruthless and unfair ruler; in ancient Greece, abenevolent dictator supported by the Assembly)

Umayyad (also Omayyad; Muslim dynasty, 632-750 AD), 18, 89

U.N. (international peace organization, 1945- ; replaced League of Nations), 178, 197, 198, 199, 204, 219

U.N. General Assembly (legislative branch, all member nations have equal voting status), 191, 219

U.N. Secretary General (chief executive; heads Secretariat [administrative bureaucracy]), 7, 191

U.N. Security Council (executive committee - 5 permanent members - U.S. Russia, China, Britain, France, plus 10 non-permanent members), 191, 219

unification movements (nationalist campaigns to unite the varied states into a nation; cf. Italy and Germany in the 19th century), 153-155

Union of Soviet Socialist Republics (see Soviet Union)

United Kingdom (18th-20th C.; union of England, Scotland, Wales, and Northern Ireland; see Great Britain)

United Nations (see U.N.)

United Nations Economic and Social Council (studies ways to increase cooperation among nations), 219

United Nations Education, Scientific, and Cultural Organization [UNESCO], 219

United Provinces of Central America (1823-1839; brief union of Central American countries after independence from Spain), 154

United States of America (U.S.; country of central and northwest North America with coastlines on the Atlantic and Pacific oceans [includes the non-contiguous states of Alaska and Hawaii and various island territories in the Caribbean Sea and Pacific Ocean]; declared their independence from Great Britain in 1776 and won a war to achieve sovereignty in 1783), 150, 158, 169, 174, 178-189, 198, 203, 204, 219, 220

Universal Declaration of Human Rights (1948, U.N. approved basis for modern ideas on human rights), 219

University of France (1802, established by Napoleon as a reform of the French system of education), 151

untouchables (class, comprising numerous subclasses, that is excluded from and considered ritually unclean and defiling by the four Hindu classes), 195

Upanishads (900-600 BC, latest portions of the Vedas, the sacred texts of Hinduism), 62

Urals (1,500 mi. long mountain range of eastern European and western Siberia form the traditional boundary between Europe and Asia and extend from the Arctic Ocean southward to Kazakhstan), 36

urbanization (relocating to the cities from the country; from farm to factory, from family homes to apartments, etc.), 215

using this book (tips for more comprehensive approach to review), 25-27

U.S.S.R. (Union of Soviet Socialist Republics; see references under Soviet Union)

Utopia (16th C. work by Thomas More on ideal human society), 117

utopian society / socialists (believers in ideal society in which the state functions for the good and happiness of all), 156, 157

V-1 and V-2 (jet-propelled bombs developed by Nazis in WWII), 176

vaccination (inoculation with a preparation of a weakened or killed pathogen that stimulates antibody production against the pathogen but is incapable of causing severe infection), 168, 221

vaisya (third of the four Hindu classes, comprising farmers, herders, artisans, merchants, and businessmen.), 94

valley (lowland between two uplands, often site of draining river), 31

Vandals (Germanic people that overran Gaul, Spain, and northern Africa in the 4th and 5th centuries AD and sacked Rome in 455), 84, 85

Varangians (Byzantine reference for Scandinavian-Norse Vikings who invaded and traded along the Volga forming the beginning of Russia), 92

varnas (Hindu social classes), 94

vassal (subordinate, knight swearing oaths of loyalty to the more powerful nobles in Medieval European feudal system), 85, 87, 106, 115, 138

Vedas (Hindu holy book from Sanskrit), 62, 73, 94

Velvet Revolution (quiet, voluntary 1992 separation of Czechoslovakia into the Czech Republic and Slovak Republic), 202

Venetian (inhabitant of Venice, Italy), 96

Venice (city of northeast Italy on the northern Adriatic Sea; became a major maritime power by the 13th century and spread its influence over northern Italy by the 15th century; lost power to the Turks, and later passed to Austria), 111

Versailles (Louis XIV's Palace outside Paris; see also Treaty of Versailles), 136, 170, 173

viceroys (governor of a region or people, ruling as the representative of a king; esp. colonial Latin America), 131

Victor Emanuel III (1869-1947; King of Italy, r.1900-1946; appointed Mussolini premier), 172

Vietnam, Socialist Republic of (country of southeast Asia in eastern Indochina on the South China Sea; ruled by China [217 BC - AD 939 and 1407 to 1428]; occupied by the French in the 19th century; independent, 1976), 48, 91, 92, 195

Vietnam War (Western powers resisted communist insurgency; French Phase: 1946-1954, American Phase: 1959-1975), 190, 195, 196

Vikings (also Norsemen; 8th-12th C. invading Scandinavian groups trading and raiding along the shores of the Baltic, North, and Irish seas and along the rivers of eastern and western Europe), 85, 92, 97

Vladimir I (956-1015, Grand Duke of Kiev), 92

Volga River (longest river of Europe; 2,300 mi.; main commercial waterway of the Russia; linked to the Baltic Sea), 36, 37

Voltaire, Francois Marie Arouet (1694-1778, French Enlightenment writer), 149, 150, 154

von Moltke, Helmuth Karl Bernhard (1800-1891; Prussian general was the strategist who designed the military victories leading to German unification under Otto von Bismarck), 155

Walesa, Lech (1943- ; led Polish Solidarity labor movement; President of Poland 1991-1995), 202

War Communism (1917-1921, Bolsheviks' initial command economic policy in Russia during the civil war), 171

Wars of Religion (1562-1598 in W. Europe, Protestant v. Catholic monarchs; in France, involved Calvinist Huguenots), 120

Wars of the Roses (1455-85; series of armed clashes between the houses of Lancaster and York, rival claimants to the English crown), 110

Warsaw Pact (1955-1991; Warsaw Treaty Organization; Soviet military alliance of Eastern European nations; a Cold War answer to NATO), 190, 201

Washington Conference (Washington Naval Arms Conference 1921-1922; limited Japanese naval power in comparison to that of Britain, France, and the U.S.), 176

Waterloo, Battle of (1815, near Brussels, Belgium, Napoleon's decisive defeat by British Duke of Wellington), 152

Watt, James (1736-1819, invented the steam engine), 157

Wealth of Nations, The (1776, Adam Smith - doctrine of laissez-faire), 157

Weimar Republic (1919-1933, weak democratic republic set up in Germany after World War I; displaced by Nazis in 1933), 173

Wellington, Duke of (Arthur Wellesley, 1769-1852; British soldier and statesman defeated Napoleon I at Waterloo; prime minister [1828-30]), 152

welfare program (financial or other aid provided, especially by the gov't., to people in need), 191

Western Europe, 13, 33, 188, 191

West Bank (territory of the Jordan River disputed among Palestinians, Israelis, and Syrians), 197

West Germany (see Federal Republic of Germany)

Western Hemisphere (North and South America and surrounding ocean areas), 32, 133

White Paper of 1939 (British limited Jewish immigration to Palestine), 174

Windsor Dynasty (English ruling family, 1901 - present; originally known by the German name Wettin—which came from Prince Albert of Saxe-Coburg-Gotha, husband of Queen Victoria; George V chose Windsor during World War I, when Britain was at war with Germany), 139

Whites (epithet [nickname] for anti-Bolshevik opposition after 1917 Revolution and during the ensuing civil war, 1917-1921), 171

WHO (U.N. - World Health Organization; main activities include information dissemination, research, technical assistance, setting of international health standards, and aiding victims of natural disasters), 191, 219

William (I) the Conqueror (1028-1087, led the Norman conquest of England [1066] and provided stability and firm government in an age of great disorder), 35, 110, 139

William III (of Orange) and Mary II (17th C. English monarchs installed after Glorious Revolution ousted King James II), 139, 140

Wilson, Woodrow (1856-1924, U.S. President; WWI peace settlement), 170

writing questions (overview of varieties on global history and geography examinations), 16-24

women's suffrage (right or privilege of women to vote), 170

women, 218-219

World Bank (specialized agency of the U.N.; officially, the International Bank for Reconstruction and Development [IBRD]; established in 1944 to assist European postwar recovery; single most important lending agency in international development), 48

World Health Organization (see WHO)

World War I (1914-1918), 37, 41, 153, 154, 168-176

World War II (1939-1945), 37, 51, 168, 174, 176-178, 188, 189, 191, 194, 195, 197, 206, 219-221

writing questions (overview of varieties on global history and geography examinations), 16-24

Wu Daozi (c. 689-760, one of the greatest Chinese painters of the T'ang Dynasty), 83

Wudi (r. 141-87 BC, Han emperor Han Wu Ti, martial emperor; formerly Liu Qi or Liu Chi), 64

Xerxes (486-465 BC; Persian king and conqueror; Darius' son), 64

Xi River (China's West River, a major trading artery to Guangzhuo or Canton), 49, 63

Xi'an (Sian Province in mountainous western China), 63

Xiaoping (see Deng Xiaoping)

Yalta Conference (1945, WWII Allied meeting), 177, 178

Yalu River (boundary between Korean Peninsula and Chinese mainland), 49

Yamato clan leaders (first emperors of Japan, c. 220 AD), 91, 92, 105, 114

Yangtze (also called the "Great River" or "Long River" - Chang Jiang) River Valley (site of early Chinese civilizations), 49

Yellow River Valley (Huang He; site of early Chinese civilizations), 49, 62

Yellow Sea (arm of the Pacific Ocean between the Chinese mainland and the Korean Peninsula; connects with the East China Sea to the south), 49

Yeltsin, Boris (1931- , Russian Federation President [r. 1990 -]; attempted social and market economic reforms with international assistance; presided over dissolution of Soviet Union), 201, 202

Yenisei River (river of central Siberia flowing about 2,500 mi. westward and north to the Kara Sea), 36

yin and yang (ancient Chinese concept representing a balance of opposing forces in the universe; yin = passive, feminine, darkness, principle, represented by the Earth/Moon; yang = active, masculine, light principle, represented by Heaven/Sun), 101 [symbol]

Yom Kippur War (1973, Arabs attack Gaza and Golan; U.S. aided Israel, U.S.S.R. aided Syria), 42, 197

Yoruba (12th-19th century W. African trading state), 108

Yoritomo, Minamoto (r. 1192-1199 - strengthened power of shogun; unified daimyo), 104

Young Plan (1929; Owen D. Young of the U.S. proposed to modify the 1924 Dawes Plan to aid Germany in paying WWI reparations), 173

Young Turks (1908 gained power and began a series of reforms), 155

Yuan Dynasty (1279-1368, following the conquest of China by Mongol tribes, Kublai Khan), 105, 106, 112

Yugoslavia (S.E. European country on the Balkan Peninsula; formed in 1918 as the Kingdom of Serbs, Croats, and Slovenes; renamed Yugoslavia in 1929; today, the Federal Republic of Yugoslavia [FRY, 1992] consists of only two republics: Serbia and Montenegro; FRY is the successor-state of Tito's Socialist Federated Republic of Yugoslavia [1946], which broke up in 1991), 7, 37, 153, 202-203, 205, 216, 217

Zaire River (central Africa, also called the Congo River), 44, 45, 46

Zambezi River (1,700 mi) long river of s. central and southern Africa rising in Northwest Zambia and flowing South and West to the Mozambique Channel),44, 45

Zapatista National Liberation Army (in Mexico, lead 1994 revolution against gov't.), 205

Zedong (see Mao Zedong)

Zemin (see Jiang Zemin)

Zen Buddhism (popular among samurai; required meditation called for much self-discipline), 115, 116

Zheng (217-204 BC; proclaimed Shi Huangdi [First Emperor] of China; united China into the Q'in Dynasty), 64

Zheng He (also Cheng Ho, 1371-1433; Ming admiral with an expeditionary fleet of hundreds of ships exploring over 30 years), 112, 128, 138

Zhou (Chou) Dynasty (c. 1027-252 BC; semi nomadic people from Xi'an; began China's bureaucracy, Confucian, Taoist, and feudal system), 61, 62, 72

Zhuangzi (c. 399-295 BC; a founder of philosophical Daoism with Laozi), 74

Zhu Yuanzhang (see Hong Wu)

ziggurat (temple tower of the ancient

Assyrians and Babylonians, having the form of a terraced pyramid of successively receding stories), 62

Zimbabwe (S. African trading city-state; 1200-1900 AD), 108

Zionism (organized movement to reconstitute a Jewish state in Palestine), 174

Zollverein (German customs union, established in 1834, stemmed initially from Prussia's desire for the economic unity of its scattered territories and helped lead eventually to the unification of Germany), 155

Zoroastrianism (religious system founded in Persia by Zoroaster [c. 628-551 BC]; set forth in the *Zend-Avesta*, teaching a universal struggle between the forces of light and of darkness), 62

Zwingli, Ulrich (Swiss, 1481-1531, spread spirit of Protestant Reformation into Switzerland, France, and Netherlands), 119

ASSIGNMENT SCHEDULE

Date Due	Page(s)	Questions	Description